AF564509

Hospitality and Tourism Management Strategies

Hospitality and Tourism Management Strategies

Billy Edeson

RANDOM PUBLICATIONS
NEW DELHI - 110 002 (INDIA)

Hospitality and Tourism Management Strategies

ISBN 978-93-51113-04-1

Published in 2014 in India by

RANDOM PUBLICATIONS

Reprint : 2016

4376-A/4B, Gali Murari Lal, Ansari Road

New Delhi-110 002

Phone: +9111-43580356, 23289044

E-mail: randomexports@gmail.com; sales@randompublications.com; info@randompublications.com

Type Setting by: Friends Media, Delhi-110089

Digitally Printed at: Replika Press Pvt. Ltd.

Preface

The subject of strategic management is often taught as a core topic at some stage during a tourism degree programme. Strategic management also acts as a key feature of postgraduate tourism degree programmes. The topic consolidates what the student has learnt in the preceding years of their degree and applies this knowledge at a strategic level to tourism contexts. However, many of the concepts associated with strategy and strategic management are abstract in nature and can often be difficult for teaching staff, let alone students, to comprehend. It is important that lecturers and students are able to access resources that enable their wider understanding of the subject matter and create opportunities where theory can be effectively applied to practice. Though there are many generic strategy resources that exist, these are predominately 'manufacturing' related, and specific subject resources focusing on tourism service contexts can be difficult to find. Indeed, there are still only a few key strategic management textbooks that focus specifically on tourism. This resource guide will thus be essential to anyone teaching a strategic management module targeted at tourism students. The guide also embraces examples from the hospitality industry so will be useful to tutors teaching on strategic management modules with a hospitality focus. The book is separated into different sections. Firstly an annotated bibliography of resources is presented. This section is further separated into the key themes that may comprise a semesterised module in strategic management.

Strategy can be explored from a variety of different perspectives and there are many definitions of what strategy is. It is important to understand these different strategic perspectives so as to gain an holistic understanding of strategy formulation and implementation. It is often the case that the opening chapter of any generic strategy textbook will include an initial definition and interpretation of strategy. An analysis of the macro environment is crucial in determining the factors which have a direct impact and/or might influence the strategic direction of an organisation. A number of different concepts can be used to analyse the external macro environment in an attempt to identify those factors, which might have an impact upon the organisation, both in terms of being a threat or an opportunity. The analysis of the immediate competitive environment is important for understanding the strengths and weaknesses of the competition and the organisation's relative position in the industry. It is upon this basis that the organisation can then go on to formulate strategies that enable a strategic advantage to be gained over competitors. A number of concepts can be used to analyse the competitive environment and these are embedded within the following resources. Once an organisation has been through the process of analysing the external macro and micro environment and has conducted a rigorous analysis of its internal resources and culture, then the organisation is in a position to formulate strategies in pursuit of a competitive advantage. The classical strategy approach often utilises Porter's (1980) generic strategy framework of focus, cost leadership, and differentiation to understand the particular strategic direction an organisation may pursue.

This book will be of interest to technicians working in the field of this subject.

I thank all members of my team who have helped in the preparation of the book. My special thanks go to "Random Publications" who have published the book.

—Billy Edeson

Contents

1

Tourism Strategies

The marketing mix-the 4 Ps-target audience-segmentation-objectives-evaluation. These and other terms are all used in the process of "marketing." In tourism and tourism related industries, success means understanding this process.

This bulletin is designed for those in the tourism industry who may not be completely familiar with marketing or who may simply wish to refresh their basic marketing skills. Covered will be important concepts used in marketing, the relationship of marketing to tourism, and a process for developing a marketing plan for tourism/recreation businesses and/or communities. It will be impossible to cover in detail all the aspects of marketing within the scope of this bulletin. There are, however, other bulletins in this series that will provide more in-depth information on the different components of a marketing plan.

What is Marketing

People hold a variety of misconceptions about marketing. Most common is its confusion with selling and advertising. Selling and advertising are actually types of promotion which is only a component of marketing.

Marketing involves much more, including product/service development, place (location and distribution), and pricing. It requires information about people, especially those interested in what you have to offer (your "market"), such as what they like, where they buy and how much they spend. Its role is to match the right product or service with the right market or audience. Marketing, as you will see, is an art and a science. According to the American Marketing Association, marketing is "the process of planning and executing the conception, pricing, promotion, and distribution of ideas, goods, and services to create exchanges that satisfy individual and organizational objectives." Simply stated it is creating and promoting a product (ideas, goods or services) that satisfies a customer's need or desire and is available at a desirable price and place. Modern marketing is a way of doing business, heavily based on the "marketing concept" which holds that businesses and organizations should:

(1) design their products/services to meet customer needs and wants;

(2) focus on those people most likely to buy their product rather than the entire mass market; and

(3) develop marketing efforts that fit into their overall business objectives.

By adopting this concept you not only provide your customers with better products, you will avoid wasting valuable time and money developing and promoting a product or service nobody wants.

Recreation and Tourism Marketing

Earlier it was mentioned that a product can be "ideas, goods, or services." Since tourism is primarily a service based industry, the principal products provided by recreation/tourism (R/T) businesses are recreational experiences and hospitality. These are intangible products and more difficult to market than tangible products such as automobiles. The intangible nature of services makes quality control difficult but crucial. It also makes it more difficult for potential customers to evaluate and compare service offerings. In addition, instead of moving the product to the customer, the customer must travel to the product (area/community). Travel is a significant portion of the time and money spent in association with recreational and tourism experiences and is a major factor in people's decisions on whether or not to visit your business or community. As an industry, tourism has many components comprising the overall "travel experience." Along with transportation, it includes such things as accommodations, food and beverage services, shops, entertainment, aesthetics and special events. It is rare for one business to provide the variety of activities or facilities tourists need or desire. This adds to the difficulty of maintaining and controlling the quality of the experience.

To overcome this hurdle, tourism related businesses, agencies, and organizations need to work together to package and promote tourism opportunities in their areas and align their efforts to assure consistency in product quality.

The Marketing Plan

One of the most important steps a business or community can take to improve the effectiveness and efficiency of their marketing efforts is to develop a written marketing plan. This plan will guide their marketing decisions and assist them in allocating marketing resources such as money and personnel time. The plan should include:

(1) the overall business objectives—what you want to accomplish;

(2) an assessment of the market environment—what factors may affect your marketing efforts;

(3) a business/community profile—what resources are available,

(4) market identification (segmentation)—the specific groups or clientele most interested in your product;

(5) the marketing objectives for each segment;

(6) the marketing strategies (or mixes) for different markets you target—the best combination of the 4 Ps (product, price, place, promotion) for each segment;

(7) an implementation plan—how to "make it work;"

(8) the marketing budget-how much you have to spend; and

(9) a method for evaluation and change.

A framework which can be used to develop a marketing plan. Each component will be briefly discussed in the remainder of the bulletin. For more information regarding different components of the plan be sure to consult other bulletins in this series.

Overall Business Objectives

Businesses, agencies, and communities should develop overall objectives and regularly monitor their progress. The objectives should provide guidance for all decisions including finances, personnel and marketing.

They should be quantitative and measurable statements of what the business or community wants to accomplish over a specified period of time. Business objectives are often stated in terms of sales, profits, market shares and/or occupancy rates. Communities frequently establish objectives relating to such things as increasing the number of tourists, developing or changing their image, facility and activity development, cooperation among tourism related businesses and increasing length of stay and local expenditures. It is important that the objectives be reasonable given the market conditions and the firm's or organization's resources. Establish a few reasonable objectives instead of a long, unrealistic "wish list." This is especially true for new businesses or communities which do not have much experience in tourism development and/or marketing.

Market Environment Analysis

The next step in developing a marketing plan is to assess the impact of environmental factors (such as economic, social and political) on present and future markets. Changes in these factors can create marketing opportunities as well as problems.

Demographic and Lifestyle Trends

Changing demographics and lifestyles are having a major impact on R/T participation. An assessment of these trends is important to understand how they will likely affect your business or community. Some of the important trends that bear watching:

(1) population growth and movement;

(2) rural community growth compared to metropolitan areas;

(3) number of adult women employed outside the home;

(4) the number of households is growing, especially non family and single parent households, but family size is decreasing;

(5) the impact of two wage earner households on real family income;

(6) the number of retired persons with the financial ability to travel;

(7) better health to an older age; and

(8) continued aging of the population (we are becoming a middle aged society).

Economic Conditions

Overall economic conditions can have significant impacts on recreation and tourism markets. A marketing strategy that is effective during periods of low unemployment rates may have to be significantly adjusted if unemployment increases.

Businesses and communities should monitor and assess the likely impact of factors such as unemployment rates, real family income, rate of inflation, credit availability, terms and interest rates. Consideration should also be given to the prices of complementary products, such as lodging, gasoline and recreation equipment.

Laws and Government Actions

As a complex industry, tourism is significantly affected both positively and negatively by laws and by actions of governmental agencies. For instance, rulings on such things as liability issues or decisions regarding building and health codes may change or possibly prevent the construction of a proposed facility. If a public facility changes the prices of its services, this could affect the service offerings of associated private businesses. These actions may have both positive and negative effects on the marketing efforts of the business and community. To avoid wasting valuable resources it is important that R/T businesses, agencies, and communities continually monitor and evaluate governmental actions.

Technology

Technological developments are increasing rapidly. New recreation products, such as all-terrain vehicles and wind surfers, provide new ways for people to satisfy their recreational preferences. New production technologies and materials offer recreation and tourism businesses ways to reduce costs and improve the quality of their products/services. Advances in telecommunications have and will continue to create new promotional opportunities. Technological innovations, in relation to jobs and the home, have resulted in increased leisure time for many people.

Competition

Businesses and communities must identify and analyse existing and potential competitors. The objective of the analysis is to determine the strengths and weaknesses of the competition's marketing strategies. The analysis should include the competition's:

(1) product/service features and quality;

(2) location relative to different geographic markets;

(3) promotional themes and messages;

(4) prices; and

(5) type of customer they are attracting.

Business and Community Profiles

Too many communities attempt to market themselves as tourist destinations without accurate information about their resources (facilities, services, staff), image (projected vs. Actual), and how well their customers are satisfied. Without this information, it is difficult to make other decisions in the planning process. Included should be such things as recreational and entertainment facilities, cultural and historic sites, overnight accommodations, restaurants, shopping opportunities, special events and activities, staff size, and transportation. Each item of the "inventory" should also be assessed in terms of quality and availability.

Market Segmentation (Identification)

Recreation and tourism businesses and communities often make the mistake of attempting to be all things to all people.

It is difficult, and risky, to develop marketing strategies for the mass market. Strategies designed for the "average" customer often result in unappealing products, prices, and promotional messages. For example, it would be difficult to develop a campground that would be equally attractive to recreational vehicle campers and backpackers or promote a property to serve both snow mobilers and nature oriented cross country skiers.

Marketing is strongly based on market segmentation and target marketing. Market segmentation is the process of:

(1) taking existing and/or potential customers/visitors (market) and categorizing them into groups with similar preferences referred to as "market segments;"

(2) selecting the most promising segments as "target markets;" and

(3) designing "marketing mixes," or strategies (combination of the 4 Ps), which satisfy the special needs, desires and behaviour of the target markets.

There is no unique or best way to segment markets, but ways in which customers can be grouped are:

(1) location of residence—instate, out-of-state, local;

(2) demographics—age, income, family status, education;

(3) equipment ownership/use—RV's, sailboats, canoes, tents, snowmobiles;

(4) important product attributes—price, quality, quantity; and

(5) lifestyle attributes—activities, interests, opinions.

To be useful, the segment identification process should result in segments that suggest marketing efforts that will be effective in attracting them and at least one segment large enough to justify specialized marketing efforts.

After segments have been identified, the business or community must select the "target markets," those segments which offer them the greatest opportunity. When determining target markets, consideration should be given to:

(1) existing and future sales potential of each segment;
(2) the amount and strength of competition for each segment;
(3) the ability to offer a marketing mix which will be successful in attracting each segment;
(4) the cost of servicing each segment; and
(5) each segment's contribution to accomplishing overall business/community objectives. It is often wiser to target smaller segments that are presently not being served, or served inadequately, than to go after larger segments for which there is a great deal of competition.

Marketing Objectives for Each Segment

Marketing objectives which contribute to the accomplishment of the overall business objectives should be established for each target market. Objectives serve a number of functions including:

(1) guidance for developing marketing mixes for different target markets;
(2) information for allocating the marketing budget between target markets;
(3) a basis for objectively evaluating the effectiveness of the marketing mixes (setting standards); and
(4) a framework for integrating the different marketing mixes into the overall marketing plan.

The target market objectives should:

(1) be expressed in quantitative terms;
(2) be measurable;
(3) specify the target market; and
(4) indicate the time period in which the objective is to be accomplished.

For example, increase the number of overnight stays by people from the Chicago market over the next two years by five percent. Remember, rank objectives by priority and carefully evaluate them to ensure that they are reasonable given the strength of the competition and resources available for marketing.

Marketing Strategy (Mix)

The marketing strategy, or mix, should be viewed as a package of offerings designed to attract and serve the customer or visitor. Recreation and tourism businesses and communities should develop both external and internal marketing mixes for different target markets.

External Mix

The external marketing mix includes product/service, price, place/ location, and promotion.

Product

Earlier we said the principal products that recreation and tourism businesses provide are recreational experiences and hospitality. The factors that create a quality recreational experience often differ among people. A quality experience for one skier might include an uncrowded, steep slope. To another it might be a good restaurant and a chance to socialize. Decisions on what facilities, programs and services to provide should be based on the needs and desires of the target market(s). They should not be based on the preferences of the owner/manager or necessarily on what the competition is providing.

Recognize that a recreational/tourism experience includes five elements: trip planning and anticipation; travel to the site/area; the experience at the site; travel back home; and recollection. Businesses should look for ways to enhance the quality of the overall experience during all phases of the trip. This could be accomplished by providing trip planning packages which include maps, attractions en route and on site, and information regarding lodging, food and quality souvenirs and mementos. Recreation and tourism businesses should also view their service/product in generic terms. Thinking of products/services in this manner helps focus more attention on the experiences desired by customers and also the facilities, programs and services that will produce those experiences. For example, campgrounds are the business of providing recreational "lodging" not just campsites to park an RV or set up a tent. Marinas should provide recreational "boating" experiences, not just slippage.

Location and Accessibility—Place

Too many tourism businesses and communities fail to recognize their role in improving travel to and from their areas. They focus instead on servicing the customer once they arrive at the site/community. A bad experience getting to or leaving an R/T site can adversely affect a person's travel experience. Ways to help prevent this include:

(1) providing directions and maps;

(2) providing estimates of travel time and distances from different market areas;

(3) recommending direct and scenic travel routes;

(4) identifying attractions and support facilities along different travel routes; and

(5) informing potential customers of alternative travel methods to the area such as airlines and railroads.

Potential businesses should also carefully assess alternative locations for:

(1) distance and accessibility to target markets;

(2) location of competitors with respect to target markets;

(3) modes of travel serving the area; and

(4) other attractions and activities that might induce travel to the area.

Pricing Price is one of the most important and visible elements of the marketing mix. When setting prices it is important to take into consideration all of the following:

(1) business and target market objectives;

(2) the full cost of producing, delivering and promoting the product;

(3) the willingness of the target market to pay for the product or service you provide;

(4) prices charged by competitors offering a similar product/service to the same target market(s);

(5) the availability and prices of substitute products/services;

(6) the economic climate (local and national); and

(7) the possibility of stimulating high profit products/services (such as boats) by offering related services (such as maintenance) at or below cost.

When establishing prices, R/T businesses should give attention to pricing strategies which may encourage off season and non-peak period sales, longer stays, group business, and the sale of package plans (combination of room, meals, and recreational facilities). For additional information on pricing.

Promotion

Promotion provides target audiences with accurate and timely information to help them decide whether to visit your community or business. The information should be of importance and practical use to the potential or existing visitor and also accurate. Misrepresentation often leads to dissatisfied customers and poor recommendations. Don't make claims you cannot live up to. Developing a promotional campaign is not a science with hard and fast rules. Making decisions regarding which type or combination of promotion types to use (personal selling, advertising, sales promotions, or publicity) is not always easy. If, however, you follow a logical process and do the necessary research, chances for success will be improved. It will be necessary to make decisions regarding:

(1) Target audience—the group you are aiming at;
(2) Image—that which your community or business wants to create or reinforce;
(3) Objectives—those of the promotional campaign;
(4) Budget—the amount of money available for your promotion;
(5) Timing—when and how often should your promotions appear;
(6) Media—which methods (television, radio, newspaper, magazine) will most effectively and efficiently communicate your message to the target audience; and
(7) Evaluation—how can the effectiveness of the promotional campaign be determined.

Internal Mix

As stated, marketing services such as recreation and tourism differ from marketing tangible products. Recreation and tourism businesses must direct as much attention at marketing to customers on site as they do to attracting them. In this respect, internal marketing is important because dissatisfied customers can effectively cancel out an otherwise effective marketing strategy.

The success of internal marketing is dependent on creating an atmosphere in which employees desire to give good service and sell the business/community to visitors. To create such an atmosphere requires the following four important elements:

(1) Hospitality and Guest Relations—An organization wide emphasis on hospitality and guest relations, including a customer oriented attitude on the part of the owners and managers as well as the employees. If the owner/manager is not customer sensitive, it is unlikely the lower paid employees will be.
(2) Quality Control—A program which focuses on improving both the technical quality (the standards associated with what the customer receives) and the functional quality (the standards

associated with how the customer receives the service). All employees who come into contact with customers should receive hospitality training.

(3) Personal Selling—Training the staff in the selling aspects of the property (business) or community. This also includes rewarding them for their efforts. By being informed about the marketing objectives, and their role in accomplishing those objectives, they can help increase sales.

(4) Employee Morale—Programs and incentives aimed at maintaining employee morale. The incentives can be both monetary and nonmonetary.

A customer oriented atmosphere usually results in customers that are more satisfied, do less complaining and are more pleasant to serve. This helps build employee morale, their desire to provide good service and their efficiency.

Marketing Budget

Successful marketing requires that sufficient money and personnel time be made available to implement activities comprising the marketing strategy. A marketing budget is a financial plan which shows the total amount to be spent on marketing during different times of the year and how it is to be allocated among alternative activities. Separate marketing budgets should be developed for each marketing mix strategy. The separate budgets should then be aggregated to develop an overall marketing budget. If the total amount is too great it will be necessary to modify the overall objectives and the target market objectives, narrow down or drop target markets, or adjust marketing mixes. The final budget should be realistic given your objectives. When deciding on a marketing budget, consideration should be given to the job that needs to be done as defined by the objectives. Basing marketing budgets on some percent of sales or what the competition spends usually leads to over spending or under spending. Decisions should also be based on the costs, projected revenues, and desired profitability of different activities, not just costs alone. Successful marketing activities will generate additional revenues which can be projected based on the marketing objectives (such as increase off season stay by 5%).

Although budgets should be viewed as flexible plans, every effort should be made to adhere to them. Revisions in the budget should only be made after careful consideration of the likely impact of the change on the marketing mix and accomplishment of your objectives.

Implementation

Many well designed marketing plans fail because they are poorly executed. Businesses, agencies, and communities can increase the likelihood of successful implementation if they:

(1) Identify specific tasks which must be accomplished;

(2) Assign people or departments specific responsibility for different tasks;

(3) Provide employees with information on the marketing plan (rationale, objectives, strategies);

(4) Develop time lines and deadlines;

(5) Adhere as much as possible to the budget; and

Evaluation

It is important that marketing efforts be continually evaluated. This will improve the effectiveness of marketing strategies by quickly identifying differences between actual results and expected performance and determining likely reasons for the success or failure to realize objectives.

A framework for evaluation would include:

(1) Determining which elements of the different marketing mixes are most important to evaluate.——It is rarely possible or cost effective to evaluate all elements;

(2) Establishing performance standards to compare against actual results.—Marketing objectives, if properly formulated, should serve as performance standards;

(3) Development of formal and informal methods for collecting data on actual results.—There are many ways different elements of the marketing mix can be evaluated. For example, promotions can be evaluated with money off coupons. Special information request forms, telephone numbers to call or post office box numbers to write to can identify the area the request is coming from. Also, formal (written) and informal surveys can be used to determine the promotional material the customer used in planning the trip;

(4) Comparison of results with objectives;

Conclusion

Customer satisfaction in tourism is greatly influenced by the way in which the service (hospitality) is delivered and the physical appearance and personality of the business. It is critical that these elements be communicated in the best possible manner to convince people to come and experience what your business or community has to offer. Equally important is the ability to generate repeat business because of your efforts. Thus, marketing becomes the method to reach potential visitors. It is a vital part of tourism management and can be done effectively and well, with sophistication and tact, or it can be done poorly in a loud, crass and intrusive manner. Hopefully, this bulletin has given you the basics for the former rather than the latter. Remember that to do an effective job at marketing:

(1) Adopt a strong customer orientation which includes regular research and assessment of their needs, wants and attitudes;
(2) Allocate sufficient resources and time to marketing;
(3) Assign formal responsibility for marketing to one person or department; and
(4) Develop and regularly update a marketing plan.

Information Supply in Tourism Management

Operators in tourism management, compared to other management sectors, are confronted with a vast field of complex aims, requiring different plans of action. The special working requirements of the services sector are a result of its business peculiarities. Problems instrategic, and frequently operational planning, are characterized by their complexity, often being intermingled, non-transparent, individualistically dynamic and requiring the achievement of multiple goals. The vast amount of information or complex weighting of the different sectors can present an insurmountable problem for human resources. As are sult there are high expectations of decision-makers' trouble-shooting abilities.

In order to solve complex problems, decision-makers need to have a factual knowledge of the industry (declarative knowledge) and the methodology used (procedural knowledge). The wealth of knowledge is drawn from two pools; that obtained from the "storage" of already existing experiences, and by generating knowledge in the respective field. Com-bining these two pools creates an arena for problem solving.

Declarative Knowledge – Decision Basis in Tourism Planning

Currently, information gains more and more importance, leading legitimately to the development of a fourth economic sector – the information sector. Information also plays a vital role in tourism for entrepreneurs and managers who spend the whole day involved in information processing. In the tourism industry there is no lack of market research data, on the contrary, there is a rather uncontrolled growth of various data sources, each having different survey purposes and survey designs. Tourism surveys of national and international market research institutes are published in ever shorter intervals and the level of itemization of market data increases rapidly. Information collected by these means has indicated data which can be organized into the following groups:

1. Information on markets and environment,
2. Information on customer behaviour,
3. Information on competition in the industry, and
4. Internal information for executive boards.

The first three information groups are predominantly non-discretionary from a manager's point of view as the information can very rarely be directly influenced by an individual company. Information from these groups are similar in nature and scope for most sectors represented in the tourism industry (hotel trade, restaurant trade, tour operators, travel agents, common carriers, pressure groups, etc.). In the fourth group however, there is a larger scope for variety. Due to high costs for primary market research many tourism managers abandon market research in general. Even the larger businesses and tourism organizations lack market research departments and employees rarely work exclusively on market research items. This results again in an inconsistent development of marketing aims and strategies, as businesses as often as not grope in the dark for their direction.

In Europe the most frequent or highly recognized of the commissioned tourism studies are either publicly financed, directly by national or local authorities, or indirectly by government agencies. This method of procuring market research, is important and often a condition for its development, as the expensive primary studies cannot be financed by the numerous small or medium-scale businesses. The resulting obligation to pass on information, created by the above mentioned research financing, has lead to a wider search-inregional tourism organizations, and other bodies representing tourism-to find means of successfully sharing and communicating information.

Traditional data resources in tourism market research are reports, records and statistics which may be presented either in printed format or are electronically driven (CD-ROM). Computer-based information systems (databases) are currently a rarity, but usually can be found either in connection with the official statistical data of a country or a region or international institutions. The information available by this method is rarely used since it ignores the special information requirements of the end-user (managers), or is simply inaccessible due to high fees, complicated application procedures or is simply not user friendly.

The lack of practical relevance, of these information systems, can be explained by their bias toward representing the economic interest of the sponsors and data collectors and/or by the universal requirements the systems have to meet in the collection, storage and search of statistical data from other industries. Market research results are mainly available in print and they can be obtained either in bookshops, online or directly from the author. From the consumer's perspective this way of passing on secondary information has a number of disadvantages:

- Due to the complex design of market research reports the surveyed data is not up to date any more.
- Data from different sources cannot be easily compared especially if it has been surveyed for different purposes.
- Information contained in reports is often of limited relevance for the particular problem.
- Presentation of data is either not detailed enough, not significant enough, or supplementary information is missing which prevents a faultless interpretation of results.
- Often only very specific data from a more comprehensive study is required and thus the cost-benefit-ratio becomes unattractive.

There is usually an overabundance of available information leaving managers to cope with determining which is the best source. Often the entrepreneur has to rely on external consultants and market research specialists resulting in additional costs.

Procedural Knowledge – Decision Basis in Tourism Planning

"The big problem with management science models is that managers practically never used them." More than 20 years ago John Little described the discrepancy between the scientific development of planning instruments, models, level of itemization and the fact that, when available, the knowledge gathered is rarely put into practice. This is caused by the numerous, often poorly documented assumptions of model architects, which was denoted as model plutonism by Hans

Albert. As a response to this problem Little suggested that the manager is included in the model. He postulated in his article on the Decision Calculus, aniline models with the following features: robustness, ease of control, simplicity, completeness of relevant detail and suitability for communication.

The communication problem is of vital importance in the every day life of managers' daily events. It is still common practice to employ various levels of change rather than continue-ally observe the changes in market share and volume. Many entrepreneurs do not even know terms such as market segmentation or market positioning and they do not regard them as essential. They keep on looking for measures to expand seasonal business but lack knowledge of methods that will measure their success. Corporate planning only takes place if external financing is required and supporting documents have to be submitted to the lender. Heuristic forecasting methods are hardly ever used, accordingly quantitative methods are never used. Models of strategic market plan-ningportfolio analyses and analyses of the lifestyle of a product-employed in other industries are hardly ever used in tourism management.

The grounds for the poor employment of methodological processes in tourism management can be divided into two groups; technological development and insufficient training. Issues related to the technological development of existing information processing and transmission systems are:

- Data required for the application of tourism models is either not up-to-date or unsuitable.
- Standard software is not able to support the relatively complex tasks in tourism management.
- Specially developed software is too expensive for single tourism businesses. Issues related to the insufficient training of tourism managers are:
- Managers have little knowledge of existing methods or available data.
- Managers are confronted with various data sources and different results and they do not know how to cope with this situation.
- Managers do not know which data sources and models are suitable.

The Transmission of Market Research Data in the Internet

Due to the vital role of tourism in many countries and regions in Europe a number of programs concerning tourism promotion have been installed. Government and private tourism organizations have been established in order to strengthen a tourism destination. Usually the aim is to increase the added value of a region. The major tasks of these bodies are:

- To provide consumers with information about the destination,
- To coordinate and implement sales promotion measures,
- Tourism advertising,
- Support in sales and distribution, and
- To coordinate and implement market research projects.

For most of their tasks (except the coordination and implementation of market research projects) these tourism promoting bodies provide efficient methods. The actual effect of the last item mentioned has been lost in the past due to inefficient instruments relating to the transmission and utilization of declarative and procedural knowledge. Now with the development of cheaper hard- and software many tourism organizations are reconsidering their promotion policy.

In almost all industries systems are being developed in order to support investment and marketing planning. Also the tourism industry has developed decision support systems and the most important applications are: (1) systems supporting marketing decisions in national tourism organizations, (2) travel counselling systems for shipping clerks, (3) systems supporting regional planning regarding the optimal selection of locations in which to invest (4) systems providing tourism portfolio analyses, (5) simulation tools for forecasting travel behaviour in certain regions. In Austria in 1982 the Austrian Society of Applied Research in Tourism (ASART) started a project aiming at the development of a marketing information system for the national tourism organization in Austria (Austrian National Tourist Office).

The first version of the tourism marketing information system (TourMIS) consisted of a database installed in a host system of the Scientific Computer Centre Vienna and an optimization programme for the advertising budget of the Austrian National Tourist Office. Though the programmes were adapted in 1991 in favour of PC-software, and hence became accessible for a greater number of people (mainly employees of tourism organizations in the federal provinces), the area-wide information supply for top managers in the tourism industry did not begin until 1999 when the internet version was introduced.

Tourism Marketing Information System

The major aim of Tour MIS is an optimal information supply and decision support for the tourism industry. The first step is to provide aniline tourism survey data, as well as evaluation programmes to transform data into precious management information. Tour-MIS predominantly comprises:

1. A database containing tourism market research data (declarative knowledge),
2. Various program modules (method-base, procedural knowledge) converting acknowledged methods/models into simple surfaces, and
3. Various administrative programmes which assist the maintenance of the database and track and control the information search behaviour of users.

The internet supports the transport and presentation of animated and unanimated pictures, sound and video recordings and text and numerical data and is expandable. A high-performance SQL-database and a functionally designed user interface for Tour MIS based on hypertext and Perl permits the development of interactive applications. The programme modules contained in the method-base are developed according to the specific requirements of tourism managers. The internet offers a number of advantages against the old PC-solution. Since changes in the database have immediate worldwide effect the speed of information transmission can be reduced to the availability of the information source. For example, Tour MIS makes the monthly projections of Statistics Austria available within only a few seconds to all regional managers of the Austrian National Tourist Office regardless of whether they are located in New York, Sydney, Tokyo or Madrid. Anybody provided with access to the internet and entitled to use Tour MIS may access data and information, make calculations or simulations send or receive data – without tiresome postal procedures, danger of loss, delays and costs. All these advantages have led to a significant expansion in the number of users.

Conditions for the Use of the System

In the beginning Tour MIS was provided with strict access control and used to be only accessible to certain users. In this respect the application did differ from traditional internet offers. However, the present concept is also not an Intranet. Unlike the Intranet which supports internal information management systems Tour MIS is not owned by a certain organization but is open to all authorized tourism organizations, societies, tourism consultants, companies, tourism training centres, pressure groups, etc. in Austria and abroad. By covering the maintenance costs, a consortium of 12 of the most important initiators of market research projects in Austria (Austrian National Tourist Office, nine provincial tourism organizations, the two special interest associations for Hotel Trade and Restaurant.

Trade of the Federal Chamber of Commerce, Federal Ministry for Economic Affairs and Labour Tourism and Recreational Commerce Section) guarantee the continuous updating of the comprehensive database. Since 2000 this initiative has provided the Austrian tourism industry with free access to overall data and functions (with some exceptions) of Tour MIS. The necessary hardware resources are situated at the Institute for Tourism and Leisure Studies at the University of Economics and Business Administration in Vienna where a major part of the necessary maintenance work is carried out.

The Tour MIS Database

In the beginning Tour MIS contained data that was strongly influenced by the internal interests of its commissioner, the Austrian National Tourist Office. In this respect international tourism statistical data, empirical tourism studies and economic indicators for the most important markets of origin for the Austrian tourism industry have been collected in Tour MIS. The PC-version, developed in the early nineties, contained more than 10,000 time series. The periodicity of information was generally based on annual data, however the most significant time series have also been recorded for periods of less than a year. Over the years the database has continually expanded. Due to the increasing importance of overseas markets further information has been required. Unequal needs of provincial tourism organizations led to additional statistics regarding the federal provinces and Vienna, being city and federal province at the same time, acquired an exceptional position. Furthermore data on the Austrian and international city tourism has been added. This information was collected at the branch offices of the Austrian National Tourist Office, transmitted by fax and data was entered manually into the marketing information system in order to be available to users. Later based on international cooperation (European Cities' Tourism, European Travel Commission) the first online maintenance agreements with local tourism organizations were initiated. The most important available data sources of Tour MIS are indicated in. Besides the basic information search functions the method-base has also been continually upgraded. In this respect the system more and more meets the requirements of an efficient decision support tool. In the next paragraphs the most important data sources and the facilities for analysis and reporting are discussed.

National Tourism Statistics Austria

One of the first data sources which was installed in Tour MIS was the official tourism statistics in Austria. Data generated from the registration with accommodation suppliers is one of the fundamental supports of the official inbound tourism statistics in Austria. Accommodation statistics are divided into two different kinds of survey: the accommodation for inbound travel and the accommodation capacity. The data on arrivals and over nights are surveyed for 50 generating countries related to 13 different accommodation types and 1,600 municipalities (= report communities) on a monthly basis.

Thus the official travel survey offers 25 million data points per annum which can be transformed into precious information for tourism managers. From the data material important information on tourism development, trends in markets of origin and accommodation types, evaluation of the competing situation can be derived. For example, for each of the 1,600 municipalities the database allows the user to regularly monitor the development of the average duration of stay, the seasonality, market shares, guest-mix structure, and, in connection with the capacity statistics, the occupancy rate.

Tour MIS presently offers official tourism statistics only at the provincial basis which nevertheless requires maintenance work of 11,700 data sets per month. The necessary data transfer from the host system of Statistic Austria (ISIS) to Tour MIS takes place automatically each time after the arrival of new data segments and in accordance with various maintenance routines.

The information supply of Tour MIS users takes place by means of predominate tables and reports created for the user in real time operations.

The content and design of tables or reports plays an important role in the user's perception of the system's usefulness and usability. Only if the information supply meets the users' needs will the system achieve its aim of providing a high-performance usage of market data and improve the information supply in tourism management.

Source Feature Evaluation Period Update Data

Statistic Austria bed nights, arrivals, capacity (suppliers and beds) 50 countries of origin (markets), 13 types of accommodation – for Austria and her 9 provinces since 1960 monthly secondary data in time series format Austrian Guest Survey 250 variables incl. intention to revisit, guest satisfaction, type of travel, means of transport, duration of stay, travel motive, expenses, selection of accommodation, activities, net income of the household, profession, education, etc. 16 countries of origin (markets) – for Austria and her 9 provinces since 1991 each third year primary data ETC (European Travel Commission) bed nights, arrivals, capacities (beds) 21 countries of origin (markets) – for 33 destinations (countries) in Europe since 1990 annually secondary data in time series format ECT (European Cities' Tourism) bed nights, arrivals, capacities (beds) 21 countries of origin (markets) – for 80 European cities since 1983 annually secondary data in time series format.

Number of visitations in Austrian attractions (Austrian National Tourist Office) number of visits for 240 Austrian attractions federal provinces of Austria since 1998 annually secondary data in time series format Austrian Hotel and Restaurant Panel 60 variables incl. net product, fixed and working assets equity and debt capital,, cash flow, profitability-ures, etc. location, size, category and type of business. Since 1982 annually primary data.

- No particular database knowledge is required by the user,
- The data transformations and calculations implemented in the method-base of Tour MIS allow for adequate problem reporting, and
- The user interface refers to a familiar technical terminology.

Especially for the requirements of the managers in the provincial tourism organizations. The comparison with the developments in other (competitive) destinations permits an evaluation of the market share development in Carinthia.

The analysis in indicates for example that Carinthia could defend its position regarding the three most important markets (Germany, Netherlands, Italy), shown in the increase of market shares, despite the fact that Carinthia experienced a severe loss in bed-nights. On the other hand an apparent success regarding the increased demand of American guests (+ 7,7%) has to be put into perspective since the other federal provinces outperformed Carinthia in this segment. Due to the comparative analysis and a simple and informative presentation of the statistics (using sorting features and different colours to distinguish between market share gains (green) and losses (red)) the data material is upgraded. The analysis presented in may be used for historical or current data, for each Austrian province, based either on arrivals or bednights for each of the 13 different accommodation types.

Competitive Analysis for Austrian Regions

The opportunities for implementing tools which use official tourism statistics for bench-marking analyses, the implementation of early warning systems and forecasting tourism trends is obvious. Due to the refinancing interests of data collection authorities and the lack of financial resources in the tourism industry, however, the data analysis for smaller tourism regions or report communities has been prevented in the past.

This factor must be regretted since it can be assumed that the evaluation of key success factors in tourism marketing will significantly improve when they are measured in smaller regional units. Also tourism managers, especially those operating on a regional level, usually have only very little influence in the organization of nationwide surveys. Therefore, many of the statistical series are based on administrative regions that are not always congruent with actual regional use and by tourists and subsequent flows.

Number of Visitations in Austrian Attractions

The collection of statistical data on leisure-time activities and especially the measurement of visitor arrivals in attractions is a rather complex project. It is rarely executed internationally on a systematic or continuous basis. The major problems lie in the delimitation of the study object and the methods of measurement. Since the early 90's the Austrian National Tourist Office has collected and distributed information on the visitation numbers in Austrian attractions. In close collaboration with the nine provincial tourism organizations a list of 240 Austrian attractions is checked for completeness and updated on an annual basis.

Number of Visitations in Austrian Attractions

Since 2001 this maintenance procedure is carried out online in Tour MIS. Here the market research specialists at the respective provincial tourism organizations enter their information into the system. Due to the newness of the database the reporting facilities are still very limited. The present tables either provide simple time series for a single attraction or list all attractions for one or more federal province(s) arranged according to frequency of visits.

Austrian Guest Survey

Since 1988 alternating each third year a comprehensive visitor survey in Austria has been carried out. The Austrian Guest Survey is one of the most important sources of information in tourism market research. It provides vital information on guest profiles, customer satisfaction, information and booking behaviour, type of travel, destination, means of transport, accommodation, activities, visitor expenditures and other current topics.

The Austrian Guest Survey is financed and coordinated by a consortium of authorities responsible for tourism promotion in Austria (Austrian National Tourist Office and nine provincial tourism organizations), the Chamber of Commerce and the Federal Ministry for Economic Affairs and Labour (Tourism and Recreational Commerce Section). Since the Austrian Guest Survey is a primary study it presents some features which complicate the information diffusion in Tour MIS compared to the above mentioned secondary data sources. The main reasons for these additional difficulties are:

(1) The much wider scope of the study,

(2) The required data analyses are more demanding, and

(3) Interpretation possibilities are limited by the sample size and characteristics.

The Austrian Guest Survey has more than 200 features which are partially modified for each survey. Considering the scope of the study and that only descriptive evaluation is possible the Austrian Guest Survey offers more than 1 million findings per survey. Traditional forms of report (market research report, press releases etc.) cover just a small part of the real investigation and evaluation potential. Thus important questions managers would raise remain unanswered although theoretically the answers exist. Data of primary analyses are available unprocessed (disaggregated data format). Regarding the Austrian Guest Survey there are 10,000 interviews per survey, all of the features being available in quantitative form. However, information processing requires the application of analytical methods ranging from calculating simple mean values to complicated data mining procedures.

The necessary methodological knowledge has to be obtained from statistics experts who create costs which, in most cases, cannot be covered by the tourism industry. Therefore, due to a lack of know-how or lacking financial support, many questions managers raise remain unanswered although data actually would be available. Contrary to a census, as found in official statistics, sample surveys do not integrate all elements of the whole picture into the study. The major aim in statistics is to draw reliable conclusions regarding to the totality from a limited number of elements. The previously mentioned evaluation procedures take more effort and interpretation depends on the features of the sample (sample size and sampling technique).

Automatic Selection of Analysing Methods

In addition the user may select only a certain part of the overall data set for evaluation (i.e. data of a certain province or market). In order to prevent interpretation errors due to unreliability of results, those values based on a small sample are only indicated after informing the user about the problem.

The analysis takes place in real time. Tour MIS provides the facilities to evaluate more than one survey, at the same time offering two alternatives: longitudinal and cross section analyses. The first application informs the tourism manager about changes in the guest behaviour over a specified period of time. Query support is provided by offering only variables surveyed unmodified over the overall selected period of time (i.e. the standard questionnaire programme). The latter application increases the sample size (for 4 surveys more than 45,000 interviews) which makes answers to detailed questions possible (assuming a particular time invariance, of course). This function permits for example reliable results about the share of side expenses of Italian guests in the federal province of Salzburg during a particular season.

Comparison of Hotel and Restaurant Groups

The database supports regional planners and tourism managers in their decisions as well as managers in the hospitality industry. The results of the past 10 years of a project which has been executed by the Austrian Society of Applied Research in Tourism and commissioned by the Austrian Hotel and Restaurant Association situated within the Austrian Federal Chamber of Commerce are presented in Tour MIS. In this project operating data and annual financial statements for hotels and restaurants in Austria are compared on an annual basis. Information collected directly from the businesses with a high level of itemization is supplemented with comprehensive, compressed data stored at cooperative industry related organizations such as the Wirts chafts for derungs institute der Austrian Federal Economic Chamberund Tourism us bank and Burges Forder ungsbank of the Austrian Federal Ministry of Economic Affair and Labour. In connection with the design and evaluation of continually repeated surveys a number of new approaches for the diagnosis and comparison of industry groups are developed. Tour MIS presently provides the following applications:

- Industry information for more than 1,300 hotels and restaurants per year since 1991.
- Various functions supporting key ratio analyses in the hotel and restaurant industry.
- The chance for hotel and restaurant managers to participate online in the most significant hotel and restaurant panel survey in Austria.

Information about more than 50 different key ratios is provided in the form of arithmetic mean and median values for 30 distinguished industry groups. Within the industry groups additional evaluations for businesses of excellent profitability (best practice enterprises) are available. For the hotel and restaurant panel database Tour MIS users are provided with the following query and analysing facilities:

- Evaluation of a key ratio for all industry groups referring to a certain year.
- Comparison of all key ratios for a particular industry group.
- Development of a key ratio uncovering the main industry developments.
- Benchmarking analysis for a particular hotel or restaurant (only provided when managers are actively participating in the study).

The quality of information based on the results of the survey is strongly influenced by the number of participating businesses. Due to the chance for interaction in the internet the first results may be obtained straight after entering business data. In this context the problem of how to prevent participants from entering incorrect data occurs. Tour MIS offers a number of plausibility controls during data entry and records data in a second, temporary database. At regular intervals experts determine which records are qualified to be stored in the general database.

Analysis of the User Behaviour of Tour MIS

How do we know that we have successfully implemented a system? Researchers have not really agreed on an indicator for successful implementation. One appealing approach is a cost-benefit study. In this evaluation, one totals the costs of developing a system and compares them with the benefits resulting form the system. In theory, this sounds like a good indicator of success, but in practice it is difficult to provide meaningful estimates. Obtaining the cost side of the ratio is not too much of a problem if adequate records are kept during the development of the system. However, an evaluation of the benefits of a computer-based information system is difficult. How can the value of improved information processing be measured? With transactions processing and some operational control systems, it is usually possible to show tangible savings. For example, many transactions systems have resulted in increased productivity in processing paperwork without a proportional increase in cost. Operational control systems, such as those used to control inventories in large hotels and restaurants, may reduce inventory balances, saving storage and investment costs while maintaining existing service levels. For systems that aid a decision maker, it is much more difficult to estimate the benefits. For a marketing information system, like Tour MIS, use of the system is voluntary. A manager or other user receives a report but does not have to use the information on it or

1. Council of the European Union, Council Directive 95/97/EEC of 23 November 1995 on the collection of statistical information in the field of tourism, Official Journal. L291 of 6 December 1995.
2. Commission of the European Communities Report to the Council, the European Parliament, the Economic and Social Committee and the Committee of Regions on the Application of the Directive of the Council 95/97/EEC on the compilation of statistical data in the field of tourism, 17 January 2001, even read the report.

In particular systems that provide aniline retrieval of information from a database can be classified as voluntary since the use of such a system is frequently at the discretion of the user. For this type of system where use is voluntary, it is generally accepted that high levels of use is a sign of successful implementation.

In this case the economic or personal success of its users is indirectly measured by the frequency of usage. Several authors have shown that the frequency of usage is determined by the perceived usefulness (textual component) and the ease of use (technical component). The acceptance of Tour MIS can be determined by means of constantly updated and aniline available access statistics. Contrary to other internet applications the accesses to websites is not counted but the number of virtually answered queries is. Results of the Tour MIS statistics are therefore not influenced by website characteristics (number of graphics or distortions due to the application of window techniques), but do represent the 'genuine user acceptance'. In addition, the comprehensive protocol system permits the analysis of queries broken down into various user groups, information sources and the type of query.

The community of Tour MIS users has continually developed. In 1998 there were only 50 registered users at the Austrian National Tourist Office and at the end of 2001 more than 1,000 registered Tour MIS users have been counted. The distribution of user groups indicates that Tour MIS is not only favoured by tourism managers (44.6%), but also by employees, students and pupils of education and research institutes (31.6% of all queries) and other non-tourism professionals or private persons (23.8%). The distribution of various user groups is present. The average number of queries per user in 2001 and therefore indicates the frequency of use for a specific Tour MIS user group. The employees of provincial tourism organizations use Tour-MIS most (92 queries per user) due to the comprehensive data material available on the federal provinces. The students, as the largest user group, show a relatively low number due to only temporal interest (for a seminar paper or a diploma thesis they need access to data material only once). The number of accommodation providers and F&B managers using the system is, considering the number of existing businesses, very low. A reason for this is probably that the most interesting information source for this user group (the Austrian hotel and restaurant panel database) is a relatively new data set that is simply not known by the managers. Overall, 34.538 queries have been processed in 2001, signifying an increase of 35.5% in comparison to the previous year (25,492 queries).

About half of all queries are made regarding the official tourism statistics in Austria. The industry appears to be very interested in the development of the major markets of origin and accommodation types in the federal provinces (on average approx. 50 queries per day). Regarding the official statistics for Austria most queries are made in connection with information concerning monthly statistics (20% of all queries). The international data sources ECT and ETC gained 18.7% respectively and they rank behind the official Austrian statistics. The significant increase of queries regarding these two international data sources as well as the tendency towards English queries, however, indicate a growing international interest in Tour MIS. The assessment of demand of information certainly needs a more detailed investigation than simply monitoring the current use of market research resources. However, in Tour-MIS 'demand of information' not only refers to the principal (statistical) sources, but also to the sort of data transformations (analysis) and formats of automatically generated reports available to the users. The functional characteristics and the design of the system have always been developed in close collaboration with the affected managers. For instance, concerning the development of the decision support tools part of the international data sources in the system, the developers have met more than 20 times in form of working group meetings and seminars with representatives (CEOs and research directors) of European Cities Tourism and the European Travel Commission. The involvement of the managers in the design and operation of the information system resulted in favourable user attitudes and perceptions of the information system and led to higher levels of use. In the beginning only a few members were able and willing to actively contribute to this project by entering their data on a regular basis. Today, more than 100 managers working in different tourism destination marketing organizations, based in more than 30 different European countries, and speaking more than 15 different languages, are obviously convinced by the significance of the project and the value of the system as they regularly and voluntarily enter their data into the system.

Conclusions

Generally speaking tourism managers benefit from access to the internet in two ways: the internet provides the opportunity to communicate and serves as a platform for new distribution channels. The present article does not deal with new distribution channels and new booking systems in the tourism industry. This undoubtedly important topic has been discussed in an number of publications and symposia. The present article introduced Tour MIS, an aniline accessible decision support tool for tourism and hospitality management which has been successfully used by more than 1,000 users for three years. According to Ritchie and Ritchie for the development of an industry supported destination marketing information system, information must be both generally accessible and widely advertised so that managers are aware of the benefits it offers. In lieu of a more preferable cost-benefit analysis, the success of Tour MIS was analysed by studying actual system use observed from various log files generated by the system. The merits of this form of evaluation lie in the objectivity of the findings, the cost-effective procedure, and the comparability of the estimates when the analysis are performed on a regular basis.

The major reason for the poor application of management science models and methodologies in tourism management is the insufficient education of practitioners and the inadequacy of problem solving features of standard software solutions. The development of simple, affordable (shareware) programs, downloadable for every tourism manager, is the first step into a new era of dialogue between research and practice. Within a short time, for internal diagnosis, forecasts and simulations on the net there will be high-performance computer languages available which are now being developed by major international software producers.

Technological progress will also offer benefits for the electronic transmission of tourism market research data. Interdisciplinary research projects will be challenged with tourism research, research in statistics and commercial information technology. For example there are still a number of problems to be solved in order to be able to jointly use ecoscopic and demoscopic tourism data within a marketing information system. These combination options require a constant standardization of information sources as well as new approaches towards the methodological processing of data gained from various studies. Another vital research initiative will be the development of information systems about themselves? Optimizing the knowledge presentation of 'service quality in information services' has been neglected in the past. By applying and accepting decision support systems the significance of this field of research will increase. Another important factor will be the role system imminent? Protocol presentations play, which are continually improved. Thus data on the user behaviour offers not only information on necessary improvements in the data processing of tourism market research results, but also on the future focus of tourism market research.

The sudden explosion of data and the growing need for information challenges basic research as far as data reduction and decision support methods are concerned. Therefore existing concepts for qualitative forecasts and market reaction models and their calibration options in a marketing information system have to be reconsidered. In this respect projects which aim at a systematic and regular compilation of experiences experts made with regard to various technical subjects (i.e. short-term development of singular markets of origin) are considered to be promising. It is their aim to provide an improved evaluation of future market developments and eventually to integrate the findings into the strategic planning of national and regional tourism organizations and businesses. Another necessary development regards already existing data collections and the processing of the European cities' statistics. In this respect this author has observed many shortcomings relating to the international comparability of the data. The improved communication possibilities provided by the new medium stimulates critical discussions and behavioural learning among all participants. Within European Cities Tourism, among other things, new initiatives to evaluate one city's major competitors have been released due to the managers' increased awareness of the importance of this problem.

The trend towards globalization in research, where the internet plays a vital role, refers also to tourism research. To those critics who refer to the internet as uncontrolled growing, complicated and in its applications too playful, supporters used to point out that one day smart and profitable applications would be found. That is where we stand now. The new areas of responsibility regional and national tourism managers are confronted with today, not only suggest shortcomings in education but also promise new opportunities for the next manager generations to acquire status.

2

Tourism Services

There is an interrelationship between the nature or characteristics of the tourism services and the marketing mix. Hence, there is a need to take into consideration the 7 key issues while determining the criteria of the Marketing Mix (4 Ps).

The Marketing Mix

The most important factor is consumer perception of price:

- Consumer may choose not to buy when offering is perceived to be of lesser value than the asking price. Hence, bookings or visits will decline.
- If price is low in relation to value offered, then demand will be difficult to manage and revenue loss could be substantial.

The marketer's task is to maintain a balance between; Value Perceived (Quality) & Price.

Price and Demand

- Price has little to do with cost, and far more to do with what customer arc prepared to pay for a product.
- How well a changed in price affect a change in total demand—price elasticity of demand.
- In a market where the product is unique, or without satisfactory substitute, or where-the product is manufactured by a company that enjoys a monopoly or near monopoly, price will be set high.
- In setting the prices, the company will want to know what levels of demand it is likely to experience at different prices. For a new product this is hard to gauge. The:

Two most common methods of assessing demand are:

b) Asking potential customers what they would be willing to pay for service

c) Test marketing the product at different prices in different regions.

How can price be used to control consumer demand?

- Maximize access.
- Restrict access.
- Control demand in time.
- Control demand in space.

Pricing Methods

Cost-plus Pricing

- A standard mark-up is added to the cost of the product.
- E.g. A bottle of wine that costs $14 may sell for $28, a 100% mark-up on cost.

Going Rate Pricing

- A strategy of going-rate pricing is the establishment of price based largely on those of competitors, with less attention paid to costs or demand.
- The firm might charge the same, more, or less than its major competitors. Some firm might charge a bit more or less, but they hold the amount of difference constant.

Skimming Pricing

- Price skimming is setting a high price when the market is price insensitive. (Higher-end market).
- To be used when:
  - o Highly differentiated product.
  - o Inelastic demand.
  - o Maximize shortrun profit when product has short life cycle or demand exceeds supply over a short time period.
  - o Premium product with added value.

Penetration Pricing

- Companies set a low initial price to penetrate the market quickly and deeply, attracting many buyers and winning a large market share.

- To be used when:
  a) Little product differentiation.
  b) Many competitive substitutes.
  c) Inferior product.

Place

- It is place that represents distribution of and access to the product.
- In tourism industries, distribution systems are used to move the customer to the product: hotel, restaurant cruise ship or aeroplane.
- Various distribution channels or intermediaries are used to market tourism services.
- Distribution channels or Intermediaries are used to describe any dealer who acts as a link in the chain of distribution between the company and its customers.

Distribution Channel Functions

(1) *Information*-gathering and distributing marketing research and intelligence information about the marketing environment.

(2) *Promotion*-developing and spreading persuasive communication about an offer.

(3) *Contact*-finding and communicating with prospective buyers.

(4) *Matching*-shaping and fitting the offer to the buyers' needs.

(5) *Negotiation*-agreeing on price and other terms of the offer so that ownership or possession can be transferred.

(6) *Physical distribution*-transporting and storing goods.

(7) *Financing*-acquiring and using funds to cover the cost of channel work.

(8) *Risk taking*-assuming financial risks, such as the inability to sell inventory at full margin.

Why do companies choose to deal with intermediaries?

(1) It is cheaper for a company to deal through intermediaries than to set up its own network of retail shops or sell its product directly in any other way By paying a commission or other agreed form of financial remuneration to their intermediaries, companies buy the use of distributive network.

(2) The system also acts as a convenience to consumers as they can choose from a range of different products under one roof,

instead of having to visit each producer's shop in turn to select their product.

(3) Through their contact, experience and specialization, intermediaries normally offer more than a firm can on its own Managing, Monitoring and Modifying Channels Channel systems will require periodic review and modification to meet changing market needs. Organizations will need to review the success of their channel systems regularly and determine is all the participants are performing at an acceptable level. It may be necessary to:

- Either expand or reduce membership at various levels or drop some existing channel members who are no longer performing.
- Change direction or consider totally new ways of looking at the business.

This is happening as the interest in call centres grows and hotels are reviewing the need for hotel representatives where call centres might be able to achieve the same results more cost effectively. Similarly, major changes are taking place in computer reservations systems with every advance in technology.

Promotion

- o Is an aspect of general marketing that promotion management deals with explicitly.
- o It includes the practices of advertising, personal selling, sales promotion, publicity and point-of-purchase communications.

Why promotional activities are carried out?

All marketing communication efforts are directed at accomplishing one or more of the following objectives:

1. Build product category wants.
2. Create brand awareness.
3. Enhance attitudes and influence intentions.
4. Facilitate purchase.
5. Promotional Mix Strategies.

Most leisure and tourism organisations use a combination of promotional activities including:

1. *Advertising:* the paid-tor sponsorship of a message in a commercially available medium. The media (press, broadcast:

television and radio, posters/billboards, cinema) task is essentially to choose and buy the most economical combination of advertising space and/or time to reach defined audiences sufficiently frequently and with sufficient impact to convey the agreed messages effectively.

2. *Sales Promotion:* Those marketing activities other than personal selling and advertising and publicity that stimulate purchasing and dealer effectiveness, such as displays, shows and exhibitions, demonstrations and various non-recurrent selling efforts not in ordinary routine. Sales Promotion can be targeted at consumers, the trade and the company.
3. *Public Relations:* PR in tourism is about how people who matter to a tourism organisation think about it and how their perceptions, attitudes and behaviour can be kept or made positive. *External PR* involves everything an organisation does that impinges on people's perceptions including: its products; its employees; its communication programmes and media coverage, its overall corporate identity; its financial reputation; its promotional activities; the buildings in which it transacts business — in short everything that contributes to the *image* of an organisation. *Internal PR* is used to build and maintain morale within an organisation through such things as good communication practices, incentive benefits, sportsman activity provision, etc.
4. *Direct Marketing:* Tourism organisations make heavy use of promotional materials mailed out or given away to customers or passed on to them by intermediaries Photographs are a crucial element of mass tour brochures. Also, maps, a critical part in tourism promotion in generating interest in a destination. One of the most difficult things to achieve in brochures aimed at the mass market is competitive differentiation.
5. *Personal Selling:* An interpersonal process whereby the seller ascertains, activates and satisfies the needs and wants of the buyer so that both the seller and buyer benefits. It is a method of influencing the purchase. The selling sequence include prospecting and qualifying, planning and delivering sales presentations, overcoming objections and closing the sale.

Product

Problems in Managing Services

The effectiveness of planning the marketing mix depends as much on the ability to select the right target market as on the skill in devising a product which will generate high levels of satisfaction. Hence, the decision depends very much on the capability of the marketers to tackle the following issues concerning tourism services:

Intangible Nature of Business

Customer cannot physically evaluate or sample most services: they tend to rely on other people's experiences with these services Customers place great value on the advice of hospitality and travel experts, such as travel agents Implications:

- Tourism marketers tend to 'tangibilize' the tourism offering in brochures and videos-visual displays of the real thing.
- Marketers tend to generate positive "word-of-mouth" among the customers.

Variability in Production Methods

Quality control of services is neither as precise nor as easy to achieve because of the human factors that are involved in supplying them All staff members cannot consistently provide the same level of service as their colleagues

- Although standardised service is an admirable target that all organisations should try to achieve it is unrealistic.
- The same standardisation cannot be provided since the actions of service staff, other+customers and the customers themselves make the experience more variable.
- Hotels, restaurants, airlines, theme parks and travel agencies are some of the 'factories' in the business. Behaviour of one customer can ruin the service experience of others.
- Implications:
    - Tourism marketer design processes to minimise differences in service encounters and provision between different outlets or between different shifts at a hotel. Example: Provision of uniforms and of similar physical surroundings illustrates evidence of standardisation.

Perishability

- Service is highly perishable-"like a running tap in a sink with no plug".
- An unoccupied seat on a train or bed in a guesthouse is lost forever.
- Services and the time available to experience them cannot be stored.

- Implications:
  - o The management task emphasises managing demand and capacity to a degree of time tuning. Example: Airlines offer stand by fares to those willing to fill unexpected empty seats at short notice.

Distribution Channels

There is no physical distribution system in tourism industry. Instead, there are many intermediaries in the hospitality and travel industry where the items are being purchased.

Cost Determination

Services are both variable and intangible. Some customers might require more attention than others.

Relationship of Services to Providers

- Some services are inseparable from the individuals who provide them.
- Example: Restaurant-whose chefs or owners have developed unique reputations for their food, personalities or both.
- Implications:
  - o Marketers attempt to devise delivery systems which ease interaction and invest in campaigns to educate staff and consumers as to how to get the best from the interaction.
  - o Training in hotels emphasises how staff can manage the interaction.

Target Marketing

- In tourism industry, we need to acknowledge that not all individuals would want to buy from us.
- Me might not have the services that they may be looking for.
- And hence, it is important to consider targeting the right market to ensure success of our business.
- Marketing is about developing the right product/service to the right market/people so that they will be satisfied with what they receive.
- Target marketing can be defined as:
  a) Seller identifies market segments (groups), selects one or more and develops products and marketing mixes tailored to each selected segments.

Market Segmention

- Involves dividing market into distinct groups of buyers who requires different products or marketing mixes.
- There is no single way to segment a market
- MaNor variables include.
  - (a) Geographic Segmentation divide market according to location e.g. nations, regions, states, countries, cities.
  - (b) Demographic Segmentation divide market into groups, based on demographic variables e.g. age, gender, family life cycle, income, occupation, education, religion, race/culture, nationality.
  - (c) psychographic Segmentation divide buyers into different groups, based on social class, lifestyle, and personality characteristics.
  - (d) Behaviour Segmentation buyer is divided into groups, based on knowledge, attitude, usage rate, and response.

Refers to the buying behaviour of final customers (individuals and households) to buy goods and services for personal consumption MaNor factors influencing buying behaviour include.

E Ypxyvi Jegxsvw

Culture comprise of the basic values, perceptions, want and behaviour that a person learns continuously in a society Culture is expressed through tangible items such as food, buildings, clothing and art. e.g. the culture shift toward greater concern about health and fitness has resulted in many hotels adding exercise rooms/health clubs. e.g. KFC, piazza and Burger King in Israel adapted their menus to make them kosher for Passover (.ewish) Subculture groups of population with shared value system base oncommon experiences and situations Social classesare relatively permanent and ordered divisions in a society whose members share similar values, interests and behaviours e.g. income, occupation, education, wealth Social classes show distinct product and brand preferences in such areas as food, travel and leisure activity. e.g. CE3, managers and directors organizations often indulge in golfing activities.

Reference Group

A personvs refer group consists of all the groups that have a direct/ indirect influence on the personvs attitude/behaviour e.g. artist, idol Family Marketers have examined the role and influence of the husband, wife and children on the purchase of different products and services.

Roles and Status: A person position in each group can be defined in terms of role and status a role consists of the activities that a person is expected to perform each role carried a status e.g. pinna parents daughter Family wife/mother Company staff.

B9=ER DECISI32 4R3CESS

This model emphasizes that the buying process starts long before and continues long after the actual purchases It encourages marketer to focus on the entire buying process rather than Nust the purchasing decision.

Problem Recognition

The buying process starts when the buyer recognizes a problem or need.

The need can be triggered by internal and external stimuli. They should research customers to find out what kinds of needs/problems, led them to purchase an items, what brought these needs about, and how they led consumers to choose a particular product. E.g. SPA Travel relaxation/need to get out of city life.

Information Search

1. The strength of drive.
2. The amount of initial information.
3. The ease of obtaining the information.
4. The value placed on additional information.
5. The satisfaction one gets from search.

Consumer can obtain information from several sources personal sources family, friends, neighbours, acquaintances Commercial sources z sales person, packaging, advertising, dealers, displays public sources z restaurant reviews, editorials in the travel section Therefore, a company must design its marketing mix to make prospects aware of and knowledgeable about the features and benefits of its products/ brands.

E.g. TRA:E0 Fair

(1) promote in newspaper (create awareness).

(2) initial information (from newspaper or a call to travel agent).

(3) obtain information from internet, visit travel agents.

(4) value (are the information of high quality trustworthy).

(5) satisfaction (are consumers happy with the search).

Evaluation of Alternatives

- o This is the stage where consumer makes an assessment of the goods/services offered and is considering the alternatives.
- o The marketer must ensure that his product/service is on the list of alternatives.
- o The buyer must be convinced of its suitability before the buyer can proceed to the buying/purchase decision.
- o The product/service must be readily available to the consumer.

Purchase Decision

- o The buyer would have made a decision by now as to which product/service is suitable to fulfil his/her needs.
- o The ideal product would have all the attributes/characteristics that the customer is looking for:
  - Then the decision to purchase is made, the product that is thought to be most suitable will be selected.
  - However, 2 factors can influence the purchase intention and the purchase decision.
    - (i) Attitudes of others (getting information from relatives/ family members).
    - (ii) Unexpected situational factors (e.g. earthquakes, flood, SARS, effect of tsunami).

Post Purchase Behaviour

- o Feelings felt by the buyer towards the product offer that has been purchased.
- o To avoid post purchase dissonance, there must be no gap between the expectations of the buyer and the actual product performance.
- o The buyervs decision to buy the product again later will depend on the buyervs satisfaction with the product performance.

Paper on Community Travel and Tourism Marketing

Every community if affected by visitors. While many communities recognize opportunities for growth in the tourism industry, options at the local level expand when travellers are included. Travellers are people away from home temporarily. In collecting data, sometimes "more than miles away from home" further defines a traveller.

This travel may result from a variety of sources: a pleasure vacation, business and convention purposes, friends and relatives, special events and festivals, sport recreation, historic sites, specific attractions, or when people pass-through headed for another destination. The cash register doesn't sort out travel purchases this way, and in reality it is impractical to separate tourists from travellers. All visitors are important to the travel and tourism industry.

Minnesota is experiencing a boom in communities organizing to attract and host visitors as a way to diversify and boost economies. The impact of travel and tourism on the local economy goes beyond first level expenditures at food, lodging, gas, entertainment, and retail establishments. Travel spending brings in outside dollars that "turn over" in the community. Even if you do not have direct contact with travellers, the money filters through the entire economy as residents re-spend travel dollars. But the increased interest in tourism translates to fierce competition in the marketplace.

Key to gaining the attention of potential tourists is development of a community marketing, not a selling approach. Marketing is a continuous, coordinated set of activities associated with efficiently distributing products to high potential markets. It involves making decisions about product, price, promotion, and distribution. Marketing focuses on providing customer benefits and satisfying needs better than the competition. It is based on the principle that consumer buying resistance will be overcome if the product satisfies buyer needs.

In contrast, selling focuses on the product offered rather than satisfying customer needs. It assumes that the main thing necessary to sell the product is to overcome purchase resistance. A statement reflecting the selling approach is "we will attract tourists to Our City because we want tourists and everyone would want to visit. Selling is only a small part of marketing. The formal marketing process involves six steps:

- Analyse your current situation.
- Identify product(s).
- Select target market(s).
- Set objectives.
- Carry out promotion strategies.
- Evaluate results.

When the structure to support tourism is in place-1) attractions, 2) services and facilities, 3) an information/direction/interpretive system, and 4) transportation linkages-communities can move to market their unique tourist and travel experiences. This publication outlines one approach for preparing a marketing that describes how you will get visitors to stop, to stay, to tell others, and to return.

Analyse your Current Situation

What does your community have that travellers want? The first step in the marketing process is to conduct an inventory and analysis of the travel and tourism industry and its potential within your area. Tourism isn't just a community or collection of small businesses with an interest in attracting visitors. Tourism is an entire "region" organizing to draw and host travellers-it's an overall view with a wide angle lens. Analysis answers the question "what is?" As a basis for "what could be?" Ten crucial questions for a community to answer on a regular basis include:

1. What attractions exist that will entice people to stop and visit?
2. What hospitality services and facilities are available?
3. What experiences are visitors having in the community?
4. What promotion methods are used? How well do they work?
5. What are the current markets?
6. What is the competition for your community?
7. How is tourism related to the community lifestyle and goals?"
8. What roles do community organizations play in tourism development?
9. What are trends that affect the tourism industry?
10. What are the community strengths and weaknesses, problems and opportunities in serving visitors?

Attractions (Question 1)

Through fate or creativity, most communities have tourist attractions that draw visitors. A community's basic assets may include:

- Natural resources, or a scenic setting;
- Human-made attractions such as racetracks, museums, or resorts;
- Historical sites;
- Cultural and ethnic resources;

- Recreation opportunities;
- Special events and festivals;
- Availability of high quality personal services such as shopping, medical care and education; or
- Local industries and economic base.

Describe each attraction, including quality. How many of each type of attraction are there? Look forward and list potential visitor resources that could be enhanced or used more fully. The Minnesota Extension Service publication "So Community Wants Tourism" outlines the range of travel attractors that determine a community's capability to bring travellers.

As you develop a community tourism campaign, it is useful to separate "core" attractions that are a prime reason for travel, from secondary "supporting" attractions that enhance a visitor's experience once they are there. There are infinite reasons to visit Minneapolis and St. Paul, but Twin Cities Attractions Council is organized to promote the plus theatres, museums, special events, and other core attractions that draw large audiences. This distinction is useful when you are selecting an image for your marketing program. The Spicer area tourism committee has developed a four-tier list of tourism assets: most important (includes Green Lake, resorts, 2 hours to Twin Cities); important (Sibley State Park, fishing, golf course); significant (fall colours, hunting, July 4 celebration); and contributing (antique shops, sailing regattas, farm tours). Spicer's marketing theme reflects this ranking.

Hospitality Services (Question 2)

The economic impact of tourism largely comes from spending in the hospitality sector primarily composed of private commercial businesses. The U.S. Travel Data Centre estimates tourist dollar expenditures on a state wide basis by category (1985):

* Food $0.26,
* Public transportation.25,
* Auto transportation.17,
* Lodging.15,
* Entertainment & recreation.09,
* Retail and other.08,
* $1.00.

It is useful to have local or regional expenditure data to track the travel industry and develop public support for this economic sector.

However, data collection requires a visitor survey, and study and questionnaire design are complex. Seek assistance from industry professionals in developing a data base that accurately represents spending patterns.

Good restaurants and sufficient overnight lodging capacity are essential. Describe the mix of establishments, their occupancy, and their services.

For example, do motels have facilities for families such as pools and playgrounds, or are they positioned to attract business meetings where evening entertainment may be a factor in the decision to make reservations? Grocery stores, specialty retail shops, entertainment and service stations also support the visitor industry.

Questions about the adequacy of public services come into play. Transportation issues such as roadway congestion, parking and signing, restroom availability, and utilities (sewage and trash disposal) assume importance as the industry expands. Plans for a proposed megamall in the Twin include construction to widen roads in the area.

Tourism Today (Questions 3, 4, and 5)

The tourism experience your community promotes now, whether or accidental, is generally a good indicator for the future. It is often easier to modify and market a travel experience that has evolved over time and is built on local flavour, than Do introduce and develop a new form of tourism that does not match local culture, environment, and heritage. Mississippi Rivertown Rendezvous, an organization promoting the towns along the river corridor from Hastings to Winona, builds upon a common heritage and landscape.

Describe the visitor experience your community offers both in terms of tangibles: the resorts, the boating, the location, as well as the intangibles. Talk about customer benefits when you think about intangibles: rest and relaxation, friendliness, excitement. Then outline and valuate promotion strategies now in use to envision future options. Through survey or observation, determine who is buying your community's experience now. Customers who have visited (even though there may have been no major promotion campaign) are a good clue about the target market your community naturally appeals to.

Outside Influences (Questions 6 through 9)

Tourism marketing occurs within a competitive marketplace that goes well beyond the community boundaries. There are many forms of competition for your customers and their dollars-but neighbouring communities generally are not one of them. A number of strong travel-oriented communities, working together on regional promotion, results in a stronger destination image, a greater variety of attractions and facilities, wider market exposure, and a healthy degree of competition that spurs improvements. The Land of Legends group-a ring of communities within 60 miles of Itasca State Park could not promote itself as a major destination without the involvement of many Chambers of Commerce. This "critical mass" of diverse attractions and quality services also enables the Land of Legends area to attract and host "fam" (familiarization) tours for travel writers and tour brokers as part of an overall marketing program.

More important, there is competition for how consumers spend their discretionary dollar. The purchase of a VCR, buying a more expensive car, or saving for a college education means less money is available for leisure and travel. You also have to be concerned with other destination areas on a national level. Consumers have worldwide choices today; you must understand your competition and their strategies to market your competitive advantages.

In promoting certain visitor experiences, assess what type of tourism is compatible with local lifestyles. For example, many residents of northwestern Minnesota enjoy the hunting opportunities. They use the same resource nonlocal hunters use. Conflicts over resource use must be negotiated before hunting is promoted as a primary visitor attraction. In other areas, emphasis on scattered small town activities is more appropriate than major new construction and facility development. The latest brochure for Southeastern Minnesota Historic Bluff Country emphasizes small-scale tourism businesses such as canoe rental, locally made arts and crafts, bed and breakfasts, and a lefsa factory tour. It is a format designed to encourage travellers to wander and explore the area, rather than directing everyone to a few major sites. In addition, specify the roles various community organizations play in development and promotion, and understand social trends that influence your market position. React quickly when they occur. For example, the move toward shorter getaway mini-vacations is radically changing travel industry strategies.

Where are We Now? (Question 10)

Summarize findings on community attractions, services and facilities, the current travel industry and outside influences in a Written summary statement. Combine relevant in an outline of community strengths and weaknesses, problem opportunities for tourism. Spend sufficient time on this step: analysis is the basis for subsequent decisions about marketing your community's unique visitor experiences.

Identify Product

What is your community marketing? One main reason people travel is to experience a new and different environment. After the situation analysis, most communities find they are faced with multiple options for attracting tourists. The challenge is to choose one dominant identity among all these alternatives. You can not and should not promote all of the community attributes equally. In a tourism marketplace where consumers are faced with diverse choices, need an "edge" to set yourself apart from the competition. You need to create a unique product with a theme or identity that characterizes major promotion efforts. Red Lake Riverlands-Red Lake Falls, Thief River Falls, Crookston, East Grand Forks-features river uses like tubing and boat tours, and nearby food and lodging services. The thirteen Iron Trail United Communities capitalize on the unique mining characteristics and strong ethnic heritage of the Range. Iron world, with its train and festival series, Hill Annex Mine and Tower-Soudan State Park are the core attractions that support the mining theme. A region-wide visitor newspaper and radio information network are part of this cooperative marketing approach.

An example from the private sector is three ski resorts that offer the same hills, the same snow, and the same lift equipment. One business bills itself as a "mountain of hospitality," another is a family resort and the third sells serious, technical skiing.

A marketing theme is the one main idea or message you want to communicate. It should be based on satisfying visitor needs. Theme development requires creativity, and there are advertising agencies that specialize in "positioning" a product in the marketplace and developing a parallel marketing campaign. Consult the Minnesota Extension Service sheet "Creating a Tourism Promotional Theme.

Select Target Markets

Who will buy the product your community is marketing? One certain way to fail is to try to please everyone. A target market is a group of individuals sharing common characteristics, toward whom marketing efforts will be directed. The process of dividing the total market into high-potential target markets is called market segmentation and involves these steps:

- Identifying and describing the different segments that make up the total market;

- Evaluating the economic potential of each segment;
- Choosing one or more market segments on which to focus.

Current visitors are a good indication of target markets attracted to your community. New prospects are likely to have many of the same characteristics unless you are planning a product shift. Target markets can be defined by several factors: geography, demographics, and behaviour.

Geography refers to potential visitors: where they live and they travel. Negative travel time and positive attraction factors are recognized widely as the two main variables that determine what customers choose to see and where they choose to go. Travel time and distance can be negative factors for potential visitors, but the power of an area's tourist attractions may be a counteracting positive factor. A destination that offers a large variety of interesting attractions has more pull, at an equal distance, than a location that offers only one or a few low interest attractions. This doesn't cancel the fact that travel to and from an area is an important part of the total experience, as "pass-through" communities have discovered. Demographics refers to characteristics like age, sex, marital status, number and ages of children and life stage (young single adult or retired) that have direct and obvious effects on travel patterns. For example, unmarried men and married couples with young children have vastly different spending patterns. Behaviour refers to how potential tourists act, such as length of stay, new us. Repeat visitors, and skills (novice expert). But market segmentation using behaviour variables also refers to why they behave as they do, their interests, and their values. There are many factors that affect travel by individual consumers: the reasons for travel, activities enjoyed during travel, a person's general interests and opinions about travel, and personal values.

For one person, travel may mean a tour of museums, monuments and other cultural attractions. Another person may travel to a meeting of a professional organization. A third person seeks amusement at a sporting event; another visits a park to fish. For different reasons they engage in different activities while travelling and value different types of attractions.

Information on behaviour can be difficult and expensive to collect. Some details are available from observing visitors analysing existing records, but most knowledge is likely to come from surveys or interviews. Work with a marketing professional about survey design to assure a representative sample if you try this method. New and even established host communities must evaluate each major target market for its economic potential. Consider your product and estimate the drawing power of the attractions. Think about proximity to metropolitan areas and the quality of the transportation network. Consider the of people travelling near your area; consult Minnesota Department of Transportation records.

Use size and accessibility of the target market as criteria. There must be enough members of the target market justify the investment in reaching them. You must be able to reach the target market through a standard form of promotion. Boaters, runners, and anglers, for example, are very accessible: they belong to organizations and read specialized publications. In contrast, young single parents less accessible market because there is no common affiliation or central source of information.

Finally, select one or more of the target markets. You can concentrate on a single target market to the exclusion of all others, or you can use a strategy where promotion campaigns are developed for two or more markets simultaneously.

It is likely you will change market segments during the season in the same way resort operators shift their marketing efforts from anglers (spring) to families (summer) to retired couples (fall). Most important, a community shouldn't try to be all things to all consumers. Primary destination areas like the Twin Cities, state offices of tourism, and major attractions such as Disneyland have the resources to accomplish that. You are much more likely to be successful if you narrow down the target market you want to reach.

Set Marketing Objectives

Now write down marketing objectives that clearly state what community wants to accomplish in its promotion campaign. Objectives keep energy and action focused on what's important. They help you track your success and judge when it is time to review and shift strategies. A good objective contains four elements:

- A specific action of interest such as increased visitation, sales volume, or awareness;
- A measurable outcome, expressed in dollars, a percentage or numbers for example, that indicates how much change will
- A time frame within which the action should occur; and
- An indication of the target market you are trying to reach. Some poorly stated objectives are "to increase visits," "to midweek

business," and "to attract more retired couples." In contrast, some examples of well-written objectives follow:

- In the next year, increase midweek (Monday-Thursday) occupancy to 55 percent by attracting business travellers.
- The Chamber of Commerce will book 500 advance reservations from vacationers travelling the Lake Superior circle route in summer (June 1 through Labour Day).
- Increase phone and mail inquiries by 20 percent from fall magazine advertising between August 15 and October 15.
- Increase retail sales on main street during a summer festival by 25 percent over last year's.

Carry out Promotion Strategies

Many communities and private entrepreneurs mistakenly assume that marketing is just deciding on a promotion strategy. They direct broad appeals to poorly defined markets through a variety of media. You can't afford to spend scarce promotion dollars in appealing to people who are not prospects for purchase of your product. Effective and efficient promotion decisions build from a situation analysis, identifying products, selecting target markets and setting objectives.

The message content comes directly from the product and the associated theme. It emphasizes both tangible and intangible aspects, focusing on customer benefits your product offers.

Carrying out promotion strategies involves taking your message to the consumer through a specific delivery system. Promotion is any attempt to stimulate sales by persuasive or informative communications to current or potential customers. The major types of promotion used to stimulate travel and tourism follow:

Advertising: Any paid form of nonpersonal presentation and promotion of ideas, goods, or services by an identified sponsor using mass media. Television, radio and print media some of the major Minnesota destinations are an example.

Personal Selling: An oral or written presentation to one or prospective customers on a face-to-face basis, including telephone solicitation and direct mail. Attendance at sports shows is a form of personal selling.

Sales Promotions: Activities other than advertising and personal selling that stimulate purchasing or create awareness. Sales promotions, including contests featuring free tickets or trips, may be geared toward the individual visitor, while other promotions may be directed toward organizations selling travel services. The Duluth contest to guess the date the first ship will enter the harbour in spring is an example.

Public Relations: A nonpaid presentation of ideas, goods or services generally using mass media. Unlike advertising there is no identifying sponsor. Travel feature stories written after a "fam" (familiarization) tour are a result of public relations efforts.

These promotional categories are known together as the promotional mix. Strictly speaking, the promotional mix refers to the relative amounts of efforts or dollars put into each major promotional category. To find its optimal tourism promotional mix, your community might look at towns comparable size and attracting power. However, do not copy programs-no two communities will be exactly alike.

Finally, the committee may be drawn from owners. The committee structure is used most often to guide tourism development. There are several ways to organize a tourism promotion committee. Some groups originate within the Chamber of Commerce because of shared goals. Others form freestanding community endeavour; the final plan must represent goals independent committees with community-wide representation.

The Minnesota Extension Service publication "Tourism Advertising: Some Basics" outlines a process for selecting an advertising strategy. The tools discussed include magazines, newspapers, radio, television, direct mail, and outdoor displays.

Evaluate Results

There is no secret promotional formula. Test and evaluate regularly. A community or business must continually monitor evaluate results, and experiment with various types of promotion. Even with an effective promotional mix now, the situation may change. Preferences and characteristics of travellers change: marketing efforts must respond.

The Minnesota Extension Service publication "Evaluating Tourism Advertising with Cost-Comparison Methods" describes methods such as cost per inquiry, cost per reservation, and return on investment. The importance of coding advertisements to track results cannot be overemphasized.

The Next Step

Working through the tourism development process is a community endeavour; the final plan must represent goals commonly agreed to by area residents and business owners. The committee is used most often to guide tourism development.

There are several ways to organize a tourism promotion committee. Some groups originate within the Chamber of Commerce because of shared goals. Others form freestanding independent committees with community-wide representation. Finally, the committee may be drawn from current leaders in existing tourism agencies, associations, businesses, and attractions. You know the dynamics of your community best to pull together a core group of individuals make things happen.

There must be periodic feedback between the committee and the community at large. In some locations, the tourism committee begins its task with a community-wide survey (by mail, newspaper, or phone) to solicit opinions about tourism development. The results advise the committee and can create a widespread base of public support early in the process. The other strategy is to be sure there is always an opportunity for community discussion at key decision points. The local media can play a major role in keeping the public informed. Here are seven steps to get started (from "Developing a Tourism Organization," 1987, a Michigan State University Extension Service booklet):

1. Select a name that creates an image and identifies the group.
2. Develop a policy statement, including a statement of purpose and bylaws.
3. Develop an action program: set goals and methods of accomplishing them.
4. Set up committees and subcommittees as needed. Some of the major tasks relate to community involvement, attractions and support services, promotion, budgets, research, and information.
5. Create community awareness and support for tourism.
6. Establish lines of communication and develop a flow of information.
7. Foster a spirit of close cooperation and coordination among the various communities, agencies, and other organizations.

Where to Look for Funding

Often good community marketing plans go unrealized or even unused because financial support could not be obtained. Funding can be a difficult obstacle. Communities that have developed a steady and reliable source of marketing funds generally have the most success. Constant scrambling for marketing funds drains energy away from the original marketing objectives. Some of the basic strategies used to raise money for tourism and travel marketing are a lodging tax, local government sources, internal organizational fundraising, private businesses, foundations, and the Minnesota Office of Tourism. Adapt these standard methods to your local situation. Minnesota Statutes permit the creation of a local option lodging tax. Home rule or statutory cities and townships with elected officials may enact a tax of up to three percent on the proceeds of a lodging facility-with a possible extension to municipal campgrounds. In unorganized townships, county officials may enact a lodging tax. Cities townships can create joint districts to better reflect the local tourism region.

Of the proceeds collected, 95 percent must be used to fund marketing and promotion of the area as a tourism or convention destination. These monies may not be used for capital expenditures such as buildings, parks, and civic centres. Lodging facilities are directly affected by the tax, so any plans for a lodging tax should include early discussions with representatives of overnight accommodations. Some communities have had special legislation passed to help fund tourism programs: two options are expansion of the tax base or increases in the tax ceiling. It is normally difficult to pass special interest legislation, but such authority can prove valuable to communities where tourism is a major industry.

Many local governments recognize the importance of the tourism and travel industry to their economies; a number of provide funding to marketing programs implemented by local groups. Monies can come from the general fund, bonding sources, special assessments, or a variety of other sources. Government support can greatly assist local marketing efforts, but funding is less stable due to changing demands for government funds, the health of the local economy, and the fortunes of local politicians.

Tourism organizations typically employ some internal fundraising strategies, in addition to outside sources. Membership dues is the most common method. Set either a standard rate or variable fees based on factors such as business size or number of employees. The organization's ability to attract members then becomes critical. Assessments above and beyond dues are another alternative. Assessments are often based on percent of gross revenue or business size. These may help to fund an overall marketing program, but are also used to pay for specific promotional efforts. Tourism organizations can also sell products, services, and activities directly to the public for income.

Examples are publications, souvenirs and merchandise, tours and tour guides, and operation of attractions, special events, festivals or auctions. Major businesses operating in the community and benefitting from travel and tourism sometimes make substantial contributions to a marketing program. An important element in obtaining this support is to thoroughly identify the benefits of such a contribution, both to the marketing program and the contributor. Direct benefits-increased sales-as well as secondary benefits-general expansion of the local economy-are important. Tax benefits may be an issue. Do not overlook the potential to build goodwill in the community.

There are opportunities to obtain project-specific grants through organizations such as foundations, the Minnesota Office of Tourism and nonlocal private businesses that will fund ongoing expenses for tourism marketing. Projects that provide promotion to an expanded region or attempt to market an area with an innovative approach are more likely to attract a foundation grant. The Minnesota Office of Tourism administers a joint venture marketing program that allocates matching funds on a competitive basis for advertising, creative marketing, and new brochure development. Private businesses beyond the specific area might also sponsor an activity if there is a connection between their product and the focus of the event. For example, dog food manufacturers could be approached for national sponsorship of a sled dog race.

Travel and Tourism Resources

Tourism USA: Guidelines for Tourism Development. 1986. University of Missouri, Dept. of Recreation and Park Administration, University Extension. Prepared for the U.S. of Commerce.

- Excellent "how to" handbook with sections on) appraising potential; 2) planning for tourism; 3) assessing product and market; 4) marketing tourism; visitor services; sources of assistance. Single copies are available for $3.00 from U.S. Dept. of Commerce, 1 4th & Constitution, Room 1 865, Washington, D.C. 20030, 202-377-0140. Managing Small Resorts for Profit. 1 985. Minnesota Extension Service, University of Minnesota.
- Contains a marketing section with articles on the market planning process, brochure development, advertising, positioning and package tours. Available for $20.00 from Bud Crewdson, Small Business Development Centre, Minnesota Extension Service, 248 Classroom Office Building, University of Minnesota, St. Paul, MN 551 08, 61 2-625-31 Minnesota Office

of Tourism, 250 Skyway Level, 375 Jackson Street, St. Paul, MN 551 0 1,-800-652-9141, 6 1 2-296-Contact for information on a joint venture marketing program. Marketing activities may be eligible for matching funds allocated on a competitive basis to any local, regional, or statewide nonprofit organization formed to promote tourism. Tourism Centre, Minnesota Extension Service, University of Minnesota, 240 Coffey Hall, 1420 Eckles Avenue, St. Paul, MN 55108.

- Offers educational programs and materials for the visitor industry on community tourism development and small business management. Contact your local county extension agent for copies of the extension publications listed in the folder. So Your Community Wants Tourism: Guidelines for Developing Income from Tourism in Your Community (CD-FO-0679, Available 1988) Creating a Tourism Promotional Theme Tourism Advertising: Some Basics (CD-FO-331 1) "Evaluating Tourism Advertising with Cost Comparison Methods" (CD-FO-3372) Tourism Brochures to Boost Business (CD-FO-3273).

Community Improvement Resources

Tourism development depends on citizen cooperation to accomplish community goals and improve the local environment. The Minnesota Department of Trade and Economic development administers four such programs that give residents an opportunity to develop expertise in identifying and using community resources-the Minnesota Community Improvement Program, the Governor's Design Team, Minnesota Main Street, and Minnesota Beautiful. Program coordinators can be reached at the Department of Trade and Economic Development, 900 American Centre Building, 1 50 East Kellogg Blvd., St. Paul, MN 551 01. The general office number is 612-297-3190.

The Minnesota Community Improvement Program (MCIP) is a community (or county) revitalization and recognition program. Citizens conduct a community analysis and set goals. They build broad support networks and document the improvement process so that MCIP judges can evaluate annual progress. The Minnesota Extension Service provides educational and technical support. Involvement in MCIP can build the skills and coalitions necessary to accomplish other specific tasks such as economic development, downtown revitalization and design, and beautification. The Governor's Design Team calls on architects, landscape designers, urban planners, artists, and other professionals volunteer their time and services and virtually descend on a community for a two-to three-day intensive design consultation and work session. Communities want the team to a fresh look and new ideas in such areas a downtown revitalized town image, and development potential. Before applying for a visit, the community should focus on specific issues and areas of need. During a visit, broad-based active citizen support and involvement is expected.

Minnesota Main Street encourages revitalization of downtowns in small and midsize cities, working with assets already inherent in the downtown tradition. Rebuilding main street's image depends on improvements in organization, promotion, design, and economic restructuring, made in operation with downtown groups.

Minnesota Beautiful supports activities that help keep Minnesota a clean and quality place to live, work, and visit. Projects include recycling, landscaping, general cleanup of waste materials and unsightly areas, tree planting, and mineland reclamation. Minnesota Beautiful offers educational materials to communities undertaking these projects, and organizes an annual conference to recognize significant progress.

Cultural Tourism Promotion and Policy in Malaysia

Malaysia is experiencing a tremendous pace of tourism development. Tourism sector has been recognized by Malaysian government as a major source of revenue and catalyst to the Malaysian economic renaissance. Tourist arrivals to Malaysia for the last ten years have shown a significant rise. In the year 2004, this country attracted 15.7 million foreign tourists generating around RM29.7 billion into the company. Major tourist market for Malaysia has been the neighbouring ASEAN nations especially Singapore, Thailand, Indonesia and Brunei. Other main traditional foreign markets include China, Japan, Taiwan and India.

Coupled with the growth in tourism is a booming interest in the 'new tourism'. Cultural tourism has emerged as a potential form of alternative tourism among both international tourists as well as Malaysian domestic travellers. Cultural tourism in Malaysia attracted great publicities with the increase in the number of incoming tourists annually. Malaysia has marvelous cultural tourism resources that are readily available to be explored such as the existence of multicultural, historical buildings, colorful lifestyles and friendly atmosphere. The purpose of this paper is to give an overview of the promotion of culture and heritage in Malaysia as well as the related strategies and policies that support the measure. It also discusses several underlying issues pertaining the cultural management in Malaysia.

Table: *Tourist arrivals and receipts to Malaysia*

Year	*Arrivals (million)*	*Receipts (RM millions)*
1995	7.46	9,174.9
1996	7.14	10,354.1
1997	6.21	9,699.6
1998	5.55	8,580.4
1999	7.93	12,321.3
2000	10.22	17,335.4
2001	12.78	24,221.5
2002	13.29	25,781.1
2003	10.58	21,291.1
2004	15.70	29,651.4

Source: *Tourism Malaysia, 2005*

Defining Cultural Tourism

Culture in tourism is an important issue. The relationship between tourism and culture can take many forms and the outcome can be viewed as negative and positive when meeting of hosts and visitors occurs and possibly leads to the transformation of the hosts' culture. The destruction of local culture as a result of tourism is well documented. However, studies by researchers' consider this as a lopsided view of the impact of tourism. Studies have shown that tourism have lead to the strengthening of local culture. Culture is defined broadly as quoted in Meethan (2001:117), "*.....as a set of practices, based on forms of knowledge, which encapsulate common values and act as general guiding principles. It is through these forms of knowledge that distinctions are created and maintained, so that, for example, one culture is marked off as different from another*".

World Tourism Organization (1985) defines cultural tourism as the movements of persons for essentially cultural motivations such as study tours, performing arts and cultural tours; travel to festivals and other related events. Essentially, cultural tourism is based on the mosaic of places, traditions, art forms, celebrations and experiences that portray ones nation and its people.

Meethan (2001:128) rightly observed that there are array of tourist activities that come under the heading of cultural tourism. However, he argues for a distinct demarcation of cultural tourism and hence a distinct profile of cultural tourists quotes;

> *"....the cultural tourists are those who go about their leisure in a more serious frame of mind. To be a cultural tourist.....is to go beyond idle leisure and to return enriched with knowledge of other places and other people even if this involves 'gazing' at or collecting in some way, the commodation essences of otherness".*

Studies of western culture by Richard (1994) described the cultural tourists were *'a high socioeconomic status, high level of educational attainment, adequate leisure time, and often having occupations related to the culture industries'.* It must be borne in mind that culture is not static but one that is dynamic and evolving. Meethan (2001: 127) draw attention to globalization of culture and also the mobilization of culture for internal and external purposes. Yamashita, Kadir and Eades (1997: 29-30) further illustrates the processes that transform culture.

Heritage tourism can be classified as a subclass of cultural tourism. Both cultural and heritage tourism become a growing segment of the tourism marketplace.

Cultural tourists appear to be motivated for different reasons than do traditional tourists. Some tourism destinations see cultural tourism as a promotion for tourism products, and this has been lamented. Millar (1989) and others suggest that heritage tourism is "about the cultural traditions, places and values that... groups throughout the world are proud to conserve." Cultural traditions such as family patterns, religious practices, folklore traditions, and social customs attract individuals interested in heritage as do monuments, museums, battlefields, historic structures, and landmarks.

Cultural Tourism in Malaysia and its Management

In Malaysia, heritage and culture has also been identified as new niche products to be developed extensively in tourism development. Cultural vibrancy is clearly manifested in the ongoing and successful "Malaysia: Truly Asia" promotional drive by the country's promotion arm, Tourism Malaysia. In this promotion, Malaysia boasts to host a wide variety of Asian ethnic groups that making it into a little Asia. Malaysia also has distinctive multicultural architectural heritage with strong Islamic, Chinese and Western influences; all of which have been portrayed in the heritage buildings.

The major heritage elements; historic building, historical sites and unique local cultures are commonly found in many historic cities throughout Malaysia. An inventory has revealed that 30,000 heritage buildings are located in 162 cities throughout Malaysia. From this figure, 69.6% are shop houses and dwellings built before World War II. The unique colonial architectural styles of buildings have played major role in the creation of historic cities such as George Town, Ipoh, Malacca, Tapping, Koala Lumpur and Kuching.

Table: *Distributions of Pre-War Buildings in Selected States in Malaysia*

States in Malaysia	***Number of Pre-War Buildings***	***Percentage (%)***
Penang	5057	24.3
Perak	3351	16.1
Johor	2323	11.2
Malacca	2177	10.5
Koala Lumpur	1763	8.4

The management of culture and heritage in Malaysia was put under the Ministry of Tourism and Culture, established on the 20th of May 1987, combining Department of Culture from the Ministry of Culture, Youths and Sports with the Malaysian Tourism Development Corporation from the Ministry of Trade and Industries. On 22nd October 1992, the ministry was renamed into Ministry of Culture, Arts and Tourism. This ministry was later divided in Mac 2004, into two ministries, namely the Tourism Ministry and Ministry of Culture, Arts and Heritage. This separation is seen as recognition of tourism as a potential number one sector of the country and a move to appreciate the value of heritage of the country.

Agencies under this ministry are the National Archives, the National Art and Gallery, the Department of Museum and Antiquities, Malaysian Handicrafts (Kraftangan Malaysia), the National Film Development Corporation (Finas), the National Art Academy, the National Library and the Istana Budaya (the Culture Palace).

Despite the move to strengthen the ministries, the separation of the cultural elements from the Tourism Ministry can give impacts on the direction of 'cultural and heritage tourism', leaving this niche area as an no-man's land!

The Formulation of National Cultural Policy

At a national conference organized by Malaysia's Ministry of Culture, Youth and Sports in 1971, the Malaysian government formulated what was to become a national cultural policy based on the following principles:

(i) The national culture of Malaysia must henceforth be based on the cultures of the people indigenous to the region.

(ii) Elements from other cultures which are judged suitable and reasonable may be incorporated into Malaysia's national culture.

(iii) Islam will be an important element in the national culture.

In the period since its implementation, Malaysia's national culture policy has become one important point of vigorous debate and political conflict. In the years since the formulation of a National Cultural Policy, and particularly in the late 1980's, the Malaysian government has been concerned to implement its basic principles by intervening directly and across the board in the cultural field. Not surprisingly, and perhaps because it has not been altogether clear and efficient about its task, government intervention in the cultural field has produced a response on the part of a variety of non-Malaya groups who feel that their cultural freedom has been curtailed.

For example, at a meeting of the Chinese guild and associations of Malaysia held in March, 1983, delegates passed a series of resolutions that were compiled in a joint memorandum to the Ministry of Culture, Youth and Sports. In April 1984, a group of the best-known Indian cultural, social and religious organizations submitted a similar memorandum. Both memoranda accused the government of having formulated a cultural policy which was Malaya-centric and undemocratic, and requested that a new policy on national culture be established which was more clearly multi-ethnic and democratic.

Law and Legislations on Cultural and Heritage Properties

The legal foundations of the Malaysian cultural policy are derived from the following acts and regulations:

i) Antiquities Act 1976 (Act 168).

ii) National Art Gallery Act, 1958.

iii) Legal Deposit of Library Material Act, 1986 (Act A667).

iv) National Library Act, 1972; The National Library (Amendment) Act, 1987.

v) National Archive Act, 1966 (Act 44), (Revised 1971), (Act A85), (Revised 1993), (Act 511).

vi) Tourist Development Corporation of Malaysia Act 1972 (Act 1972).

vii) Broadcasting Act 1988 (Act 338), Broadcasting (Amendment) Act, 1997 (Act A977).

viii) Cinematography Film-Hire Duty Act 1965 (Revised 1990), (Act 434).

ix) (Perbadanan Kemajuan File Nasional Malaysia Act 1981 (Act 244), Perbadanan Kemajuan File Nasional Malaysia (Amendment) Act, 1984 (Act 589).

x) Perbadanan Kemajuan Kraftangan Malaysia Act 1979 (Act 222).

xi) Theatres & Places of Public Amusement (Federal Territory) Act 1988 (Act 182).

xii) Bernama Act, 1967 (Revised 1990), (Act 449).

xiii) Entertainment Duty Act 1953 (Revised 1973) (Act 103).

Efforts to preserve the heritage buildings in Malaysia are supported by various acts and legislations. The prominent acts have been the Town and Country Planning Act of 1976 or the 172 Act, The National Land Code (Kanun Tanah Negara), the Street, Drainage and Building Act 133, the Antiquities Act 1976, as well as local legislations such as the Malacca Enactment No. 6 (1988). Act 133 for instance stipulates that "No person shall erect any building without a prior written permission of the local authority".

This provision is supported by Section 18 of Act 172 which states "All land/building use shall comply with the local plans (structure and local plans). Any development shall obtain planning permission. And if there is no development plan prepared for the area, the owner/ developer of the land shall inform their plan to the adjoining landowners (Act 172,).

To date, a guidelines on the Guidelines on the Conservation of George Town Inner City details out specific recommendations pertaining extensions, renovations, revitalizations of heritage buildings within the prescribed zones.

At present, any erection of buildings is loosely bonded by both Acts (133 and 172). Section 16 of 133 defines erections of building includes 'renews or repairs of any existing buildings in such a manner as to involve a renewal, reconstruction or erection of any portion of an outer or party wall to the extent of one storey height". Further, all building that fall within the definition of development, stipulated in Act 172 also requires planning permission. The Guidelines is in concordant with Part Vll of Act 133 that gives the State Authority to make bylaws or in respect of every purpose which is deemed by him necessary. In regards to the preservation of buildings, the State Authority, among other things, has the right to make by laws in:-

(i) The construction, paving, width and level of arcades and footways;

(ii) The construction, alteration and demolition of buildings and the methods and materials to be used in connection therewith;

(iii) The minimum timber or other building material content in any building.

Issues

The promotion of culture and heritage in Malaysia faces several underlying issues that both are related to the complexity of the society living in Malaysia. Among the issues are:-

Whose Culture?

Despite the fact that Malaysia is proud of its multiculturalism, promoted worldwide as the 'Truly Asia', the question remains on whose culture should be promoted at the forefront. As discussed above, Chinese and Indians have continuously felt that their cultures are not well represented in the tourism brochures produced by the government.

Similar sentiment was raised up during the nomination process for the listing of Penang and Melaka into the world heritage city. Malays in Penang especially feel that the listing do not benefit them and the island's Malaya history is not taken into consideration.

Some also feel that the listing of the 12000 heritage buildings where many of them are colonial buildings—is just another post colonization of the country, lamented on why we have to glorify the colonial past!

3

Hotel Organizing Systems

Introduction

One of the main problems that each enterprise faces is to organize the efforts of the people working on common goals. Most of the solutions to this problem originate from the time before computers became available for practically any company. However, it's a general practice even now, that the developers follow the old management scheme when the company is being computerized, whereas modern computers offer unique opportunities for implementing new, far more effective approaches to management.

We discovered the limitations of existing management schemes while computerizing a small trading company. Our objective was to develop a system able to assist the office workers in all aspects of their routine work. One of our tasks was a conventional one-to support such activities as taking orders, delivering goods, making a phone call, etc. The other one was more ambitious-to register all completed activities and to help plan new activities based on the completed ones.

We realized very soon that our second objective could not be achieved within the functional management scheme adopted in the company. To cope with our task we started to consider the company's activity as a number of processes (such as "processing an order", "closing a deal") without regard to the way these processes were being managed. As a result a new approach to management was developed which we call a process-oriented management. This approach can be described as a project management without project managers, a project manager's functions, e.g., planning, controlling the execution of activities, etc., being distributed among the workers involved in a particular process.

The main point with the process-oriented management is that it permits a company to gain full control over all the processes within the frame of the existing, often functionally-oriented, organizational structure. This type of management facilitates also the communication between the workers involved in the same process, and it provides them with actual information on the state of the process, as well as on all activities performed and planned. Below, we present the main ideas of the process-oriented management, and the requirements for a computer system needed to support it.

We tried our best to do that in a very informal way to make it easily understood by all concerned. It should also be mentioned that the author is not a specialist in the field of management, but he worked with experts on management throughout the project. The paper reflects a fresh view of an application developer not spoiled by the experience of the pre-computer management era.

The rest of this paper is organized as follows. In section 2, we outline our view on the management of routine work. In section 3, we present the main principles of the process-oriented management. We look at existing approaches to management of the routine work-the function-oriented management and project-oriented management, and then move on to describing the ways of transforming the project-oriented management into the process-oriented one. We discuss the process-oriented management without regards to computer systems, however, this type of management can't be implemented without computers.

Requirements for a computer system designed to support the process-oriented management are discussed in section 4. In section 5, we discuss the major issues of the development and implementation of such systems. In section 6, we present a short summary of our practical and research work that lead to the development of a process-oriented approach to management.

Management of Routine Work

It's generally recognized that the main objective of management is to ensure a successful achievement of a company's goals at minimal costs. A company has several different types of goals to achieve at any given moment-long-term, short-term, etc. As we are concerned with the management of routine work, it's the "conventional" everyday goals that are of primary interest to us; we call them "operational" goals. A typical operational goal for a trading company is, for example, to "drive" an incoming order through a delivery to receiving payment within certain time limits. A typical operational goal for a hospital is to administer the appropriate treatment to a patient that would lead to his discharging from the hospital. A typical operational goal for a software development company is to build a software system according to the specifications. But for the section of technical support of such company, a typical operational goal is to process a bug report so that the bug is fixed or/and a work-around solution is found.

Though operational goals may be quite unsophisticated, they, nevertheless, constitute the backbone of any business, as they have to be achieved on a day-to-day basis to ensure the proper functioning of the company. The character of operational goals depends on the type of business, but they have a number of common features:

- operational goals pop up more or less regularly;
- there is, usually, a standard procedure for achieving the operational goals of a given kind, which doesn't mean, of course, that a particular goal can't be approached in a different way if needed;
- there is often a set time limit for achieving an operational goal. If the goal is impossible to achieve within the time limit, it is discarded in a standard way.

To achieve an operational goal, a series of activities should be completed. For example, a series of activities aimed at getting payment for an incoming order includes delivery of goods and sending an invoice to the customer. This series may include more items in certain circumstances, for example, if the ordered goods are out of stock, they should be produced or ordered from the suppliers. The activities aimed at achieving an operational goal are not, usually, executed immediately one after another, e.g., if the ordered goods are out of stock, it takes some time to get them from the suppliers. The execution of these activities is a process that continues over some period of time. The main objective for management of operational goals is to ensure that this process results in achieving the goal.

Different activities concerning the same goal can be completed by different workers from different divisions. Another objective of management is, therefore, to coordinate the work of all workers participating in the process of achieving an operational goal.

A Race Towards a Process-Oriented Management

Approaches to management of operational goals may be divided in two types-function-oriented and project-oriented. The function-oriented management (Fn-management) is usually used in the environments where a lot of relatively simple operational goals pop up very frequently. The Fn-management implies that operational goals are handled in a routine manner by the staff where each member has his own function in achieving operational goals. A manager does not coordinate the execution of activities for each goal, workers just react on the incoming documents, phone calls, etc., by completing activities they are assigned, and forwarding the received or newly composed documents further to their colleagues.

The project-oriented management (Pj-management) is usually used with more sophisticated goals such as construction or software projects. The Pj-management implies that a process for a new goal is planned in detail before the work on it starts, and there is someone (e.g., a project manager) who supervises all the work being done.

Fn-management is most cost-effective, but it works poorly when a process of achieving an operational goal deviates from a standard pattern, as it lacks control over individual processes. Pj-management gives full control over an individual process, but it's inefficient when a lot of coexisting processes are involved. There are working environments where one or the other type of management fits well. But in most environments a combination of these two approaches would be the way to obtain both full control over all processes and efficiency.

Below, we discuss our proposals for integration of the Fn-and Pj-managements. The result is a new type of management which we call the process-oriented management, or Pc-management, for short. This name highlights the main objective of the Pc-management-to control the processes, in contrast to Fn-management that places the emphasis on the execution of activities, and the Pj-management that emphasizes plans. We describe the Pc-management here in the following way. We consider an environment typical for the function-oriented management-a trading company, and try to introduce the project-oriented management in it. The process-oriented management is presented thus as a result of tailoring the project-oriented approach to fit a different kind of environment. We find this way most convenient for discussing our ideas, but it's not, naturally, the only possible one.

The Pc-management is based on the notions of "orgobject", "history" and "dynamic and distributed planning", which we can now turn our attention to.

Orgobjects

The Pj-management involves developing a detailed plan for achieving a project's goal before the work on the project can start. This plan is premised on certain assumptions that may turn out wrong after the project is under way. The plan should then be adapted to the changed conditions. For this purpose, a clear picture of the current state of the project is required to figure out what should be done to complete the project.

A project often involves developing some product that is a physical object, e.g. a software system, a building, etc. This product comes into existence in some form already at the earlier stages of the project, e.g. a half-ready software system or a building under construction. This half-ready product serves as a good representation of the current state of the project. As the half-ready product can be studied without regards to how it has been produced, the plan can be revised without going into details of the project's history.

In cases where the Fn-management is involved, there is no half-ready product to represent the current state of achieving an operational goal. A kind of an abstract object that contains all information on the current state of the process would be helpful here. As it would serve as an organizing device for achieving the goal, we call it an "orgobject".

For example, an orgobject representing a process of "Get payment for an incoming order" may be a record that contains information on: the name and address of the buyer, a description of each kind of goods ordered, the quantity and price per unit of each kind, the quantities of goods already delivered; the amount of money invoiced; the amount of money received. Having this orgobject, the conditions for the successful achievement of the "get payment" goal could be formulated as follows:

- have the numbers representing the quantities of 'goods ordered' and 'goods delivered' equal for each goods kind,
- have 'money invoiced' equal to the sum of 'ordered' multiplied by 'price per unit' for all goods kinds, and
- have 'money received' equal to 'money invoiced'.

As the process develops, the corresponding orgobject should change so that it reflects all the time the current state of the process. As soon as some activity is completed, the orgobject representing the process is to be modified. Thus, in the above example, after the delivery (full or partial), the quantities of the goods delivered are modified; if the customer has changed the order, the types and quantities of the goods ordered are modified, etc. To ensure that the orgobjects are always up-to-date, the routines for every type of activity should list not only the operations required for completing the activity (e.g., packing and shipping for delivery), but also instructions for the appropriate modifications of the relevant orgobjects. Thus, the current state of an orgobject reflects the overall result of all activities completed earlier, and shows what actions should be taken to achieve the goal. To return to our example, if the quantity of the goods ordered is greater than the quantity of the goods delivered, the missing goods are to be delivered. If, on the other hand, the quantity of the goods ordered is less than the quantity of the goods delivered, then the customer should be asked to return some of the goods. Other examples: if the amount of money invoiced exceeds the payment received, then the customer should pay the difference. If the amount of the money received exceeds that of invoiced, then a credit note should be issued.

History

The current state of an orgobject contains only the result of the completed activities, but not a list of them, e.g.: the quantity of the goods delivered, but not the number of separate deliveries; the amount of money invoiced, but not the number of separate invoices, etc. This is OK if all goes as it should. But if something goes wrong, e.g., some goods sent off did not arrive, then the information on all activities performed is vital when figuring out what actions should be taken. This information can be collected through logging all the activities completed in the frame of the given process.

Let's consider the following logging scheme. Every time a worker executes an activity, he/she doesn't physically change the previous state of the relevant orgobject. He/she makes a new record instead which contain the new state of the orgobject and leaves the former one unchanged. For example, after a delivery, a new record is made containing the same information as the previous one except the information on the quantities of the goods delivered. The latter is updated according to the packing list.

The record on the previous state of an orgobject is placed in a special file containing the history of the given orgobject. The worker who completes an activity composes also a report where he/she records: the kind of activity completed, the name of a person who completed it, the date, time, comments, etc. This report is saved together with the previous state of the orgobject in the history file.

Given two consequent states of an orgobject and an activity report, we can reconstruct exactly what happened during the activity execution. For example, in case of delivery, we know exactly by whom and when the goods were delivered, and in what quantities. Thus, our log provides an easy access to the information on both the activity performed, and the state of events before and after it was performed.

Dynamic and Distributed Planning

As it was mentioned above, the Pj-management involves designing a detailed plan for each new process. If we try to apply the same to a Fn-management environment, two problems would arise:

- as Fn-processes are often trivial, their plans would be trivial too, e.g.: 'delivering goods'-'invoicing the buyer'-'getting payment'. It would be meaningless to record such plan for every process (and there are many in this kind of environments),
- unpredictable external events that often occur in Fn-management environments would demand revising the whole plan, e.g.: a customer has changed his order-additional delivery can be required, an invoice is to be sent later than it was initially planned, etc.

Dynamic planning is our answer to these problems. Dynamic planning involves planning only the first few activities at the first stage. As soon as one or several of these are completed, new activities are planned with regard to the emerging state of the relevant orgobject (and standard routines adopted in the company). For example, after a delivery, another delivery is planned if not all ordered goods have been delivered, or invoicing is planned if all goods have been delivered.

The use of dynamic planning is fully beneficial in case of processes that follow a standard pattern. Otherwise, the usual planning is preferable. In case the character of the process (standard/deviating) is difficult to foresee, dynamic planning can be used at first, followed by conventional planning if necessary.

Another poser when trying to introduce the Pj-management in an Fn-environment is how to supervise a process. In cases where the Pj-management is involved, there is usually a project manager who supervises the execution of planned activities, and corrects the plan if needed. In an environment typical for the Fn-management, a project manager supervising each process would result in significant overheads. A solution to this can be described as "distributed planning". Distributed planning implies that the worker who has completed a planned activity himself plans the subsequent activities. Moreover, he/she can assign these new activities not only to himself, but to other people too. For example, a worker who completes a delivery himself plans invoicing to be completed by another worker.

Distributed planning doesn't exclude the possibility of a centralized supervision of a process. In fact, a supervisor may intervene at any time and correct the plan if needed. Moreover, any member of staff can consult the supervisor in case he/she has some problems with his/her work on a particular process. He/she can do it by planning a special activity, e.g., "asking for help", and assigning his/her supervisor to complete it.

Let's have a look at the issue of implementing dynamic and distributed planning. Above, we considered orgobjects and plans as separate entities. Now, we put a plan inside the orgobject representing the corresponding process. As a result an orgobject besides the information on the current state of the process (e.g., on the customer, goods, delivery and payment) will also include a list of planned activities (e.g., delivery, invoicing, etc.), each of them containing information on what should be done, who's to do that and when. Thus, a plan becomes part of an orgobject. Consequently, we can treat correction of the plan as one of the operations of changing the orgobject in the course of completing an activity. In section 3.1, we've already mentioned that instructions for modifying orgobjects should be included in the working procedures for each type of activities. To ensure proper dynamic planning, these instructions should embrace modification of the process's plan. In a simple case, a worker who has completed an activity modifies the relevant orgobject by removing this activity from the list of planned activities. In more complex cases, he/she adds new activities to the list, and/or removes some other activities from it.

Being an integral part of the orgobject representing a process, a plan is subjected to the logging we described above. As a result, all acts of replanning are registered in the same way as other modifications of orgobjects. Thus, for example, the name of a person who modified the plan is recorded, which may prove to be useful in case of conflicts.

Advantages of the Process-Oriented Management

The main advantage of the Pc-management is its flexibility. The Pc-management permits to choose the optimum approach to coping with each process, and within the same management scheme. Thus, simple processes that follow a standard pattern are dealt with in a completely decentralized manner, whereas some more sophisticated case will be dealt with by centralized individual planning and supervising. Moreover, the same process may be treated differently at different stages. For example, it may be started as a standard one, but later it can be planned and supervised individually. As a result, full control over all kinds of processes is gained and efficiency is not sacrificed.

Another important thing is that the Pc-management is not bound to any particular type of organizational structure. It can be used both in case the same member of staff completes all the activities required for achieving an operational goal, and in case each activity type is assigned to a particular worker. This permits to preserve the same management scheme when the organizational structure is changed, e.g., in case of a company's expansion.

Some other advantages are as follows:

1. Orgobjects provide a perfect insight into the company's state of affairs. The information stored in the orgobjects is of great help to the management staff as it permit to quickly evaluate the state of a process (without going into its history). It also helps to give prompt answers to customers' questions. This kind of information is not easily obtainable when traditional managements schemes are used. Thus, when the Fn-management is used, only the information on the executed activities of a given type is easily accessible, and when the Pj-management is used, only the information on the state of the plans execution is easily accessible.
2. Histories of orgobjects permit to easily trace all the activities completed on a given process, which helps to devise plans for complicated cases. They are also a very important source of data for all kinds of statistical analysis, and other types of information processing required for decision-making.
3. The company's staff becomes goal-and process-conscious, as it is easy for any person to overview all the activities (one's own and those of others) completed in a process he/she is involved in. The history of old orgobjects is useful for "learning by example", which may help a worker to find solutions in difficult cases. The goal-and process-consciousness isn't easy to acquire with a traditional management scheme. Under the Fn-management, a worker doesn't see how a process he/she's in is accomplished. His/her personal goal becomes to complete as efficient as possible the activities he/she is responsible for. That

may result in, e.g., a seller concentrating on making telephone calls most of which don't get him to closing a deal.

4. The Pj-management emphasizes following the schedule, which becomes the main goal of the workers engaged in a project. There is a danger that the workers do not keep their eyes open for changes in the surrounding world, which is, e.g., the main reason why large software projects often produce out-of-day systems.
5. As all the information on the past is being stored, the management staff is in a better position concerning various kinds of conflicts, internal conflicts among workers engaged in the same process, and external ones, e.g., with customers or suppliers.
6. Distributed planning is a very powerful tool for coordinating the work which makes unnecessary the intensive communication (exchanges of documents, phone calls, etc.) among the workers engaged in the same processes. They get the required information from the current states of orgobjects and their histories.

An Orgsystem Wanted

Let's imagine you are fascinated by the Pc-management and decide to implement it in your company. A lot of orgobjects start circulating around, each accompanied by a huge history file. You don't find the one you need, you never know which of the orgobjects contains the planned activities assigned to you, and when these activities should be completed. You strove for a better order and got yourself into a mess. And, as if that were not enough, you have a lot of extra work to do. You should construct a new state of an orgobject for each completed activity, and remember to put the new activities on the list and assign them to yourself and others. You wanted to improve the efficiency, but it sinks instead. There is no need to worry, there is a means to restore the order and efficiency, and that's, naturally a computer system. It's primary aim is to make you happy with the Pc-management doing away with the chaos, that's why we call it an "organizing system", or orgsystem for short.

Let's have another look at the Pc-management, this time supported by an orgsystem. Orgobjects do not circulate between various members of the staff who are to work with them, they stay in the same place together with their history and plans, and are easily accessible to all workers involved. All planned activities assigned to a given individual appear immediately in his/her personal calendar, so that each worker knows exactly what activities he/she has to complete and when.

An orgsystem provides the means to increase the efficiency by:

- assisting workers in executing each activity,
- providing an extremely user-friendly interface.

These two features are a key to successful implementation of an orgsystem. Without them people would not be motivated to use the system, consequently the Pc-management wouldn't work. Let's look at these features in more detail.

Level of Help

All operations needed for executing an activity under the Pc-management belong to one of the two groups:

- external operations-operations that affect the "external world", and
- maintaining operations-operations aimed at maintaining orgobjects.

The character of external operation depends on the type of activity, e.g., packing and shipping for delivery, programming and testing for developing a software module, etc. Maintaining operations are the same for all activities.

They include:

- updating the information contained in the relevant orgobject,
- correcting the plan,
- logging the preceding state of the orgobject.

An orgsystem assists a worker to complete both the external operations and the maintaining ones.

1. *External Operations:* Level of help which is possible to offer for completing the external operations depends on the type of activity. For example, programming and testing of a software module are usually performed inside the computer, and they are already fully computerized. Here, an orgsystem should just integrate the existing tools for software development, e.g. editors, debuggers, etc., so that a proper tool is invoked when a user chooses to execute these operations. Packing and shipping are not that easily computerized, not now anyway. But even there, an orgsystem can be helpful to some extent by, e.g., making up a packing list. It's important to give a hand in

completing the external operations for each kind of activities. There's a risk otherwise. If some activity is left without the orgsystem's assistance, a worker who completes it can easily forget to make the appropriate changes in the orgobject concerned. In that case, the completed activity will still remain on the list of planned activities and the orgsystem will keep reminding the worker to complete it. There is also a danger that the same activity will be completed several times.

2. *Updating:* Modification of an orgobject can often be done on the basis of the information collected in the process of executing the external operations. For example, an "order" orgobject contains the information on the quantities of the goods already delivered. This information should be updated after each separate delivery. The new quantities can be easily calculated based on the packing list that was made at the previous step, which permits an orgsystem to update the orgobject without assistance from the users.
3. When correcting a plan, a worker is prompted by the system on the appropriate activities to plan next; in simple cases the plan is corrected by the system itself. This is possible, as an orgsystem possesses two type of knowledge:
   - on the working procedures used in the company, which helps to plan new activities, and
   - on division of responsibilities between different divisions, sections, and workers, which permits to correctly assign new activities.
4. Logging includes two operations:
   - saving the old state of the orgobject, and
   - making a report on the activity completed.

Saving the old state of an orgobject is done by an orgsystem without any user assistance, but an activity report needs a human participation. Even there, an orgsystem helps by automatically supplying the information on what activity has been executed, by whom and when. The rest of the report, e.g., comments, is of course the responsibility of the worker.

User-interface

Conventional computer systems are designed as a set of functions operating on a common database, the main facility of the user-interface being multilevel menus. This type of the user-interface provides the user with a quick access to a function he/she wants to complete. It reflects the objective of a conventional computer system which is to help workers to cope with single activities like updating information, printing a report, etc. An orgsystem objectives are much wider, which brings about the need for a completely different kind of user-interface. An orgsystem's user-interface permits end-users to freely choose between the object-oriented and activity-oriented way of working with orgobjects, as well as easily switch from one to the other. The object-oriented approach is applied when a user wants to work with a particular orgobject for a longer time. In this case, he/she may need to look at the object's current state and its history, as well as to plan and execute various activities involving the orgobject. The activity-oriented approach is applied when a user wants to complete the same activity for a number of orgobjects. In this case, the dialogue designed for a given activity is repeated for all relevant orgobjects.

The object-oriented way is particularly useful when one worker is responsible for many activities involving an orgobject. It is also the way that management staff can use when there is a need to evaluate the state of a particular process and to devise a plan for a difficult case. The activity-oriented approach is preferable if a worker is responsible for only one type of activities. It's also the right approach to completing simple activities that do not require much human assistance, e.g., printing an invoice, etc.

Another distinguishing feature of an orgsystem's user-interface is that it maintains personal calendars. A personal calendar is a list of activities assigned to a particular worker. The point is that these activities are included in different orgobjects and the calendar permits a perfect overview of a persons' many tasks. The orgsystem offers a variety of ways to use the calendar. A user can browse through his/her calendar, or some parts of it, e.g., to see all activities planned for a particular day, all activities of a certain type, etc. When browsing, he/she can start the execution of his/her activities (activity-oriented approach), or move to the orgobject where a particular activity belongs and start working with this orgobject in the object-oriented manner.

To maintain its user-friendly character, an orgsystem's user-interface should satisfy a number of general requirements. Most important are the following two:

- easy access to all information required for working with orgobjects. For example, when working with an orgobject representing an order, a user should have access to all information related to the customer who ordered goods: his address, previous contacts with him, etc.;

- consistency. There should be standard procedures for navigating to an orgobject, for getting information (e.g., a company's address), for planning, for starting the execution of activities, etc. These standard procedures should be the same for all types of orgobjects and activities.

Joys and Hardships of an Orgsystems Developer

There are, naturally, technical problems to solve in the development of an orgsystem. The system requirements discussed in the previous section must be met. However, an orgsystem designer's greatest problem is that he starts the development in an environment initially not based on the Pc-management, which makes both design and implementation of an orgsystem far from trivial tasks.

Orgsystems Design

An orgsystem designer should begin with:

- identifying the company's operational goals,
- figuring out what processes are used to achieve them, and
- designing orgobjects to represent these processes.

His/her next task is to review all the working procedures and tailor them to fit the Pc-management scheme (by adding maintaining operations to each activity). This is often a tough job, as there are seldom some written descriptions of the working procedures, and if they exist, they are far from complete. The only way to cope with the job is to try and get the missing information from the company's workers.

The workers would, naturally, know nothing about orgobjects, but they know their job. The conditions in which an orgsystem designer works are similar to those of a linguist who studies a language that exists only in the spoken form. Linguists have special methods permitting them to get the necessary information from the native speakers without teaching them any linguistic notions. Moreover, it's considered a wrong practice to teach informants linguistics, as it may only spoil them. An orgsystems designer needs similar methods that would permit him to redesign the company's working procedures without introducing the workers into the world of orgobjects, distributed planning, etc. We believe that rapid prototyping is the right method. As soon as a designer has identified the company's operational goals and processes, and designed the orgobjects to represent them, he/she should make a prototype of the system and let the future users test it. To be able to use prototyping, an orgsystem designer needs appropriate application development tools. These tools should allow him to quickly produce a sketch of the system that has "look-and-feel" of a real system, but lacks processing routines and database access. It's this sketch that we call the prototype of the system. Working with it, a user can navigate among orgobjects in the same way as he would do that when the orgsystem is ready. He can modify existing orgobjects, create new ones, and see how to start different activities. But he can't save the information or see the results of the completed activities.

After the future users have accepted the prototype, the designer can stepwise add database access and processing routines, which would be also done with the help of the above mentioned application development tools.

Orgsystems Implementation

Implementing an orgsystem means introducing the Pc-management in a non-Pc-management environment. This may be achieved in one of two ways:

- by substituting all the old working procedures in the company at once, or
- by gradual introduction of the new working procedures.

The first approach may suit small companies whose workers often switch from one activity type to another. An orgsystem would help to do these switches very quickly, and it would help the workers, who usually have a lot of different things to do, to preserve the order in their affairs. The staff of a small company would easily understand the advantages of using all facilities provided by an orgsystem: object- and activity-oriented ways of working, personal calendars, easy access to the history, etc. However, in case of large companies, the second approach may be the best choice. Large companies usually, have a lot of workers who are involved only in one or several activities for each process. These workers may believe that an orgsystem is too complex for their simple tasks. It would be difficult for them to see the advantages of the object-oriented user-interface, and their earlier experience of traditional computer systems can only make the things worse.

Luckily, an orgsystem provides a means for working in the activity-oriented manner, which would put the workers competing simple activities at ease. There would be no problem to teach them to use the orgsystem in the activity-oriented way, because it resembles their old manner of doing things. Later, the workers could be taught the object-oriented way as well, which would give them better possibilities to take the initiative and find solutions for difficult cases. But even if most of the office workers continue to use the activity-oriented approach, there would always be some key people who benefit from the object-oriented approach, e.g., management staff.

Conclusion

Orgsystems-What's been Achieved so Far?

The notion of the Pc-management came into being when the author together with several colleagues developed an application for supporting sales and marketing activities of a trading company. The system was called "DealDriver" to highlight that it helps the workers to "drive" the deals to the end which is receiving payment. Deals were thus the first type of orgobjects designed. The work on the project started in spring 1989, and the first version of DealDriver was ready in summer 1990. Since then, Dealdriver has been successfully used at our home office to support one of IbisSoft's business activities-reselling of professional software.

The DealDriver project, gave us some valuable insights into the problems of orgsystems development which are summarized in our internal reports. We developed also an experimental version of application development tools to support orgsystems development. These tools were later used for building both prototypes and functioning systems in a number of other application fields, e.g., hospital administration.

Next two subsections discuss some theoretical and technical aspects of orgsystems development. The reader who is not interested in such issues is invited to look over these.

What are the Related Research Fields?

Orgsystems development belongs to an application field called groupware. This is a multidisciplinary field where social scientists and computer scientists work together. Some of the computer science fields related to our work are as follows:

- the behaviour of dynamic objects, where the orgobjects belong, is being formalized by the theory of object-oriented systems;
- methods of storing and accessing structured information, which are vital for orgsystems development, are the subject of the database theory. Particularly related to our work are the

theories of semantic databases, object-oriented databases, and temporal databases;

- methods of planning for robots are one of AI's (Artificial intelligence) favourite research problems. The results obtained there may in some cases be directly applied to the management field. For example, the difference between classical and reactive planning corresponds to the difference between the pure Pj- and Fn-management.

What Makes the Systems Work?

The main ideas of the Pc-management originate from our previous research work on the CHAOS project (CHAOS stands for Concurrent Human-Assisted Object Systems). The project's objective was to work out a formal model for describing distributed interactive systems. This model is based on the notions of objects and connectors.

Objects are used to represent the elements of the "real world", (e.g. people, companies, projects, etc.), whereas connectors are the active elements of the system whose task is to make changes in the objects. A connector may be thought of as a little computer connected to one or several objects. As soon as some of these objects change, the connector changes all the other objects to restore the consistency of the system.

Thus defined, the model has a purely reactive nature, i.e. changes in objects are made as a reaction to changes in other objects. But objects in our model can be complex, i.e. they themselves can contain connectors, which means that a reaction can result in adjusting the system configuration to changes in the environment.

The CHAOS model fitted the management field so well that all we had to do was to use another set of terms. Thus, complex objects became orgobjects, connectors became planned activities, and the principle of reactive reconfiguration of the system was called dynamic and distributed planning. Some of the results of applying the CHAOS model to management field were virtually the same as those from the research works based on the theory of planning. However, being more general than the theory of planning, our model provides a better framework for management automation as it covers all aspects of management not only the issues of planning.

The CHAOS model is abstract, but the approach taken in the DealDriver project was very pragmatic. The objective of the project was to create a working system, not to speculate on the management automation issues. This project differs in many ways from similar research projects. Below we list the most important differences:

1. *Computer Environment*: We worked with PC computers under MS DOS in stand-alone and network versions, whereas research projects are often completed on Unix-based workstations. We used text-based terminals, not a graphic-based windowing environment with a mouse, icons, etc. This environment was chosen because it was the one an average company could easily afford.
2. *Development Tools*: Research workers often choose programming languages popular among computer scientists like Lisp, Prolog, Smalltalk, etc. These languages have a sound theoretical basis (e.g., function theory, logic, etc.), but require a lot of programming when they are used for the development of an application. We made a point of getting the maximum available help with programming by employing commercially available application development tools. We chose JAM from JYACC as a front-end tool, and Btrieve from Novell as a record manager. These tools were of great help to us, as we had limited resources for completing the project (in terms of time and manpower).
3. *Design Principles*: Researchers are often far too interested in the technical issues, such as methods of software design and programming, etc. We concentrated on user-interface issues instead. Our only principle of programming was: a program should work and permit to easily make necessary changes. All programming was done in C-language, and though our system was object-oriented in a very high degree, we didn't use any object-oriented extension to C.

Thus, two factors contributed to the successful completion of the DealDriver project:

- the use of a powerful abstract model, and
- a pragmatic approach to system development, and we strongly believe that both of them are obligatory for the development of a computer system of a totally new kind.

We are also convinced that there is no need to wait 10-20 years, which it usually takes for new research ideas to be implemented in application systems. New ideas can be implemented today and with the means available now.

4

Prospects and Challenges for Tourist Transport

Introduction

The relationship between tourism and transport by developing the concept of a tourist transport system as a means of analysing the processes shaping the provision and consumption of transport services by tourists. Throughout the book, transport is emphasised as a dynamic and active element in the tourist's experience of travelling because it is a vital part of the process of tourism. Some of the first-generation tourism textbooks (e.g., Mathieson and Wall 1982) regarded tourist transport an essential part of tourism but not worthy of study in its own right. In fact, a number of subsequent texts continue to view transport as a passive element in the tourist experience (Ryan 1996) and it remains a descriptive feature of most texts.

In the scope of multidisciplinary research on tourism and transport is reviewed in terms of the concepts and methods of each discipline (economics, geography, marketing and management) use to analyse tourist transport. However, the different philosophical backgrounds of researchers from these disciplines mean that their approach to tourist transport is not easy to synthesise into a holistic framework. Moreover, the tendency for researchers to retain their disciplinary training–whether in economics, geography, marketing or management–has simple contributed to the growing body of knowledge on transport and tourism. For our understanding of tourist transport systems and the tourist's experience of travel to grow, a greater degree of coherence and a theoretical basis needs to be developed. This means that research will need to be interdisciplinary in nature. Interdisciplinary research requires people from different disciplines to collaborate and focus on a specific research problem, where different questions are asked about the topic without each researcher losing sight of the problem under consideration. This may help to integrate the contributions which different disciplines can make to the analysis of tourist transport systems in order to achieve a more holistic understanding of the operation, management and use of transport services by tourists.

Although there is not space within this introductory book to undertake a comprehensive review of transport and tourism, it has sought to focus on how the consumer, provider and other agencies (e.g., national governments) interact in different transport systems. The concept of a tourist transport system was developed as a framework in which to understand the interrelationships between different elements in such systems. Using a system approach to the analysis of tourist transport also highlighted the importance of *inputs* to the system (e.g., the demand and supply) as well as *controlling influences* (e.g., government policy) and *outputs* (the tourist travel experience) and the effect on the environment. The book has also sought to identify a number of process which characterise the tourist transport system. For example, deregulation and privatisation is a process now affecting tourist transport systems in North America, Western Europe and Australasia (Button and Gillingwater 1991) as well as communist states such as China (Tapling 1993). Within the existing literature, the discussion of tourist transport systems has remained fragmented and dependent upon generalised and empirical studies or extremely specialised studies of both tourism and transport. The interface between tourism and transport has not been integrated into a holistic framework. Wilst tourism is now regarded as a complex phenomenon by educators and researchers, its frequent association with transport has meant that social science researchers have failed to integrate these issues in a framework where the complementarity between tourism and transport could be explored further. The tendency within tourism research to focus on typologies of tourism and tourists has led to a critical separation of the tourist from the mode of transport they use. This has the effect of contributing to the separation of tourism and transport research , with tourist motivation to travel viewed in isolation from the process of travelling. The result is that tourist travel is divided into two discrete elements (transport and the tourist) rather than being conceptualised as a continuous process using a systems approach. But what are the process shaping tourist transport in the new millennium?

Tourist Transport Provision in the late 1990s and the New Millennium

One of the overriding themes affecting the tourist transport system is globalization especially in those sectors which deal with the management and logistics of international travel (Lovelock and Yip 1996). Globalization inevitably produces 'winners and losers's in the pursuit of business and four distinct processes are associated with it. There are :

- *Deregulation,* where the entry barriers to many sectors of the tourist transport business have been removed and large oligophilies are challenged the new entrants (Pearce 1995b). As the example of the US domestic airline industry illustrates, in newly deregulated indicters, competition increased at a rapid pace. However, there is debate within the American domestic airline industry as to whether consumers have been the main beneficiaries, with lower prices. Goetz and Sutton (1997) explain that the benefits of deregulation have accrued to those passengers travelling on trunk routes, while business travellers and passengers travelling to/from more peripheral locations have experienced higher fares.
- *Technological change,* which has revolutionised the organisation, management and day-to-day running of tourist transport businesses with the introduction of information technology (IT). IT has also helped reduce some of the costs of business operations. The introduction of CRSs and GDSs have certainly assisted with the globalization of the supply of tourist transport services. The introduction of the Internet has also had a major impact on the supply of transport services (Macdonald) Wallace 1997). In fact many of the world's airlines now have Internet sites and as Whitaker and Levere (1997) show, some are being used for bookings, but 'the scope and standard of airline-related material on the Internet varies drama-tically'. In fact the evolution of Internet sites and their use in marketing has now moved beyond a tool simply to advertise and sell tourist transport services. This traditional use, based on sales and marketing, is reflected in the UK express coach network site—http://www.national-express.co.uk. However, there is evidence that some companies are developing a more holistic approach to transport and tourism and using the Internet to address the impact of competitive force such as rival carriers. The company's Internet site –http://

www.redfunnel.co.uk contains the traditional sales and marketing function. But it also moves into a tactical marketing role where bookings can be auctioned and place-marketing is undertaken in relation to the main destination they serve–the Isle of White. The website provides ideas for theme itineraries and the main attractions to visit which complement the tourism marketing activities of the public sector . This is certainly leading the way in providing a seamless tourism experience facilitated by technology and the activities of the transport operator. Some airlines also often sophisticated system allowing passengers to plan book and pay for their flights other can master little more than sketchy corporate information .

- *Regional change :* The highest costs for air travel remain in Europe and North America whereas in other trading blocs such as ASEAN, lower costs exist. For tourist transport providers in the global economy, it can mean airliners are competing on a different cost basis as Halon (1996) observes in terms of regional wage rates and remuneration of airline employees.
- *Hypercompetition:* Within the global marketplace, tourist transport provider are facing pressures continually to improve products and to remain competitive. In some case, organisation and constantly struggling to remain in business as experience in the international airline industry suggests. As the privatisation characteristic of the 1990s and deregulation seem set to continue, established industry leaders and find their position challenged or destroyed by fierce completions. According to D'Aveni (1998), this hypercompetition is typified by :
- Rapid product innovation.
- Aggressive competition.
- Shorter product life cycles.
- Businesses experimenting with meeting customers' needs.
- The rising importance of alliance.
- The destruction of norms and rules of national oligopolies.

D'Aveni (1998) identifies four processes which are fuelling hypercompetition :

- Customers requiring better quality at lower prices One of the innovations airlines have pursued to develop improved quality at lower prices is in-flight catering (Jones 1995)

- Rapid technological change, especially the use of IT.
- the rise of aggressive large companies willing to enter markets for a number of years with a loss-leader product in the hope of destroying the competition and capturing the market in the long term.
- Government policies towards barriers to competition are being progressively removed. This is evident in the tourist transport sector throughout the world, albeit to differing degrees depending on the political persuasion and commitment to deregulation.

At first sight, D'Aveni's (1998) processes are not particularly different from those listed under globalization (e.g., deregulation, technological change, consumer preferences and regional change). But the fundamental different lies in the business strategy of hypercompetitors. As D'Aveni (1998) argues, hypercompetitors tend to destroy the existing competencies of businesses. Those affected by such change are often trapped by an inability to think laterally and to adopt new competencies. Even when new competencies are introduced, businesses often have difficulty in diffusing them throughout their organisation. Some belatedly look towards the concept of 'change management' but this can sometimes be too little action too late. Often firms are so severely affected by hypercompetions and their action, that their reponses are bound by age-old relactions based on previous rules of completion, However, the hypercompetitor can only remain in a competitive position while it retains the advantage. According to D'Aveni (1998), hypercompetitors enter the market by disrupting the competition in some of the following ways :

- By redefining the product market, thereby redefining the meaning of the quality while offering it at a lower price. This is the strategy adopted by EasyJet in the UK which entered the market with low-cost air travel from Luton Airport to challenge the market leaders (e.g., BA, British Midland and KLM UK).
- By modifying the industry's purpose and focus by bundling and splitting industries. BA's response to EarJet was to reduce fares in the short term, but then it provided a splitting action by establishing a similar low-cost operation based at London Stansted, with lower landing fees. This avoid eroding profit margins and using high-cost airline capacity from Heathrow and Gatwick. In other words, BA can operate a loss-leader small business to compete head on which FasyJet on equal terms. A similar response occurred in New Zealand in the mid-1990s

when Air New Zealand established a low-cost airline (Freedom Air) to compete with the Hamilton-based airline Kiwi Air.

- By disrupting the supply chain by redefining the knowledge and know-how needed to deliver the product to the customer.
- By harnessing the global resources from alliances to compete with the non-aligned businesses. This in particularly acute in the airline industry although to data the term 'hypercom-petitor' has not been used to describe the business strategy of key players.

The process of globalization and hypercompetition are powerful forces affecting the tourist transport sector and a number of themes emergy which are worthy of further discussion :

- The role of the consumer.
- The growing significance of service quality.
- The introduction of Total Quality Management Systems.

The Tourist as a Consumer

Much of the rhetoric and hype associated with the rapid expansion of popular business books and the elevation of individuals to 'guru' status in the 1980s and 1990s is characterised by one consistent theme : that businesses need to understand the customer and to get near to them as 'end-users'.

Swarbrooke (1997) reiterates the importance of consumer behaviour research in tourism, since from a tourist transport perspective it allows businesses to plan infrastructure developments, identify product opportunities, set price levels for products and identify market segments and the best marketing medium to promote the product. Consumer behaviour research also allows businesses to modify their product and its delivery to align it more closely with consumer expectations. For the tourist transport business, understanding how tourists make their purchasing decisions and the factors affecting their choice of product is critical. In particular, the travellers' predisposition towards certain forms of transport will obviously affect their overall satisfaction with the product. For the tourism sector in general, Swarbrooke (1997) identifies a number of weakness in consumer behaviour research in the UK which are particularly relevant to the transport sector (although the exception may be the major airlines who commission in-house research that emains confidential and commercially sensitive). The main weaknesses are :

- An absence of reliable and up-to-data a feature emphasisted.

- A lack of longitudinal studies to trace the evolution of consumer behaviour in tourism through time.
- The methodologies and techniques used to collect data on consumer behaviour in tourism remain relatively crude and unsophisticated.
- The most robust data collated by private sector companies remains inaccessible to researchers.
- Methods of segmenting the market remain outdated due to a reliance on the lifecycle concepts and age, despite major societal and value changes which have questioned their validity in the late 1990s.
- Cross cultural differences in tourism markets and a predisposition towards using specific tourist transport mode remain poorly understood. The research identified by Lumsdon (1997), in prt, addresses some of these issues in relation to cycling.
- There are few media available to disseminate results to the practitioner audience.

As a result, consumer behaviour is one area which tourist transport operators will need to focus on if they seek to understand what motivates tourists to travel and to select specific modes of transport.

Tourist transport systems are likely to be affected by various opportunities and constraints on tourist travel in the late 1990s and beyond. For example, congestion of airspace in developed countries such as North America and Western Europe (French 1994, 1997b) will remain a persistent problem for policy makers and transport planners in late 1990s and new millennium. At the same time the demand for long-haul travel is developed for transports provides and tours operators if cohstraints cannot be covercome, Environmental issues will also feature more prominently in tourist transport systems as a new generation of travellers, having become familiar with green issues in the 1980s, emerge as consumers of tourist transports services. Understanding the relative importance of these factors in shaping the tourist's desire to travel on different modes of transport will be a major challenge for service providers, as the sustainability debate (Weiler 1993) focuses on more environmentally sensitive and novel modes of transport.

Increasingly, the patronage of tourist transport service is going to depend upon the ability of providers to differentiate their services on the basis of image market positioning and reputation for service quality. The 1990s are emerging as the decade of the consumer in relation to tourist travel, the providers responding to legitimate requests for higher standards of comfort, reliability and courtesy as part of the travel experience. The new millenium is also set to see a continuity and intensity of these processes of change, while the discussion of globalization and hypercompetion indicates the pressure on transport provides will intensify, Passengers are now recognised as customers and their rights and needs are beginning to gain a higher profile in the provision, quality and management of tourist transport services.

Service Quality Issues in Tourist Transport

The concept of service was introduced in the context of marketing. While that discussion provided a broad overview of the importance of service issues in tourist, transport, it is evident from the processes affecting the tourist as a consumer, that service quality is assuming a greater role in their purchasing decisions any travel behaviour. Irons (1994) argues that services are relationships and that whether that relationship is a transient one or a longerterm proposition, it needs to be conducted in a professional and consistent manner. As Irons (1994 : 13) shows,

> Such a relationship will be based on a series of contacts or interactions. It is from these interactions with the organisation that consumers form their perceptions... to assess value, decide to buy, repeat purchase or recommend to others.

Such interactions are also repeated within the organisation and Irons (1994) expresses this process as a triangle Irons explain the triangle in the following way:

- An organisation need to associate its internal culture with the one it portrays externally and this underpins the relationships evident.
- Within the organisation, power needs to be devolved so that the relationships can be developed and the appropriate skill and know-how is provided at the point where costumer satisfaction is met.
- The organisational values and culture need to be clearly understood by all employees so that they affect their actions and activities in relation to customers.
- Managers need to lead the process, empowering people at the various levels in the organisation to achieve customer-related

targets. In other words, managers need not only to exercise a degree of control in the management function, but also to lead the organisation in this era of the consumer.

- A customer focus is critical rather than a focus first on the product and then its purchasers.

To create a service culture in an organisation, Irons (1997) identified the following key points :

- Service businesses need to identify what the priorities are for the customer. Irons (1997) cites the example of Southwest Airlines in the USA which saw a set or priorities–reliability, low fates, personal treatment–and set about 'rigorously building the airline around meeting these needs and cutting out those things the customer did not want's.
- Organisations need to develop a clear vision of 'what they stand for and where they aspire to go...This vision should be for the customer, for the staff and for the owners'.
- Organisations and employees need to communicate so that they understand what is to be achieved, why, how and the role of employees in the corporate vision.
- The organisation needs to learn from its experience through problem-solving and how this can benefit its vision.
- The service culture needs to be led from the top in the organisation rather than through passive forms of managerialism.
- It is at the point of interaction between the market and the consumer that value can be created.
- Service delivery is an integral part of the process for service organisations and it should drive the business.

While the principle outlined by Irons (1994, 1997) may be useful in outlining how businesses may create a service culture, at a practical level the service requirements of the tourist transport sector need to be examined in more derail. This is because in certain sectors of the tourist transport business, service qualities offer particular challenges to operators because of the nature of the service interaction. It should also be emphasised that in some case, tourists' expectations are rising beyond the reach of mass transport providers and their ability to meet these needs.

Within the literature on tourism and transport there are comparatively few systematic reviews of service quality. While studies reviewed on rail travel highlighted the experience of InterCity prior to privatisation, few other reviews exist. Those studies which have been undertaken have largely focused on the airline sector (e.g. Ostrowski et al 1993, 1994; Van Borrendam 1989(. Probably the most influential publication to date is that by Witt and Muhle-mann (1995) which not only reviews the previous research in the area, but also identifies the idiosyncrasies and conditions which influence service quality in airlines.

Service Quality : Conceptual Issues

Ostrowski et al (1993) argued that service quality issues were comparatively poorly developed in the airline industry, based on a survey of 6,000 travellers using two US airlines. They concluded that there was considerable scope for improvement. Hamill (1993) places this in the context of changes in the aviation sector in the 1990s, with deregulation and privatisation forcing companies to become more customer-oriented. This process is continuing in the late 1990s in Europe with liberalisation (Graham 1998), since Lufthansa prepared itself for privatisation in 1997. By January 1998, at least four other European flag carriers had prepared for privatisation (Air France, TAP Air Portugal, Alitalia and LOT of Poland). Hamill (1993) also points to the strategies pursued by some airlines, where the use of computer reservation systems (CRSs) was seen as improving service. Yet this development has no direct impact on the actual service encounter and such a perception is futher evidence of the need for a focus on service quality issues.

Witt and Muhlemann (1995) explore the problem of establishing a working definition of service quality. Gronroos (1984) introduced the idea of a *technical quality* dimension (the customer interaction with the service organisation) and a *functional quality* dimension (the process through which the technical quality is delivered). As a result, the consumer's perception of service is a result of the service dimension combining technical and functional aspects. In contrast, Gummesson (1993) argued that four qualities affected customer perceived satisfaction. These were:

- design quality,
- delivery quality,
- relational quality,
- production quality.

A further model of quality was developed by Zeithmal et al (1990) which was based on gap analysis and focused on four dimensions :

- customers not knowing what to expect,
- inappropriate service quality standards,
- a service performance gap,
- company promises not matched by delivery.

To evaluate quality, Zeithmal et. al., (1990) used ten dimensions which were reduced to five elements :

- tangibles,
- reliability,
- responsiveness,
- assurance,
- empathy.

which are combined in the SERQUAL model used to evaluate customers' perceptions of quality. While SERQUAL and measures of perceived quality were certainly dominant elements in the research agenda in the late 1980s and early 1990s Witt and Muhlemann (1995 : 34) argue the 'the succe-ssful organisation will be one which establishes a total quality culture' based on total quality management (TQM). But what is TQM, where does it originate from and how will it affect tourist transport providers?

Total Quality Management

It is widely acknowledge that the 1980s was many service providers and North America respond to a perceived 'quality' crisis posed by products and services offered by rivals in the Pacific Rim (Deeming (1982). Many service providers responded with corporate strategies focused on quality issues as a method of retaining market share. Yet if the late 1980s were characterised by a business environment committed to quality, the 1990s were dominated by total quality management (TQM) as a more sophisticated form of recognising customers' needs as an integral part of an organisation's goals. TQM developed as a corporate business management philosophy and it even has an academic journal—TQM—devoted to research in this area. Why should this be of interest to the tourist transport system in the 1990s? The growing concern for consumers, quality and total supply management in the tourist transport system is part of the move towards TQM among service providers. Furthermore, TQM is likely to assume a greater role in academic and commercial research on tourist transport in the 1990s.

TQM is an all-embracing approach which enables an organisation to develop a more holistic view of consumers, quality issues and service provision as an ongoing process. Yet one of the principles of TQM—the concern for quality—is explicitly dealt with in detail in this book. One difficulty is in establishing a universal definition of quality which could be applied to tourist transport system. Dotchin and Oakland (1992) provide an excellent review of this issue, citing the work by Townsend and Gebhart (1986) which distinguishes between the subjective evaluation of quality be the customer (quality of perception) and the provider's more objective assessment (quality of fact). Chearly the meaning of quality will very according to the context and the perception of who is establishing what can be deemed as quality, as the discussion of conceptual issues of quality showed. While the journal TQM contains many interesting discussions of this issue, opeationalisings TQM in a tourist transport context requires organisation to work towards specific goals forcused on an agreed concept of quality. Corporate commitment is required so that TQM permeates all areas of the company's business. TQM also provides an organisation with the opportunity to monitor and implement internal procedures and to control supplies using established quality standards such as BS 5750.

One of the real challenges for TQM in tourist transport systems is to establish what the customer considers as excellece in service provision and the design of service delivery systems to deal with individual tourists' requests requirements and needs. Many corporation involved in tourist transport provision are trying to make individual tourists feel more valued as customers but, until delivery systems are able to deal fully with this issue, operators will be unable to claim success in TQM. It is at the strategic policy and planning stage that organisations may need to agree on how to improve continuously and strive for quality in service provision so that the tourist's travel experience is enhanced. One challenge is to ensure that the process of travel is not perceived as such a mundane and stressful experience for some tourists.

Implementing a TQM strategy is no easy task for organisations where it may involve a change in corporate culture. Nevertheless, a number of critical factors characterise success in TQM in service provisions. Senior management set on developing a policy for TQM will need to follow certain principles and management strategies. The ideas developed by Irons (1994, 1997) on developing a service culture, while TQM is a more systematic attempt to ensure quality is dealt with in a consistent manner. Witt (1995) cites Oakland's (1989) route to implementation as a series of steps which are outline. Oakland (1989) explains that the CEO of any organisation must begin by *understanding* the concepts of TQM and the route to implementation. This then needs to be followed by *commitment and policy* to set out what the organisation hopes to achieve from its quality strategy. Following this, it may be necessary to alter the *organisational structure* to fit which the new ethos. In terms of *measurement,* the inputs (raw materials), output (product), performance of employees and any costs of failure need to be quantified. Even though it is often hard to measure intangible elements in a service, the SERVQUAL survey tool might be used. The process of *planning* is the next step, to assess the nature of the service process, who it serves, when and where. This is a good point to use the results of the SERVQUAL survey to plan changes to the delivery of the service. The next stage is called *system,* where a quality manual is produced to explain how the company undertakes its quality policies, with the management system in place. This is also an opportunity to specify the nature of the product being delivered and how it is produced. The term *capability* refers to be next stage where the organisation can assess whether it has the ability to meet each customer's set of requirements or if modifications are needed. This is followed by a *control* function to ensure the service is delivered in a consistent manner within acceptable tolerance levels, on each occasion. Since service delivery often involves more than one person, the role of *teamwork* needs to be considered. This may also involve the use of quality circles in the organisation, where employees work in teams to solve problems and promote a commitment to quality. To ensure a continuous improvement in quality, *training* is essential. At the top of the steps is TQM *implementation.* Porter and Parker (1992) notes that management behaviour and their willingers to carry through such programmes is often the key to the successful implementation of TQM.

However, interest in TQM is not substitute for the organisation and logistical skills involved in coordinating and managing rourist transport systems. Conveying large numbers of people over short and long distances for pleasure and business is a complex process requiring a great deal of planning and organisation on a day-to-day basis as well as in the longer term. Adding a concern for quality provision in this process makes the delivery of service a more complex undertaking and it is not surprising that service interruptions occur due to the sheet volume and scale of people handled in tourist transport systems. But when things do go wrong, companies and their front-line staff must be empowered to deal with incidents, or systems must be in place to deal with crises when they occur. Whether a tourist transport provider prefers a gradual improvement approach to quality or a TQM approach, it is worth considering some of the impediments to quality improvements in relation to the airline sector.

Quality Issues in the Airline Industry

Witt and Muhlemann (1995) identify two persistent problems to meeting travellers' requirements :

- How may a quality service be defined, what factors influence the customer's experience and how may these factors be identified?
- How may performance or delivery of the product be measured or contoured, given the intangible nature of services? (Witt and Muhlemann 1995 : 35)

Witt and Muhlemann (1995 : 35) identify the following five factors which may pose particular problems :

- The mixed nature of airline markets where leisure and business travellers may be mixed on any flight, each with different requirements
- Lack of direct control over factors contributing to the traveller's experience, including:
  - ticket purchases from travel agents, which can involve mistakes in ticketing.
  - experiences at the airport (e.g. air traffic control problems and weather conditions)
  - the impact of airline alliances, where partner airlines may not have harmonised standards of service to ensure a consistent quality throughout the journey regardless of the carrier.
- Congestion and slot availability, where large carriers dominate the main slots at a time when air travel in Europe and North America is becoming more congested
- Restrictions versus deregulation, where spatial inequalities occur in service provision depending upon the traveller's location in the system and choice of route, as Goetz and Sutton (1997) observe in the USA
- Differentiation in the product, where the airlines seek to segment the market and attract more travellers through the use of marketing tools such as frequent flyer programmes (Mason and Barker (1996 ; Beaver 1996).

Some airlines, such as SAS, have implemented quality management systems moving hear to TQM and BA is a further example of an airline which has attracted a great deal of attention in the research literature for its focus on quality. KLM is also implementing a full TQM scheme (Van Borrendam 1989). However, as Witt and Muhlemann (1995 : 39) suggest, 'Singapore Airlines is probably the best known for customer focus'. Aside from quality issues, there are a range of other themes likely to affect tourist transport in the next millennium.

Government policy, planning and investment in infrastructure assume a significant role in facilitating the efficient movement of people for the purpose of tourism. In this context, the London Tourist Board's (1990) *At the Crossroads: The Future of London's Transport* reaffirms the essential relationship between transport and tourism dealt. The London Tourist Board study is unique in this respect since it recognised that :

- An efficient transport network is necessary for tourists to gain access to a destination such as London; tourism would not exist without a transport network as it is part of the tourism infrastructure.
- An integrated transport network with convenient transfers between different modes of transport is essential, with reasonably priced travel options.
- Within the destination, tourists need a choice of transport to transfer between the port of arrival and their final destination.
- Investment in public transport provides social, economic and environmental benefits for both residents and tourists alike. Investment in transport infrastructure is a long term proposition and is unlikely to yield tangible benefits in market economies in relation to tourism. Yet without it, tourism would not be able to develop.

As the London Tourist Board Study notes, the development and long-terms prosperity of tourism depends on transport both to make destinations accessible and to facilitate tourist travel within the destination area. Efficiency, safety and ease of travel and convenient interchanges are likely to be viewed as important performance indicators by users of tourist transport systems. These principles apply to the wider context of tourist travel and making the travel experience more rewarding is one major challenge for all parties involved in providing tourist transport systems.

Withing the airline sector, concerns with dropping yields and moves to secure, the loyalty of economy travellers contune to face many companies. In terms of consumer behaviour, economy class travellers tend to seek the cheapest fare, which means a great emphasis on securing the loyalty of commercial passengers, regardless of whether they travel economy or business class. Even some of the British railway companies, such as Midland Mainline, which operates London to the East Midlands/South Yorkshire services, have recongnised this. Their introduction of a premium business service follows the same principle for securing the commercial traveller. Many of the world's airlines have turned to the creative flair of advertising agencies to appeal to their prestige markets such as the business traveller. For example, in August 1997 Air New Zealand launched a new advertising campaign designed by Saatchi and Saatchi. At the same time, a database marketing company worked with Air New Zealand to identify its Koru Club and Air Points members. A 'teaser' was then set to select a few members and encourage them to watch the advertisement when it was first screened, motivated by a prize opportunity. The chosen few then received a follow-up mailing some weeks after the advertisement extrolling the virtues of flying Air New Zealand. At the same time Air New Zealand customer support staff also received a newsletter to explain the focus of the campaign on business travellers, highlighting what they needed to do to show that Air New Zealand is unique.

What such campaigns show is that the marketing activities are selective and based on the concept of hand-picking. While the airline continued to use powerful national icons, such as the Koru image which is displayed on the tail of every aircraft, it is apparent that the targeting of high-yield travellers is now becoming the key focus for airlines. Such activities are likely to continue in the transport sector, as businesses seek to improve yields.

In a similar vein, airlines are also securing software which will improve yields. For example, Air New Zealand already uses Sabre Technology solutions in yield management and flight planning systems. In December 1997, Air New Zealand was in the process of signing a contract with Sabre to build a new Internet site and to introduce new software to replace its flight operation and crew management system. This illustrates that IT is enabling tourist transport operators to remain competitive and hopefully to reduce operational costs.

Transport operators are also turning to new solutions to reduce other components of their operational costs. For example, in May 1997 Cathay Pacific launched new Airbus A340 services on its Auckland–Hong Kong route–Airbus Industries claims that the fuel cost per seat of the A340 is 40 per cent of that for a Boeing 747. This was part of a US9 billion fleet replacement programme for Cathay Pacific. Fleet replacement costs represent a perennial problem for many airlines. The capital cost of fleet replacement means more innovative solutions need to be sought such as lease-buy schemes, manufacturer funding and straight lease schemes. This frees airlines from major sunk capital counts over and above those needed to service debt repayment on leases. Even so, cash -rich airlines such as Singapore Airlines continue to purchase aircraft and options on future aircraft rather than seeking leasing options.

***Table** : The potential for cost reductions among airlines.*

Cost items	*Route network*	*Cost drivers Fleet composition*	*Company policies*
Aircraft crew costs	XXX	XXX	XXX
Engineering overheads	X	XXX	
Direct engineering costs	X	XXX	X
Marketing	XXX		X
Aircraft standing	XXX	X	
Stations and ground services	X		X
Passenger services	X		X
General and administrative costs	X		X
Fuel		X	
Airport and en route costs	X		
Direct passenger service			X

Notes: XXX Significant cost reduction potential
X Some cost implications

A recent study by Seristo and Vesalainen (1997) offers a number of insights into the actual cost and revenue factors associated with airline operations. This is important in an age of cost-competitiveness, especially when airlines have been trimming staffing levels (Alamdari and Morrell 1997) and salaries in the 1990s to remain afloat. Yet as Sersto and Vepsalainen (1997 : 11) argue, 'for many a carrier even more critical measures will be needed to achieve sustainable profitability', which is also relevant to the wider tourist transport sector. In the analysis of cost derivers in 42 of the world's airlines, a number of variables were examined:

- The fleet composition of airlines.
- The flying personnel used, particularly the number of flight crew per aircraft.

- The route network.
- Cost drivers, operating expenses and profitability in terms of :
  - the composition of traffic,
  - route structure,
  - salaries/remunerating levels.

Using quantitative research methods (e.g., factor analysis), the variable were analysed and a model was built. This model highlights how various factors and variables were interrelated and as a result, it identifies the cost items and the factors where cost reductions were possible. Such analyses highlight that transport operators will need to focus on systematic appraisals of costs in a climate of increasing customer expectations, competitiveness amongst providers and declining yield per passenger through time. One strategy which airlines have followed is the pursuit of cost savings by divesting themselves of non-core activities such as in-flight catering operations. In June 1997, for example, Air New Zealand sold its catering business and planned to involve IBM in running its computer centre in a contracting-out of specialist non-core activities. These changes were identified in the company's 'Project Save' in the 1997/98 financial year, which is expected to save up to NZ$100 million in operating costs. Such savings are also expected to liberate capital to be reinvested in core business activities (Hanning (1997).

Interest in environmental factors such as sustainability in tourist transport seems set to continue as a powerful theme embracing tourism well into the next millennium. A growing interest is the use of public transport inrastructure to support tourist travel (Charlton 1998) is evident, with initiatives such as the Devon and Cornwall Rail Partnership, which has attracted leisure travel to offset losses in the non-leisure local rail market. Such rail tourism projects certainly have the potential to offer an alternative to the ingrained role of the car in recreational and tourist travel (Page 1998). Public transport certainly has a valid role to play in achieving sustainable tourism objectives in local areas. Such initiates not only make a contribution to the reduction of congestion and environmental pollution in areas of natural beauty, but also offer access opportunities for but disabled, cyclists and casual travellers in place of the car. Even in urban areas, the development of public transport system may offer the tourist more opportunities to enjoy the urban environment without the stress of parking and driving a car is congested cities. Brooks (1995) documented the reintroduction of historic Victorian trams in Chrstchurch, New Zealand, where the five vintage trams cover a 2.5 km inner city track. By 1997 it was obvious that they were not profitable. While the trams undoubtedly offer an attraction for the tourist, like those used in Blackpool and Fylde in Lancashire, UK, it is evident that transport systems may sometimes need to be subsidised to generate tourist business for other sectors of the urban economy (as is the case with the tourist tram service in Melbourne) (Page 1993a, 1995b). Yet this seems to run somewhat contrary to the political policy-making environment of the late 1990s where transport users, particularly tourists, need to pay the economic cost of transport.

Within an international context, there is also evidence to suggest that with the globalization of the airline industry and other transport sectors there is a growing need for an agency to ensure fair competition. According to downs and Tunney (1997), European completion law for the air transport industry may 'become the foundation stone for global competition rules for aviation' (Downes and Tunney 1997 : 76) The World Trade Organisation is seen as the most likely body to ensure competion rules are upheld. At the same time tourist transport providers are facing an operating environment where increased health and safety regulations (Caves 1996) and airport risk controls as well as measures such as the EU's (1995) *Protection of Tourists* (European Parliament 1995) place a greater onus on the operator and package to provide accurate information to travellers. These types of measure are likely to encourage transport operators to consider the tourist experience within the context of ever-increasing demands for quality improvements.

One worrying trend in the airline sector is the rise in 'on-board incidents' where violent passengers disrupt the flight. Skapinker (1998b) reports that while BA only encounters 10 to 15 such incidents a year, they can endanger the lives of hundreds of people. It is likely that their is only the tip of the iceberg and it is certainly a concern for both airline employees and passengers alike, as the authors found when observing such an incident. One of the contributory factors is alcohole consumption and BA now empower the staff to prevent drunk passengers from boarding and to stop serving passengers who appear drunk on board. Airport delays and inadequate information may lead to increased alcohol consumption and at least one Asian airline has even issued cabin staff with restraints to prevent disorderly conduct. Although such events usually occur on long-haul flights, airlines are imposing heavy fines on passengers, especially where pilots divert to eject passengers. It is just one additional issue with which airlines now have to deal. Managing such situations in an appropriate manner can also result in commitment and customer loyalty if the emphasis is on the enhancement of a quality experience for all passengers.

5

Hotel Environment Management

The Caribbean hotel industry is positioned to reinvent itself in a way that improves profitability, enhances guest relations, builds bridges into the local communities, and preserves the Caribbean's natural beauty.

Over the past 2 years, this trend has been translated into results in Jamaica in the form of the Environmental Audits for Sustainable Tourism (EAST) project, sponsored by the Jamaica Hotel and Tourist Association and funded by the United States Agency for International Development (USAID).

This paper presents a case study of the USAID/Jamaica EAST project demonstrating the power of becoming an environmentally friendly hotel through the adoption of an environmental management system (EMS), a comprehensive organizational approach designed to achieve environmental care in all aspects of operations.

Partnering environmental protection with cost-saving environmental improvements and best practices, the EAST project is a model for the hotels and tourism destinations in the Caribbean region and beyond for environmental assessments and actions, as well as voluntary environmental audits that can lead to the GREEN GLOBE International Certification.

Introduction

A "quiet revolution" is taking place in the Caribbean-one less visible than the construction of new hotels and the building of new cruise ships. Nevertheless, its advent is profoundly changing the nature and shape of the tourism and hospitality industry, in every hotel guestroom, housekeeping, laundry or maintenance facility, and in every tourism destination that elects voluntarily to join the environmental movement. This revolution is environmentally sustainable tourism. The Caribbean hotel industry, particularly, is positioned to reinvent itself in a way that improves profitability, enhances guest relations, builds bridges into the local communities, and preserves the Caribbean's natural beauty. Over the past 2 years, this trend has been translated into results in Jamaica in the form of the Environmental Audits for Sustainable Tourism (EAST) project, sponsored by the Jamaica Hotel and Tourist Association and funded by the United States Agency for International Development (USAID).

USAID/Jamaica EAST Project Description

In 1997, the Jamaica Hotel and Tourist Association, Government of Jamaica, Jamaica Manufacturers Association, and a number of tourism-related public and private-sector industry organizations committed to undertake the Environmental Audits for Sustainable Tourism (EAST) project. With funding from the U.S. Agency for International Development, Hagler Bailly implemented a program of environmental audits within a corporate environmental management system aimed at the tourism and hospitality industry in Negril, with a smaller component focused on manufacturing industries in Kingston and St. Andrews. The project is a model for environmental action and voluntary audits for the tourism sector, combining promotion and outreach, training, audits, and investment.

The objectives of the EAST program are:

- to develop greater awareness and understanding of the benefits of environmental systems and audits among hotel and restaurant owners and allied tourism businesses;
- to upgrade the technical skills of Jamaicans who are expected to conduct the audits and advise on environmental management systems;
- to assist a select, representative number of tourism-related establishments in carrying out environmental audits, and
- to help finance in the tourism industry, on a cost-sharing basis, selected audit recommendations in order to demonstrate the financial benefits of the systematic application of environmentally friendly practices and, thereby, encourage others in the tourism industry to do likewise.

The activities of the EAST project include:

- institutionalizing environmental management in the tourism industry;

- performance monitoring of EAST demonstration hotels;
- environmental assessments, audits, and certification; environmental awareness and training; regulatory assistance in environmental licensing;
- audits and technical assistance in the manufacturing industry;
- targeted environmental investment fund feasibility and financing; performance awards programs, and international human resources exchange programs.

An important next step for Jamaica is to sustain and expand this improved level of environmental management among government and private-sector organizations.

East Findings and Results

The following is a discussion of some of the EAST findings and results. When Hagler Bailly began in June of 1997, the awareness was quite high in Negril (the target area for the EAST project) due primarily to the influx of questionnaires and surveys sent by European tour operators such as Tui and British Airways Holidays. These inquiries were from European markets interested in buying the export products, e.g., traveling to destinations supporting environmental best policies and management practices. Hagler Bailly started with a survey of hotels in Negril to ask hoteliers why they choose to become "environmentally friendly." The results showed a genuine concern about the impact their operations have on the physical environment and an appreciation for how this can be translated into cost savings. Interestingly, the government's enforcement of environmental laws and standards ranked lowest. This told us that hoteliers were interested in measurable results and that they would respond better to incentives than to government intervention. Initially, however, when we asked individual hoteliers what they thought "going green" implied, the most common answer was to replace plastic straws with paper straws. The obvious next question, since none of the respondents had achieved the "environmentally friendly" status, was what are the perceived barriers to becoming a green hotel. The results pointed to the up-front cost of learning how to make the transition, and then to the financing to implement it.

Hotel Environmental Management System

One of the most critical elements of becoming an environmentally friendly hotel is the adoption of a new culture that extends throughout the hotel organization, and between the hotel and its guest, local community, and even its vendors. We call this an environmental management system (EMS).

An EMS is defined as a comprehensive organizational approach designed to achieve environmental care in all aspects of operations. The International Standards Organization (ISO) 14000 series is an international standard for EMS. The World Travel and Tourism Council's GREEN GLOBE international certification has developed an EMS standard specifically for the travel and tourism industry.

An effective EMS can help a hotel assure its guests of its commitment to environmental management as partners in programs such as recycling, linen and towel reuse, etc. It can set specific and realistic performance objectives and targets, and allow the hotel to monitor to see if the objectives and targets are being met. As mentioned earlier, it can enhance a hotel's image in the marketplace and help reach nearly 43 million Americans, as well as hundreds of thousands of environmentally aware tourists from Europe and elsewhere interested in visiting environmentally friendly destinations and staying in accommodations with environmental policies and programs in place.

Most importantly, an EMS can improve efficiency and reduce operating costs. In fact, the savings alone should be sufficient for any hotel to commit to implementing an EMS. Few hotels today have what we would consider an EMS. This is not to say that there are no hotels implementing environmental programs such as water conservation and composting, but it is typically not done as part of a larger management system, nor is it integrated with other environmental programs. There is a growing demand to have an EMS that meets international standards such as ISO 14001 and GREEN GLOBE. An EMS evaluation, because of its broad-reaching implications, will begin to encompass other concerns such as health, safety, and security, emergency preparedness, compliance with discharge and emissions standards, and employee training.

What constitutes an EMS? The principal components of an EMS, as defined by GREEN GLOBE, include the following: an environmental policy that clearly communicates the organization's commitment to maintaining the social, cultural and physical environment; an action plan to guide the property's actions and expenditure of resources; the implementation or operations of the EMS that encompasses all of the property's actions relative to the environment, including awareness and training, staff procedures, incentive programs, and community outreach among other things; corrective action or monitoring to ensure that the EMS performs as expected, allowing for responsive actions to capture things such as leaking toilets and chemical spills and review, typically by senior management, to determined how to improve the EMS and the level of compliance with the hotel's environmental policy.

EMS and Environmental Programs

Many will say, we already have hotels in the Caribbean that are operating in an environmentally responsible manner. That is to say that the hotel is currently composting much of its organic solid wastes, or that guestrooms have low flow showerheads installed. We call these environmental programs. An EMS is the integration of those programs under a comprehensive organizational system. An EMS takes the following approach to addressing its environmental issues (or aspects as they are referred to in the standards).

- First, an assessment is done to determine what improvements can be made, how much they cost, and what types of changes in consumption or waste generation can be expected. The assessment also allows you to establish a baseline against which change can be measured.
- Next, the hotel sets objectives such as to reduce water consumption for the entire property by 10%. Each objective is supported by a set of specific targets, such as introduce towel and linen reuse program by June 31st, or install low-flow showerheads in guest rooms and staff locker rooms by August 1st.
- The individuals, or departments, responsible for achieving the targets are identified in an action plan. It is important to remember that the greatest improvements are made through changes in staff procedures.
- Finally, the impact or results, in terms of changes from the baseline, must be measured and documented. This provides the necessary feedback to determine whether the EMS is working.

The EMS can be viewed as the integration of multiple environmental programs. Environmental programs are typically designed to address a specific environmental problem or issue such as recycling or composting solid waste; or are focused on a specific department such as a linen reuse program in housekeeping and laundry. In some instances, particularly for smaller hotels, environmental programs may involve multiple properties, such as sharing the cost of a bottle crusher for glass recycling.

East Environmental Management Audit Findings

Hagler Bailly designed a specific audit protocol that combines the attributes of an energy audit, an environmental audit, and a management audit —the EAST Environmental Management Audit. We tested the audit protocol on the full range of hotel properties, from 15 rooms to over 200 rooms. The audits covered the following areas energy use, water use, wastewater generation and disposal, solid waste generation and disposal, use of chemicals, and management and staff practices. Summarized below are some of the general findings of the EAST audits.

Inefficient use of Water: Leaking toilets accounted for 40% of the daily water use in one 35-room hotel. The cost of the leaks was US$600 per month. In another property, a defective drain valve on a washing machine increased laundry water use by more than 1 million gallons per year equivalent to US$6,000 of wasted water.

Inefficient use of Energy: Loose louvers and doors and poor insulation force air conditioners to work continuously in order to keep guest rooms cool. This mode of operation increases energy consumption and shortens the air conditioner's service life.

Excessive and Unnecessary use of Chemicals: Instead of manually cleaning the kitchen grease trap, a property used 420 gallons/year of sulfuric acid (or Drano) to do the job. This cost of this dangerous habit exceeded US$6,000 per year.

Excessive Solid Waste Generation: A 25-room property spent US$1,700 per year to purchase large plastic trash bags. Many properties place all yard waste in plastic bags and pay to send this material to the dump. Organic wastes from kitchen and landscaping accounts for up to 50% of a property's solid waste and can be easily composted.

Staff not Participating in Environmental Programs: In 90% of cases, housekeepers automatically replace all used guest towels in properties that have towel reuse programs.

Poor (or no) Monitoring: Approximately 70% of audited properties had no effective utilities monitoring program. Water and electricity bills are simply received and paid. A 20,000-gallon per day leak went undetected for more than a week because the property didn't check the water meter daily. There was considerable variation in water use among 14 properties we audited ranging from 15 to 70 rooms. To provide a common base for comparison, we calculated each hotel's consumption in terms of Imperial gallons per guest night. The results are shown in table below. The most efficient of the hotels used just one-third the water per guest night of the least efficient.

Table: *Water Use in Properties Audited by EAST Imperial gallons/Guest Night*

Most Efficient Hotel	116
Average Efficient	216
Least Efficient	351

A similar comparison was also done among audited properties for electricity consumption. The results are shown in table below. Again, the most efficient hotel used only one-quarter of the electricity per guest night of that of the least efficient hotel.

Table: *Electricity Use in Properties Audited by EAST KWH/Guest Night*

Most Efficient Hotel	8.7
Average Efficient	21.4
Least Efficient	32.9

Detailed Analysis of Efficiency Improvements in the EAST Demonstration Hotels

The water and energy use indices of a hotel are affected by occupancy rates as well as by its conservation efforts and investments in efficient technologies. As a general rule, water and energy indices rise during low occupancy months and drop during high occupancy months. Given the influence of occupancy and conservation efforts on efficiency, the monitoring data collected from the properties should be analyzed in greater detail to ensure that efficiency gains result from improved environmental practices rather than better occupancy rates. This higher scrutiny is particularly important, for example, in the case of a hotel that reduced its water and electricity use indices by more than 25% while simultaneously increasing its occupancy by 16%.

Figures below present the result of a more rigorous data analysis, and show how the hotel's monthly water and electricity use indices varied with respect to occupancy before and after its involvement with the EAST project. Since the water and electricity use indices are consistently lower "after" the EAST audit, regardless of the actual occupancy levels, these graphs prove that the property's water and electricity savings are due to improved conservation practices rather than higher occupancy rates. The vertical distance separating the "before EAST" and "after EAST" trend lines represents the actual water and electricity savings achieved through the property's conservation efforts at any given occupancy level.

Recommendations for Improvement

So what did it take to improve performance in a typical Jamaican hotel?

Most of the recommendations made in the EAST Audit reports have the following characteristics. They have low implementation costs, rapid payback periods, and they are relatively simple and easy to implement.

The EAST auditors also found that the greatest environmental and financial benefits can be achieved by improving: frequent monitoring, particularly utility bills; management supervision, oversight to ensure that programs are operating effectively; staff practices, training, and providing incentives for staff to implement programs, and preventive and routine maintenance, particularly of energy-and water-using equipment. In the breakdown of EAST audit recommendations for a typical hotel, the following was evident. Over three-quarters of the recommen-dations cost less than US$10/guest room, 19% of the recommendations cost between US$10-50 per guest room and only 3% cost more than US$50 per guestroom.

Payback period is defined as the length of time required before the savings from a measure equal the cost to implement the measure. In terms of payback period for EAST audit recommendations: 62% of the recommendations had a payback of less than 2 months, another 36% had payback periods of between 2 months and 1 year, and only 2% had payback of greater than 1 year. Another way to break down the EAST audit recommendations is by area of activity (or department) in the hotel.

Our auditors identified that the largest, by far, can be found in the maintenance and engineering department. We should note that more often than not, the problems lie in insufficient resources resulting in shortages of staff, parts, and supplies, and unwillingness to pay repair bills to fix a problem properly. Guest rooms (or housekeeping department) and restaurant and bar (or food and beverage department) accounted for 15 and 16 percent of the recommended actions, respectively. This is mainly due to the high degree of energy and water used in these areas.

Advantages of a "Green Hotel"

During our visits to Jamaica, we became aware of one small hotel in Port Antonio-Hotel Mocking Bird Hill-that has made considerable strides in improving environmental performance. For purposes of the following example, we will refer to Mocking Bird Hill's consumption levels as that of a "green hotel." Using the average from the 14 EAST hotels audited for both water and electricity; we show the difference relative to the "green hotel."

Looking now at an illustration of the cost advantages of a green hotel, let's assume a 50-room hotel, with 60% occupancy, and 2 guest per room. Over the course of a year, the water savings are over 3.6 million gallons, or savings of US$21,829 in water bills. The electricity savings are 186,000 kWh per year, or savings of US$23,886 in electricity bills. Total savings, for both water and electricity amounts to US$45,715 per year.

The savings can greatly improve a hotel's profitability. For example, if it takes US$10 of revenue to generate US$1 of profit, savings of US$45,715 in utility costs would have an impact equivalent to US$457,150 in additional revenue. Assuming average revenue of US$100 per guest night, the savings represent the equivalent to additional 4,571 guest nights worth of revenue.

Cash Flow Associated with "Going Green"

So how would the investment and savings look over an extended period of time? Most of the costs are incurred in the first 9 months. These include the cost of an external audit, energy and water savings equipment, and training of key staff. After the first year, the costs are only associated with preventative maintenance and preparing for the annual GREEN GLOBE certification. Over a 3-year period, the initial investment of US$40,000 will yield approximately US$112,000 in savings, or a net profit of about US$70,000.

Implications for the Jamaican Hotel Industry

Just to illustrate the point further, we asked the question: "What would becoming a green hotel mean for Jamaica as a whole?" Here we have used the Jamaican Tourist Product Development Company (TPDCo) hotel data for 1996, assumed 60% occupancy and 2 guests per room like the earlier example. Obviously, this over-simplifies the hotel industry, but the point is valid. For all of Jamaica, the difference between an industry comprised of green hotels and one comprised of average hotels is over 930 million gallons of water per year. The green hotel industry will use 77% less water than the average, and 86% less than the inefficient hotel industry. The reductions in water consumption also translate directly to the volume of wastewater coming from the hotel industry. We can do the same simulation for energy or specifically electricity consumption. For all of Jamaica, the difference between green hotels and the average hotel industry is over 47 million kilowatt-hours per year. The green hotel industry will use a third less electricity than the average, and two-thirds less electricity than the inefficient hotel industry.

Service Quality Measurement in Hotel Industry

In order to achieve rationality the models of business excellence also, in a way, determine whether the criteria have been met, but the evaluation of business excellence is based not only on the fulfilment of the set criteria but also on the determination of the level up to which the criteria have been fulfilled (systems of points).

When analyzing the quality of service it is desirable to analyse the largest possible number of companies supplying the same type of service. As we already mentioned, if a company carries out a research and finds that the results are negative, it can interpret this information in the wrong way and conclude that it provides services in a totally wrong way. On the other hand, when analyzing a large number of companies, it is possible to compare data and obtain a realistic picture of the position of an individual company compared to others regarding quality. The upper part of the model includes phenomena tied to the consumer, while the lower part shows phenomena tied to the supplier of services. The expected service is the function of earlier experiences of the consumer, their personal needs and oral communication. Communication with the market also influences the expected service. Experienced service, here called perceived service, is the result of a series of internal decisions and activities.

The management's perceptions of the consumer's expectations is the guiding principle when deciding on the specifications of the quality of service that the company should follow in providing service. If there are differences or discrepancies in the expectations or perceptions between people involved in providing and consuming services, a "service quality gap" can occur, as shown in image 1. Since there is a direct connection between the quality of service and the satisfaction of clients in hotel industry, it is important for the company to spot a gap in the quality of service.

The first possible gap is the knowledge gap. It is the result of the differences in managing knowledge and their real expectations. This gap can lead to other gaps in the process of service quality and is, among other things, caused by:

- incorrect information in market researches and demand analysis;
- incorrect interpretations of information regarding expectations;
- lack of information about any feedback between the company and the consumers directed to the management;
- too many organizational layers that hinder or modify parts of information in their upward movement from those involved in contact with the consumers.

The second possible gap is that of standard. It is the result of differences in managing knowledge of the client's expectations and the process of service provision (delivery).

This gap is the result of:

- mistakes in planning or insufficient planning procedures;
- bad management planning;
- lack of clearly set goals in the organization; and
- insufficient support of the top management to service quality planning.

Conclusion

So what does this all mean to the Caribbean hotel industry? First, it is a "win-win" proposition. You can improve your market share while reducing your operating costs. Second, it is neither rocket science nor is it untried or untested. The audit recommendations are relatively simple and proven to work right here in the Caribbean. Third, you have no choice.

Resorts throughout the Caribbean countries and hotels all over the world have recognized the advantages of going green. International certification programs like GREEN GLOBE are driving the industry toward improved performance. This means that instead of getting the marketing advantage of being a leader, those that fail to make the transition may soon be termed as "brown hotels." Know anyone who would prefer to stay in a brown hotel rather than in a green one?

We should also look at what it means to different stakeholders such as the government and local communities across the Caribbean. The reduced water, wastewater, and energy consumption levels of a green hotel industry translate directly to reduced shortages and lowered needs for infrastructure in water supply, wastewater treatment plants, and power plants. The same holds true for solid waste and the need for sanitary landfills.

So the more important question becomes, what are the hotels waiting for? Governments should begin laying out the necessary incentives and standards to move the industry in this direction. Banks should open special lines of credit to finance the improvements. And Caribbean Hotel Association, Caribbean Tourism Organization, and the tourist board of each island should find ways to link the marketing of Caribbean hotels directly to the computers of those millions of so-called "eco-tourists" in the U.S. and Europe who are beginning to plan their next family vacations.

6

Human Resources Development in Hotels

Employment and Globalization in the Hotel, Catering and Tourism Sector

This report has been prepared by the International Labour Office as the basis for discussions at the Tripartite Meeting on Human Resources Development, Employment and Globalization in the Hotel, Catering and Tourism Sector.

At its 273rd Session (November 1998) the Governing Body of the International Labour Office decided that the Meeting would be included in the programme of sectoral meetings for 2000-01. At its 274th Session (March 1999) the Governing Body decided that the purpose of the Meeting would be to exchange views on policies and methods of human resource development, employment creation and globalization in the hotel, catering and tourism sector; to adopt conclusions that include proposals for action by governments, by employers' and workers' organizations at the national level and by the ILO; and to adopt a report on its discussion.

The Meeting may also adopt resolutions. The Governing Body also decided that the Meeting should be tripartite, that it should be composed of 75 participants and that the following 25 countries should be invited: Austria, Barbados, Brazil, Canada, China, Costa Rica, Dominican Republic, Egypt, France, Greece, India, Italy, Japan, Kenya, Republic of Korea, Lebanon, Mauritius, Morocco, Netherlands, Poland, Portugal, South Africa, Spain, Switzerland and the United States. In the event that a government declines the invitation, an alternate will be invited from the reserve list which was established at the same time: Argentina, Chile, Croatia, Hungary, Mexico, Namibia, New Zealand, Philippines, United Republic of Tanzania, Thailand, Tunisia, Turkey, Viet Nam, Zimbabwe. The Governing Body also decided that 25 Employer and 25 Worker participants would be appointed on the basis of nominations made by the respective groups of the Governing Body. They do not necessarily come from the above list of countries.

The Meeting is part of the ILO's Sectoral Activities Programme, the purpose of which is to facilitate the exchange of information among constituents on labour and social developments relevant to particular economic sectors, complemented by practically oriented research on topical sectoral issues.

This objective is being pursued inter alia by holding international tripartite sectoral meetings with a view to : fostering a broader understanding of sector-specific issues and problems; promoting an international tripartite consensus on sectoral concerns and providing guidance for national and international policies and measures to deal with the related issues and problems; promoting the harmonization of all ILO activities of a sectoral character and acting as the focal point between the Office and the sectoral ILO constituents; and providing technical advice and practical assistance to the latter in order to facilitate the application of international labour standards.

The report attempts to illustrate how the issues of globalization, employment and human resources development in the hotel, catering and tourism sector are linked to the strategic objectives of the ILO and to its overall conceptual framework of decent work. At its 87th Session (June 1999), the International Labour Conference agreed that in future the ILO should focus its work on four strategic objectives:

- to promote and realize fundamental principles and rights at work;
- to create greater opportunities for women and men to secure decent employment and income;
- to enhance the coverage and effectiveness of social protection for all; and
- to strengthen tripartism and social dialogue.

All of the ILO's strategic objectives are closely linked to strengthening the social dialogue framework. Promoting a participatory process that gives a voice to those most directly involved in the world of work is an essential part of the conceptual framework of decent work. More especially, it provides the means of integrating the strategic objectives into a coherent approach for decent work initiatives with the full involvement of the social partners at the country level.

The report points to recent developments in the hotel, catering and tourism sector and highlights factors driving the internationalization of tourists' travel and of tourism services, including information technologies, as well as the internationalization of hotel and tourism enterprises. Without neglecting the huge subsector of small and medium-sized enterprises, it describes typical features related to the composition of the labour force and to working conditions. It raises questions concerning the difficulties faced by the sector in attracting and retaining skilled workers in enhancing the skills of newcomers to the labour market in order to stabilize the sector's labour force, while increasing the productivity of enterprises and the quality of services. Particular emphasis is put on new forms of management entailing new skills requirements, with a general tendency towards increased worker responsibility in an environment of flat hierarchies, multiskilling and teamwork. Some institutions, achievements and shortcomings of social dialogue in the hotel, catering and tourism sector are described in a perspective which also points to opportunities for increasing its scope and effectiveness. As for the causal relationships between globalization, employment and human resources development, it would be difficult on the basis of the available information to draw conclusions concerning such relationships more than is done here. On the other hand, other factors such as technological and educational progress or changes in tourism demand have also been highlighted.

Hard data on the hotel, catering and tourism sector are not easy to come by as it is rarely singled out from the services sector in general. Data specifically on tourism depend on accounting which covers a broad range of economic activities geared towards consumption by tourists. Only a few countries can provide systematically collected tourism data and little attention is given to labour issues.

The report draws on a wide variety of sources for information, including government institutions, intergovernmental organizations, trade unions, employers' organizations, companies, international non-governmental organizations, and individual scholars. The sources used are certainly not exhaustive but probably quite representative.

The report was prepared by an ILO team composed of Dirk Belau, Senior Specialist on Hotels, Catering and Tourism, Sectoral Activities Department (coordinator), Tom Higgins and Rajendra Paratian, with contributions from external experts, Lionel Becherel, Chris Cooper, Auliana Poon, Laennert Rijken and Klaus Weiermair. Editorial assistance was provided by Bill Ratteree, Sectoral Activities Department. The report is published under the authority of the International Labour Office.

General Developments in the Sector

Delimitation of the Hotel, Catering and Tourism (HCT) Sector

When the ILO Governing Body created the ILO Industrial Committee for the Hotel, Restaurant and Tourism Sector, which subsequently became the Committee for the Hotel, Catering and Tourism Sector, the sector included:

a. hotels, boarding houses, motels, tourist camps, holiday centres;
b. restaurants, bars, cafeterias, snack bars, pubs, night clubs, and other similar establishments;
c. establishments... for the provision of meals and refreshments within the framework of industrial and institutional catering (for hospitals, factory and office canteens, schools, aircraft, ships, etc.);
d. travel agencies and tourist guides, tourism information offices;
e. conference and exhibition centres.

Statistics are being organized according to the International Standard Industrial Classification of all Economic Activities (ISIC), the latest edition of which is ISIC Rev. 3. In that classification, the sectors most relevant for the ILO definition of the sector are Hotels and restaurants (division 55) and Activities of travel agencies and tour operators, Tourist assistance activities (class 6304).

Other organizations concerned with tourism, including governments, intergovernmental organizations and NGOs, often use much broader definitions of the term than that used by the ILO. They subsume under it all services and products consumed by tourists, including transport. In the ILO denomination of the sector, the part referring to "tourism" only covers travel agencies and tour operators. Hotels and catering, including restaurants, are considered by most organizations to belong to the "tourism characteristic industries" and therefore subsumed under tourism, although in some countries only a small part of their services is for tourists. However, the fact that the ILO definition of the sector thus differs considerably from the concept of tourism used by other organizations does not prevent most concerns about the development of tourism from being shared by those organizations. One such concern is the sector's potential to provide employment. Nevertheless, the ILO's focus on labour issues is unique as it includes all working and employment conditions in the HCT sector.

Tourism Satellite Accounts

As an economic concept, tourism is defined in "demand side" terms, as it comprises all services and goods consumed by tourists as well as all investments made to satisfy that consumption. A tourist has been defined by the United Nations as a traveller or visitor. The credibility and international comparability of "tourism statistics" depend heavily on: (1) a consensus regarding the choice of "tourism characteristic industries", i.e. those industries on which tourism demand has the most important direct impact, and an estimation of the "tourism ratio" of their output; as well as (2) the methods used to calculate the indirect effects on the output of many other industries. Statistical presentations differ in whether they include such indirect or induced effects in the measurement of tourism in the economy. Probably the most inclusive choice of industries is the one adopted by the World Travel and Tourism Council (WTTC), a private organization. It takes into account industries whose "tourism ratio" is low but whose products and services represent high value, such as the construction and operation of transport infrastructure.

The demand side nature of tourism is the basis of a methodology for Tourism Satellite Accounts (TSAs) developed by the World Tourism Organization and OECD and adopted by the United Nations Statistical Commission early in 2000. The ILO has been cooperating with those organizations in accordance with the mandate given to it by the Tripartite Meeting on the Effects of New Technologies on Employment and Working Conditions in the Hotel, Catering and Tourism Sector in 1997, with a view to providing a methodology for the production and presentation of tourism-relevant labour statistics to supplement the TSAs. A proposal has been formulated by the ILO for a tourism labour accounting system (TLAS) within that framework, based on its work on a general labour accounting system. A detailed "employment module" presenting labour-related issues was already attached to the TSA by the OECD, but this module does not provide the necessary framework for linking the different units, variables and classifications used when collecting labour statistics from many different sources.

Some early efforts towards TSA presentations have already been made by a number of pioneer OECD countries on the basis of figures from national accounts systems as required in the methodology adopted by the United Nations Statistical Commission in 2000. The World Travel and Tourism Council (WTTC) has been producing Tourism Satellite Accounts using a simulation method and based on a non-systematic variety of statistical sources. Relevant figures from some pioneer countries are presented in box 1.1. Because of differing definitions only very broad comparisons can be made between countries.

Tourism Economy

The Caribbean is the most tourism oriented region in the world. It is estimated that in 2000, tourism employed 3.1 million people either directly or indirectly, thus accounting for 13.4 per cent of total employment. Direct employment in the tourism characteristic industries alone amounts to 5 per cent of total employment. Visitor expenditures contributed an estimated US$17 billion, or 18.4 per cent, to export revenues. Countries whose international tourism receipts exceed 5 per cent of GDP or 10 per cent of export revenues are considered to be "tourism countries" for the purposes of the World Trade Organization.

Tourism is expanding in almost all countries including the developing countries. In fact, mass tourism involving domestic and regional travel is becoming an important phenomenon in several developing countries of Asia, Latin America, the Middle East and Africa, where the proportion of the population actively participating in domestic and regional tourism is predicted to grow considerably. In particular, regional tourism originating from China is expected to change the Asian tourism industry profoundly within the next one to two decades.

Employment in Hotels and Restaurants

This reflects a large number of small entrepreneurs and their non-remunerated family members. In some countries, this proportion is increasing as paid employment is growing more slowly than total employment, although in general growth rates for both are high.

Importance of International Tourism

Tourism across national borders represents a variable but generally large proportion of total tourism. Especially in a number of developing countries a significant proportion of gross domestic product is generated by activities designed to satisfy international tourism, which thus represents an important export activity in many countries. Globally, the World Tourism Organization (WTO) predicts that the number of international tourists will reach almost 1.6 billion by the year 2020 (as opposed to 565 million in 1995), and that international tourism receipts will exceed US$2,000 billion. The estimated growth of world international tourism arrivals of 4.5 per cent per annum will pose enormous challenges and opportunities for those regions and countries seeking to benefit from tourism while avoiding its negative impacts.

The top ten tourism destinations in the world in terms of tourism receipts are the United States, Spain, France, Italy, United Kingdom, Germany, China, Austria, Canada and Greece. Eventhough tourism is a global industry, the majority of receipts still accrue to the Americas and Europe, reflecting both the fact that closeness to origin of the travellers still matters and the fact that countries in these regions have had the time, resources and demand needed to develop their tourism industries.

For many countries, international tourism is an indispensable source of foreign currency earnings. According to the World Tourism Organization, tourism is one of the top five export categories for 83 per cent of countries and the main source of foreign currency for at least 38 per cent of them.

In 1998, international tourism and international fare receipts (receipts related to passenger transport of residents of other countries) accounted for roughly 8 per cent of total export earnings from goods and services worldwide. Total international tourism receipts, including those generated by international fares, amounted to an estimated US$532 billion, surpassing all other international trade categories.

As a by-product of the rapid fall in the real costs of long-distance travel, the developing regions of the world participate fully in the worldwide growth of international tourism. However, market shares vary strongly from one county to another and within very short periods, reflecting the economic or security crises affecting different countries or regions.

A Changing Tourism Industry

Mass tourism in and from the industrialized countries is a product of the late 1960s and early 1970s. Since then a number of interrelated developments in the world economy, such as overall economic growth and various other socioeconomic changes, government policies, technological revolution, changes in production processes and new management practices, have converted part of the industry from mass tourismto so-called "new tourism". The latter connotes the idea of responsible, green, soft, alternative and sustainable tourism, and basically refers to the diversification of the tourism industry and its development in targeted, niche markets. Competition in the new tourism is increasingly based on diversification, market segmentation and diagonal integration.

The identification and exploitation of niche markets has also proven to be a great source of revenue within new tourism, suggesting that further diversification and customization can be expected in the years to come. Market segmentation – as exemplified by ecotourism, cultural tourism, cruise and adventure tourism – is clearly in evidence and is experiencing great success. New niche markets are constantly being identified in an attempt to diversify the industry further.

Customization has also begun to play an important role in the industry. Tourism players are attempting to gain a competitive edge by catering for the individual needs of clients. The tourism product has thus been transformed over time from being completely dominated by mass tourism to an industry that is quite diversified and caters more to the individual needs of its participants.

Changing Consumer Preferences

Today, new consumers are influencing the pace and direction of underlying changes in the industry. The "new tourists" are more experienced travellers. Changes in consumer behaviour and values provide the fundamental driving force for the new tourism. The increased travel experience, flexibility and independent nature of the new tourists are generating demand for better quality, more value for money and greater flexibility in the travel experience.

The new consumers also reflect demographic changes – the population is ageing, household size is decreasing and households have greater disposable income. Changing lifestyles of the new tourists are creating demand for more targeted and customized holidays. A number of lifestyle segments – families, single parent households, "empty nesters" (i.e. couples whose children have left home), double-income couples without children – will become prevalent in tourism, signalling the advent of a much more differentiated approach to tourism marketing.

Changing values are also generating demand for more environmentally conscious and nature-oriented holidays. Suppliers will therefore have to pay more attention to the way people think, feel and behave than they have done hitherto.

In recent years the niche market has become an important factor in the tourism industry reflecting the need to diversify and customize the industry and ensure the sustainability of the product. The main niche markets (sports travel, spas and health care, adventure and nature tourism, cultural tourism, theme parks, cruise ships, religious travel and others) hold great potential and are developing rapidly.

The growth of the cruise tourism sector is an interesting case in point. Between 1980 and 1999, the cruise industry grew at an average annual rate of 7.9 percent. The Caribbean is the most important geographic market for the cruise industry, accounting for over half of all cruises taken in 1996. Since 1984, cruise visitor arrivals have increased every year except 1987 and 1989. In addition, between 1996 and 2000, the growth rate for cruise arrivals is expected to far exceed that of stay-over arrivals.

The rapid growth and development of the cruise tourism industry opens key opportunities but also poses a number of threats to their Caribbean destinations. The environmental and economic impacts of cruise tourism are increasingly the subject of discussion. Moreover, given the pace and magnitude of its development, the cruise industry is directly competing with land-based tourism and, as a result, poses a growing threat to hotels and other land-based resorts and businesses in the Caribbean.

Technology in Tourism

On the demand side, consumer preferences for flexible travel and leisure services provide a strong impetus for new tourism. On the supply side, technology plays an important complementary role in engineering new tourism. The applications of technology to the travel and tourism industry allow producers to supply new and flexible services that are cost-competitive with conventional mass, standardized and rigidly packaged options. Technology gives suppliers the flexibility to react to market demands and the capacity to integrate diagonally with other suppliers to provide new combinations of services and improve cost effectiveness.

In the travel and tourism industry a whole range of interrelated computer and communication technologies is being introduced. The system of information technologies (SIT) comprises computerized reservation systems, teleconferencing, video text, videos, video brochures, computers, management information systems, airline electronic information systems, electronic funds transfer systems, digital telephone networks, smart cards, satellite printers, and mobile communications. Each technology component identified in the SIT – for example, computers – can be and usually is fully integrated with the other components. For example, computer-to-computer communications allow hotels to integrate their front offices, back offices and food and beverage operations. This internal management system for hotels can in turn be fully integrated with a digital telephone network, and they then together provide the basis for linkage with hotel reservation systems which can be accessed by travel agents through their computerized reservations terminals (CRTs). Computerized reservations systems have emerged as the dominant technology among others being diffused throughout the travel and tourism industry.

In the United States, travel agents are using satellite printers at corporate offices to issue tickets directly at the point of demand. Interactive automated ticket machines (ATMs) have also been introduced. These consist of a computer with an attached printer that enables passengers to research schedules and fares, make reservations, purchase tickets and obtain boarding passes without the intervention of a human agent.

The Internet is a global network connecting millions of computers. As of 1999, the number of Internet users was above 200 million worldwide, and that number is growing rapidly, involving more than 100 countries. It is estimated that there were 63 million World Wide Web users in Europe in 1999. The United Kingdom, with almost 13 million Internet users, currently registers the highest number of users among the European countries. Use of the Internet for travel booking and planning is increasing rapidly. The rapid diffusion of information technologies throughout the travel and tourism industry is expected to improve the efficiency of production and the quality of services provided to consumers, and to generate increasing demand for new services.

Globalization

The driving forces of globalization impacting upon travel, hospitality and tourism.

Liberalization of Air Transport

The air transport industry, which is located mainly in the industrialized regions and in the newly industrialized countries, is a key determinant in the development of tourism. It is expanding twice as fast as the general output of the world economy, with further growth potential expected over the next two decades. In the developing countries, air transport accounts for nearly 80 per cent of international tourist arrivals. In 1998, the industry provided 28 million jobs worldwide, and by 2010 the number of people travelling by air could exceed 2.3 billion each year, with over 31 million jobs provided.

Today, liberalization of air transport largely means market access for private carriers and cabotage rights. The liberalization of air transport, traditionally pursued at the bilateral level, is now being carried to the level of multilateral trade agreements. The recent trend towards the liberalization of air transport notably through the proliferation of open skies agreements, has thus raised the issue of air transport liberalization as a discipline to be debated in the framework of the General Agreement on Trade in Services (GATS).

Multi-bilateral negotiations are already under way on an open skies agreement between the European Union and the United States. If they succeed, 70 per cent of the world's international air traffic will be covered by the agreement. It is expected in that case that the agreement will serve as a model for other international air services agreements.

The formation of international alliances is an important development in the field of aviation. Airline alliances have become widespread and are still evolving, with partnership relationships becoming more intertwined and complex. The major airlines in the Americas and Europe are the most active in securing alliance agreements.

The main motivation behind such alliances is the need to minimize costs while maintaining the quality of global services and extending connections throughout the world. Alliances can take various forms including: cooperative arrangements; wide-ranging strategic alliances, most notably the so-called "megaalliances"; groupings and concentrations at national level, as in the case of the United States; purchase or franchising of small regional companies by major operators to carry their customers to hub airports; and regional civil aviation markets.

Other trends which characterize the changes under way in the context of airline liberalization include: partial or full privatization and restructuring of government-owned airlines; partial foreign ownership of airlines; equity investment in foreign carriers; updating of airline alliances by cancelling outdated or non-performing agreements; airline consolidations at the national level; joint ventures, either between airline companies or between airline companies and equipment manufacturers or independent maintenance companies; and outsourcing with no provision of maintenance service.

Some Results of Airline Liberalization

Recent privatization initiatives have ended the protection of national airlines by governments in a number of developing countries. However, the possibility of the market becoming dominated by a single private company is perceived as a serious risk. In some cases, developing countries that have liberalized their air transport sectors as part of a policy to promote tourism have found themselves dominated by one or two foreign airlines. Some bankruptcies and closures have taken place in countries where distressed national airlines were not or could not be rescued by governments. In this context, a review of the GATS annex on air transport services is intended to draw international attention to the need to design a system that enables developing countries to compete effectively in the world market for air transport.

With regard to the liberalization of air transport as a whole, the trend is increasingly for each State to choose its own pace of change, using bilateral, regional or multilateral mechanisms. In developed countries there has been a clear tightening of competition policies to prohibit governments from providing subsidies. It is well known that many bilateral agreements have resulted in inefficiency as they were based on market access restrictions, price control and protection of money-losing carriers.

Full liberalization of air services as implemented in 1997 in Europe boosted the development of "low-cost" services and their integration in the European aviation scene. Although these services still account for a rather small share of the passenger market, their marketing impact is increasingly being felt throughout the industry. It is estimated that around 25 per cent of passengers on United States domestic services use "low-cost" airlines, as compared to approximately 5 per cent in Europe. Another result of liberalization is that new route opportunities have opened up, stimulating new demands without tampering with major carriers' shares and therefore creating new opportunities for fare reductions. Some major European flag carriers have already created their own "low-cost" airline subsidiaries (examples are British Airways/Go and KLM/Buzz). The low-cost market as it stands has considerable growth potential. Europe's low-cost airlines are finding plenty of untapped markets. Both Ryanair and easy Jet have placed orders for significant numbers of additional aircraft to almost double their capacity over the next four years to meet this new demand. The challenge for low-cost carriers is to strike the right balance between maintaining low costs, low prices and high aircraft utilization and establishing a presence at a certain minimum number of airports. A further development of the concept of the low-cost airline sector has been the advent of "seat-only" sales on charter airline flights, rather than as part of a package holiday. This has resulted, for example, in the formation of the European Leisure Group (ELG), an alliance of European charter and scheduled airlines.

Liberalization of Trade in Services

Negotiations on tourism services and existing commitments under the GATS.

The General Agreement on Trade in Services (GATS) became part of the "New World Trade Order" under the aegis of the World Trade Organization as established by the Uruguay Round in 1994. The functioning of GATS is based on the interplay of fundamental standards in commercial law, procedural regulations for their implementation and specific commitments in which member States document sector-specific limitations or concessions. GATS has universal coverage and includes a comprehensive definition of trade in services comprising four "modes of supply".

They are: cross-border movement of services; movement of consumers; commercial presence; and the presence of natural persons, and to these modes the three principles of liberalization enshrined in GATS as shown in box 2.1 are to be applied. GATS thus provides a framework for the progressive liberalization of trade in services through commitments made by the World Trade Organization member countries concerning the abovementioned principles and their applications to one or more modes of supply. Future negotiations under GATS will provide an opportunity for developing countries to address trade barriers to their services.

The tourism sector had already undergone various forms of liberalization before the Uruguay Round. It is also considered to be one of the service sectors most liberalized through sector-specific commitments made by signatory States. The number of commitments by the World Trade Organization members made so far in tourism under the GATS is rated as the highest of all sectors. Of 127 GATS signatory States, only eight have not made commitments in tourism and travel-related services. In the hotels and restaurants subsector, which offers the greatest potential for far-reaching liberalization within tourism, it is mostly low and lower-middle-income economies (LIEs and LMIEs according to the World Bank classification) in Africa and Latin America that have liberalized market access for foreign investors in the "*commercial presence*" mode: 64 per cent of all signatory States belonging to the group of LIEs and 75 per cent of LMIEs, but only about half (48 per cent) of the group of high-income economies (HIEs) have "no restrictions" to that mode. On the other hand, it is not surprising that "*presence of natural persons*" is the least liberalized mode of supply: in 117 of the 119 countries signing commitments in travel and tourism-related services, there are restrictions on the movement of hotel staff. Sixty-eight countries refer to their non-sector-specific commitments which mostly offer only temporary stay for business visitors, intra-corporate transferees and professionals. This mode is the key starting point for future moves to shift liberalization away from declaring countries' restrictive measures towards removing those measures. It is expected that the next round of GATS talks will have important repercussions on destinations in terms of tourism marketing, investment and ownership, training and other aspects affecting the structure of the industry.

The case for a more specific treatment of tourism services under the GATS has been the subject of debate since the conclusion of the Uruguay Round. Significantly, UNCTAD has come up with conclusions and recommendations with regard to the future round of negotiations on trade in tourism under the GATS, including a recommendation and a proposal for an annex on tourism services called for by the World Trade Organization. So far, tourism is not among the specific sectors referred to by the six annexes of the GATS and other related instruments. Only an ancillary service to tourism (airline computer reservation services), is included in an annex on air transport services.

Possible impact of GATS on air traffic services, tourism services production, free movement of people, market access and labour markets.

Most air traffic services are not covered by the Agreement's disciplines. The main organizations responsible for air transport are now examining ways in which the GATS could contribute to future air transport liberalization.

The GATS provides a framework for negotiating temporary entry of service personnel into the territory of other parties. The movement of natural persons is a necessary condition for developing countries' participation in the world market for services. Developing countries have given priority to making commitments under the GATS relating to the movement of natural persons (mode 4 of the GATS), partly taking into account their competitive labour cost advantage. However, commitments in this mode are largely linked to commercial presence, and firms without such commercial presence are discriminated against by having to face visa restrictions such as the so-called economic needs test, which is discretionary and non-transparent. Those restrictions are serious barriers to trade in services and negate the opportunities for market access otherwise extended in the commitments. Increased movement of natural persons also raises the question of the need to strengthen international standards regarding the licensing, accreditation and certification of service providers. The World Tourism Organization, for example, is developing a range of quality standards to be applied at tourism destinations.

Recognition of diplomas and professional qualifications is another precondition for the movement of natural persons abroad. This calls for the harmonization of diplomas and mutual recognition agreements between countries. Several countries have notified mutual recognition agreements under GATS Article VII.4. It is hoped that the GATS will increase the recognition of qualifications across borders.

Considerations within the framework of the GATS may also become relevant for the migration to the richer countries of persons who overstay their tourism visas and take up work. Many of them work in hotels or restaurants where in some countries they form a significant proportion of the labour force. Globalization will give rise to increased migration pressures in the years ahead, as a recent ILO study has shown. The increased scale and diversity of global communications systems and their declining costs, which are rapidly narrowing telecommunications gaps, have helped to make international migration easier.

With regard to the movement of consumers, tourism is an example of the services sector where consumption abroad is particularly relevant. Nevertheless, the movement of tourists is in some instances constrained by the difficulties associated with the delivery of visas, hard currency regulations and insufficient availability or inadequacy of air transport services to and from tourist-receiving countries. GATS negotiations are expected to address these problems.

Specific commitments made under the GATS to encourage greater participation by developing countries in world services trade relate to three main areas: first, the strengthening of the domestic services capabilities of developing countries through access to technology on a commercial basis, which is normally achieved through the employment and training of local personnel in foreign-owned hotels; secondly, improving the access of developing countries to distribution channels and information networks. In the tourism sector, this means access to computerized information and reservation networks managed and owned by entities in the industrialized countries; thirdly, the liberalization of market access in sectors and modes of supply of export interest to them (GATS, Article IV). According to GATS Article XIX., developing countries can attach additional conditions to such access aimed at achieving the development objectives of Article IV, namely the strengthening of their domestic services capacity and improvement of their access to distribution channels and information networks. The liberalization of services is likely to have both positive and negative impacts on the labour force in relation to wages and employment. Increased competition by better equipped hotel and restaurant companies from abroad may in the short term lead to job losses in local enterprises. However, foreign firms will employ local people, increasing local employment and contributing to a higher standard of living.

Economic Integration

The world economy is currently witnessing two distinct trends – globalization and regionalization – and within this context States as well as companies are pursuing a variety of different strategies in order to become more competitive. Shifting patterns of production and consumption across the world are also reflected in the rise of new international tourism destinations, particularly in the East Asia and Pacific region. This has given rise to increasing regional, intra-regional and interregional competition and to new challenges in terms of investment needs and human resources development, especially with regard to training and labour mobility. The impact of trade blocs on the hotel, tourism and catering sector can be gauged by the strategies adopted to create an environment conducive to tourism development. The European Union has launched a wide range of initiatives and activities through a varietym of programmes in such broad areas as sustainable development, dissemination of information, training and enterprise promotion.

The main thrust of social policy in the European Union is the improvement of labour market conditions with a special focus on those excluded from the labour market and the unemployed. European Union labour laws and social policy are having a positive impact on the tourism sector. Of importance here is the Maastricht Social Protocol which has benefited seasonal and part-time workers and small businesses. Other policies that have proved beneficial to the development of tourism include the free movement of workers across Europe, harmonization of qualifications and tax incentives for education and training.

The North American Free Trade Agreement (NAFTA) benefits the travel and tourism industry in many ways. It promotes demand for direct air and charter/tour bus travel in the region, guarantees that tourism companies will receive national treatment in all three countriesand maintains high quality of tourism services by encouraging the expansion of telecommunications links between the United States and Mexico.

Mercosur is, in economic terms, the world's fourth largest trade bloc, covering a population of 205 million people. Economic integration, through the practice of free trade with no tariff or pre-tariff restrictions between the member States of the bloc, has led to increasing cross-border flows of labour, goods and investment. MERCOSUR's concern is to tackle labour relations, employment and social security issues and the short-term negative effects of integration on labour in the member States.

Tourism development is a priority on the agenda of the Association of South-East Asian Nations (ASEAN). Its development strategy incorporates: promotion of sustainable tourism development; preservation of cultural and environmental resources; provision of transportation and other infrastructure; simplification of immigration procedures; and human resources development. A plan of action on ASEAN cooperation in tourism shows the emphasis that is being placed on investment in human resources development, with a special focus on tourism education and training with a view to upgrading the skills needed to meet the demand for improved service quality and professionalism in the tourism and travel industry and thereby sustain ASEAN's overall competitive advantage. Cooperation in tourism education and training is being intensified through the sharing of resources, skills and training facilities provided by tourism training institutions through technical assistance and experts.

Information and Communication Technologies in the HCT Sector

Computerized reservation systems (CRSs) have been developed by large air carriers since the 1970s to process flight reservations, but have evolved and expanded over time to provide other air transport-related services. Each airline has its own CRS and they are interconnected through global distribution systems (GDSs). A huge number of Internet on-line reservation systems act as a kind of virtual agent, most of them having direct links to one or several CRS/GDS.

The CRS and GDS systems have become the main distribution and marketing tool in the international tourism trade and have greatly enhanced the efficiency of travel agents' business operations. They cater to the needs of different market segments, including management of air and land transport services, the hospitality sector and entertainment services, as well as other ancillary services which make commercial transactions and risk coverage feasible. As a result, they have become increasingly important and are extensively used by all suppliers of tourism services.

There is some concern that developing countries' suppliers may well be left out because GDSs can present major barriers to entry owing to their unfavourable access conditions (their operational costs, problems of access for small service suppliers, the fact that they are owned by large air carriers). A number of African and south Asian countries are poorly represented in these systems because of structural handicaps such as the low level of tourism development in general and their underdeveloped hospitality sector. The poor representation of small service suppliers in GDSs adversely affects the dissemination of information on their tourism products, thereby holding back their sale and marketing of tourism services. This leaves such suppliers, especially SMEs, at a competitive disadvantage compared with those who are represented in the major GDSs. GDSs in many developing countries, particularly in Africa, are established in the form of joint ventures with local partners – for example, the national carrier – but operate within a de facto monopoly. This leads to excessive user fees and hinders their potential for developing tourism.

Travel agents in developing countries are at a disadvantage with regard to the use of modern technology compared with their counterparts in developed countries because of poor information network infrastructure and the shortage of professionals to manage, operate and maintain the system. Human resources assume importance in the operation of GDSs and other electronic media, and this calls for staff training in mastering the systems and their application to marketing, through specific training programmes provided by both the public and private sectors.

Emerging Use of the Internet for Marketing and Sales

Deregulation, globalization and radical shifts in leisure and tourism behaviour on the demand side have driven the tourism industry towards information-oriented activities, as seen in the introduction of IT systems in a wide range of spheres in the tourism and leisure sector. The increasing use of the Internet for destination marketing, direct sales and bookings has given rise to electronic tourism markets and at present tourism is among the most important application domains in the World Wide Web.

The development of websites has made possible the direct delivery of comprehensive travel information about tourism suppliers to potential travellers. Text-based websites with photos and graphics linked to websites of tourism suppliers at the destination is another innovative approach to marketing. Developing an effective travel website has now assumed importance for obvious reasons. International tourists are increasingly using the travel websites on the Internet that were launched by most international companies in the late 1990s. However, the real volume of Internet bookings can only be estimated and estimates from market research companies are contradictory. According to one estimate, between 33 and 50 per cent of Internet transactions are tourism based. Available evidence show that as yet only a tiny percentage of business travellers are booking on-line. On-line sales in Europe, for example, represented only 0. 1 per cent of the European travel market, and in 1999 only 1 per cent of the world's airline tickets, hotel and other bookings were purchased over the Internet, although the proportion of airline and other ticket sales through the Internet is expected to grow sharply over the next three to four years.

The Internet helps to make travel products globally accessible at much lower cost – without transaction costs and the costs of intermediaries – and has comparatively low entrance barriers with regard to financial resources and human know-how. For many suppliers, tourism marketing efforts are increasingly focusing on Internet users. A new business environment and new ways of doing business have sprung up as a result of the accessibility and relatively low cost of the Internet which is bringing businesses and consumers, buyers and suppliers on-line. Internet and Internet protocol technology is the driving force behind the growth of e-business. The Internet will have repercussions on business in the areas of e-commerce, e-working and e-procurement. A recent global survey of more than 500 business leaders lends support to the idea that e-business will be a key factor in competitive advantage in the future.

In the sphere of air travel, attempts are frequently made to bypass traditional travel agencies by direct booking via the Internet or corporate implant offices. Customer demands are becoming more technology driven, such as the demand for professional travel and billing management in place of mere ticket issuing. Advances in technology in the hotels and tourism industry, as exemplified by readily available information to guests and employees, faster service delivery, shorter cycle times and more dynamic markets, also require prompt action from service suppliers if marketing opportunities are not to be lost. Strategies of growth and concentration through mergers and acquisitions are becoming increasingly important from the mediators' perspective as a response to cost and performance pressures in international business travel. In addition, traditional kickback contracts are increasingly being replaced with new performance-oriented arrangements.

All aspects of business are being reshaped by the Internet and its related technologies, intranets and extranets. Hospitality enterprises will need to focus on providing customers with real-time access to rates and product information. The Internet also provides hotels and restaurants with opportunities to redesign the way in which they interface with employees and suppliers.

The high growth in global commerce accompanied by the emergence of electronic commerce driven mainly by the Internet has raised concerns about the need to regulate cyberspace by setting standards to regulate the use of the Internet for all aspects of travel and other fast-growing categories of electronic commerce. The primacy of the rules of the network economy will significantly lower transaction and communication costs, thus allowing more flexible pricing. The regulation of the Internet through the enactment and implementation of cyberlaws and privacy standards will most probably be perceived as an encouraging initiative which will guarantee safety and security in Internet business transactions, especially in shopping and travel accommodation bookings, where the Internet is most frequently used. As a way of managing the increasing volume of guest information, the introduction of data warehousing and data mining technologies is becoming increasingly important. Hoteliers and restaurateurs have already expressed marked interest in these technologies as means of exploiting the advantages which can be derived from, for example, increased guest loyalty and market share. By using data warehousing and data mining as well as the Internet, the hotel industry can provide higher levels of personalized services and value.

The Internet is turning out to be the most sought after amenity in hotel rooms, providing communications access, information, entertainment and education. It enables more self-service oriented transactions to take place, especially in the area of reservations booking. Information technology impacts on all aspects of the hotel organization value chain and transcends all departmental and geographical boundaries. Decisions on technology-related issues need to be made at top management levels of companies, and this means that qualified information technology personnel are needed at those levels.

Another key issue is the source of investment capital required to fund information technology initiatives. Lack of capital seriously hinders the implementation of information technology and competition for fund sourcing.

The Internet has brought about some very significant technological changes that enhance its capabilities and viability and its potential to drive electronic commerce. Besides introducing new and innovative business models in both the business-to-business and business-to-consumer markets, the Internet has shortened the value chain and put pressure on all players, especially intermediaries, by giving rise to the so-called "disintermediation" process, that is, the elimination of intermediary organizations such as travel agencies and global distribution systems (GDSs).

Online service and ticketless travel have significantly reduced the need for travel intermediaries, as a result of which travel agents in the United States, for example, have seen a reduction in commissions paid to them by airlines.

The use of information technology in the tourism industry is determined by such factors as the scale and complexity of tourism demand and the degree of expansion and sophistication of new tourism products. Tourism plays an important role in a significant number of developing countries, many of which enjoy a competitive advantage. Current changes in the hotel and tourism industry in the context of globalization, as described in this report, show that there are more opportunities in the field of e-commerce than in any other existing technology which developing countries can exploit to their advantage in order to improve the marketing of their tourism products. However, in the developing countries, tourism development is constrained by a number of factors which have been summarized by UNCTAD.

Computer software represents one of the largest segments of services delivered through the cross-border mode of supply, with a growing number of developing countries using the Internet both to market and to deliver these services. The Indian software industry is a case in point. Electronic commerce facilitates access to new markets, as well as being cost saving and time saving. However, its effectiveness depends to a large extent on the establishment of a sound telecommunications infrastructure; in most low-income countries, that infrastructure is inadequate. A wide range of factors prevent the great majority of developing countries from accessing foreign markets through the Internet. Those factors include monopoly pricing for long-distance telephony, uncertainty about the regulatory environment, lack of human resources, lack of awareness among developing country companies of the relevance of the digital economy, and the high cost of setting up, upgrading and redesigning a significant e-commerce site. The status of the developing countries' readiness for e-commerce is an important issue. Providers of tourism services must also have the capacity to invest in or have access to the physical infrastructure for logistics services and information technologies. The major obstacle to increased use of e-commerce in developing countries is the lack of pervasive low-cost telecommunications, broadcasting, Internet services and associated infrastructures, especially in rural areas. At the same time there is a need to involve more hotel and tourism enterprises from developing countries in the actual use of information technologies and information networks. If African businesses fare better than consumers in terms of accessing e-commerce, they nevertheless face the same infrastructure problems, although progress has been made in the development of e-commerce activities.

The shortage of IT specialists on the market, especially in the developing countries, is a serious impediment, given the rapid growth in Internet use. The demand for IT skills is increasing and the need for retraining of existing employees in both the public and private sectors in hotels, tourism and catering is clearly felt.

One solution would be for developing countries to take advantage of forthcoming GATS negotiations to ensure access for their suppliers to the most important generating markets, and they could make use of certain mechanisms provided for in the GATS which might enhance the contribution of trade in services to development. They could also seek commitments with respect to the training of personnel and access to the distribution channels which are essential to tourism exports, as provided for in Articles IV and XIX of the Agreement.

Consolidation Strategies

Since the mid-1990s, multinational hotel companies entering foreign markets have devised a wide range of management strategies or methods in response to competitive challenge such as the rapid development of information technology, sophisticated demands from well-informed and knowledgeable travellers and the rise of electronic business-to-business market-places and to seize the opportunities opened up by the network economy. Within each company, core competencies are being developed and renewed through rapid information technology development, international expansion and market cooperation, relationship management, development of customer-oriented products and services, structural re-engineering (involving, for example, organizational restructuring and continuous training of employees and management), new marketing initiatives and campaigns, and quality control.

Within the context of international expansion and market cooperation, companies have had recourse to a number of competitive methods which merit attention. The growing number of alliances is changing industry structures and the level of competition has shifted from the individual company level to alliance groups level. The last five years have witnessed nine major mergers and acquisition transactions in the international hotel market-place. For example, Hilton and Hilton International have merged their sales forces, integrated their logos and marketing efforts, and shared their reservation systems in a strategic alliance considered to be the largest since 1996. Hilton has also allied with Patriot American Hospitality for market expansion. Starwood has established a strategic alliance with Discovery Hotel Group in Asia to open Four Points Hotels in China. Choice International has done the same with Flag International in Asia.

There are other goals and objectives which strategic alliances can fulfil in order to assist multinational hotel firms in strengthening their market positions, improving partnership relations and supplying diversified products and quality services to their customers. These goals and objectives include: acquisition of new information and communication technology (Hyatt and Starwood with Microsoft's Expedia, Hyatt with MSN network, Carlson and Bass with WizCom to link to global distribution systems); distribution of products and cross-marketing between food-service providers and hotels (Ramada with Bennigan's Restaurants, Marriott, Hilton, Bass with Pizza Hut); distribution and cross-promotion of bank credit cards and financial services between banks and hotels (Bass Hotels and Resorts with Visa and American Express, Marriot with Visa and Chase Manhattans processing system, Hilton, Starwood, and Accor with American Express); consolidation of transportation and hotel services (Carlson and Bass Hotels and Resorts each with more than 20 airlines, Marriott with United Airlines, Starwood with British Airways and Alitalia, and Shangri-la with Canadian Airlines); copromotion of hotels and films and media (Marriott, Choice Hotels and Cendant with new films, Bass with ESPN and Discovery Channel, and Best Western with Sci-Fi Channel and E-Entertainment Channel).

Management contracts are popular competitive methods that are being used by international companies. A good example is that of Nikko Hotels International which through its expansion into Croatia acquired 21 management contracts in 1998. Some well established international companies provide their expertise by leasing out management teams to run local firms. The contracting company benefits from the knowledge and experience of the international company and from its reputation for quality and good service. Quoting figures from Ankomah (1991), Becherel and Cooper point out that in 1979, 72 per cent of all hotels insub-Saharan Africa operated under a management contract; in Asia the figure was 60 per cent, in Latin America 47 per cent, but only 2 per cent in Europe. It can be assumed that these proportions have increased with globalization.

Franchising – a contractual agreement whereby one company allows another to sell and use its products for a fee – presents a number of advantages upon which many multinational hotel companies rely for their growth and expansion. From a local human resources perspective, franchising offers the advantage of recruiting local management and staff with the added benefit of the expertise of the franchiser and any good international practice. This method of market entry is favoured by some of the international hotel corporations. Their international reputation guarantees licensees a ready-made market. In Europe, for example, franchising accounts for 1.5 million jobs, the majority in France, Germany and the United Kingdom. Many franchise agreements have been signed in the past five years. What is more, companies which have not in the past espoused franchising as an expansion tool have started to use it to the full. This was the case with Hyatt and Marriott in 1995 and 1996.

Many joint ventures or partnerships were set up between 1995 and 1996. Some examples are: Choice International with Friendly Hotels in the United Kingdom; Cendant with Mark's Hotel International's cooperation agreement in India; Accor with NH Hotels in Spain, Starwood with Hotel Pelikan in Germany and Demeure Hotels in Europe; and Sol Melia with European Travel.

The emergence of branding is another new issue in the hotel industry which is linked to merger and acquisition activities. With the evolution of the hotel industry towards a more consumer-oriented service, it is the brand rather than the company which assumes importance. In the United Kingdom hotel industry, for example, branding has become very topical and operators are increasingly recognizing the value of brands in delivering profits. The brand is thus turning out to be a fundamental element in defining the market, so much so that it is the name of the brand under which a hotel trades that carries weight, rather than its ownership and management structure.

The emergence of a multiplicity of new brand names worldwide in the last five years – Cendant's Wingate Inn, Accor's Studio 6, Hilton's Garden Inn, and others – bears testimony to its increasing importance. All these developments indicate the extent to which new products and services – including the other new competitive methods and customer-oriented technologies mentioned earlier – that have been launched by multinational hotel companies are being developed in an attempt to sustain their respective competitive advantage.

Vertical integration is another strategy that plays a dominant role in particular segments of the tourism industry. For a long time, tour operators have been establishing backward and forward linkages in the areas of service production. Their backward integration includes hotels and charter airlines. These operators also control all stages of distribution via far-reaching forward integration of retail distributors and travel agencies, marketing and package tours sales. This is also true of airlines which extend their level of integration far into the field of primary tourism and travel-related services via their charter airlines which have interests in tour operators, retailers and travel agencies. By contrast, hotels and hotel chains hardly pursue vertical integration strategies at all.

Tour operators and travel agencies are becoming increasingly involved in the process of horizontal integration, which in the recent past has attracted attention through spectacular takeovers like that of Thomas Cook by the German LTU group in 1993, or through joint ventures. An expansionist strategy of diagonal integration is geared to the provision of the broadest possible array of tourism-related service markets by a company, with a view to cutting costs, making the most of synergies between individual markets and achieving systems gains. This includes, for example, the joint use of computerized reservation systems by carriers and travel agencies under the umbrella of a holding company or cooperation between credit card suppliers and tour operators or travel agencies offering the special insurance services of a holding partner.

In the accommodation industry, an impressive amount of consolidation took place in the 1980s, bringing more and more hotel brands under fewer and larger corporate umbrellas. Consolidation offers certain advantages such as cost reduction in the areas of reservation systems, loyalty programmes and staff training and other fixed costs associated with hotel management. Available figures reinforce the impression that the forces of consolidation are indeed gathering momentum. In the institutional catering sector, franchising and management contracts are also used as management strategies by institutional food-service companies.

Compass, which is among the largest institutional catering companies in the world, employing 125,000 workers in 44 countries, is a case in point. It owns, manages or franchises hotels (Forte, Meridien, Posthouse, Heritage and Travelodge). Its food service brands include Burger King, Sbarro, Upper Crust, Caffe Ritazza, Delimento, Little Chef and Harry Ramsdens. In Canada, the institutional catering sector is dominated by large international groups. Sodexho is the largest institutional catering company, employing 212,000 employees worldwide since it purchased the institutional catering services of Marriott – Marriott Services. Another example is Aramak, an American company which employ 140,000 employees in 11 countries based in North America and Europe.

One pertinent issue frequently referred to by the developing countries is the need to reduce the risk of "leakage" of foreign exchange earnings. The developing countries in particular are usually unable to make the most of the economic and development potential of tourism, firstly, because of the high import content of construction materials and equipment and consumable goods needed to cater to the needs of international tourism and, secondly, because of the repatriation of income and profits earned by expatriates. The latter is in fact a major obstacle to tourism development.

Nevertheless, a number of advantages can be derived from international companies in terms of capital investment and know-how and technology, management and marketing expertise, training and consultancy. For example, under the "Build Operate Transfer" model, there may be conditions attached such as the requirement to train local staff or build facilities for the community. This enables countries lacking the skills base and expertise needed at all professional levels to run, develop and operate tourist establishments for an international clientele to benefit from the transfer of expertise and technology.

In a globalized economy, skills become an important determinant in competitiveness. The changing composition of the workforce and work patterns resulting from globalization processes in the industry have brought about new challenges in human resources development. Training policies in the hotel, tourism and catering sector will need to be reviewed in a new climate of empowerment and retention of staff. This is particularly the case in many parts of the world where there is an acute shortage of qualified staff to fill positions created by an expanding industry. An internationally focused human resources policy calls for a change in personnel policies and strategies which implies, among other things, management commitment to transnational strategies, the development of IT skills and procedures to support transnational operations in a number of ways such as knowledge and information transfer, and an awareness of the different national policies on health and safety, occupational standards, dismissal, discrimination and workers' rights.

Impact of Technology on SMEs

Globalization has brought about a range of opportunities and challenges which have put additional pressures on SMEs. In addition to having to cope with the effects of globalization, they need to adapt to new business conditions in terms of product positioning and product development facilitated by information technology, with all its potential benefits in terms of market access for SMEs. The potential of SMEs for achieving economies of scale is very limited and the use of computer reservation systems (CRSs) has not spread significantly, quite apart from the fact that SMEs are already disadvantaged because of their high average unit production costs. SMEs are forced by market conditions to install new systems and train their staff to use tourism-related technologybut find it difficult to invest in training or staff development, mainly because of limited investment resources and the fact that many SMEs in the hotel, tourism and catering sector are managed by a generation of staff have had no formal training in the sector. In a globalized market, SMEs need to pursue new survival strategies. The tourism sector at the destination has to cope with the increasing problem of seasonality encountered by many coastal resorts. Competitive advantage then depends on organizational competencies and capabilities. Local SMEs have to face a number of conditions imposed by large overseas companies. Large tour operators strongly influence the way in which hotels operate at their featured destinations and the prices that they charge, particularly in mass market beach resorts and in short season resorts (e.g. ski resorts); they may also impose conditions on local suppliers, such as compliance with environmental protection standards.

In developing countries, SMEs play an important role in employment creation but are hampered by low productivity levels, poor product quality and lack of access to credit and training. The impact of capital outflows from developing countries resulting from e-commerce is another issue which needs attention. The need to develop competition policy-related disciplines in this area is also clearly felt, in view of the need to establish safeguards to prevent abuse by dominant suppliers. Such issues arising from e-commerce might be addressed in future GATS negotiations.

The global hotel market encompasses a wide range of types of accommodation – full-service hotels, bed and breakfast inns, suites, self-catering short-term apartments and time-share properties. Distribution and intermediation are increasingly recognized as factors critical to the competitiveness and success of the tourism industry in general and of small and medium-sized tourism enterprises in particular. The latter need to develop effective distribution channels either to meet the needs of their independent clientele or to provide direct booking mechanisms to reduce their dependency on tour operators. Hospitality organizations and hotel chains already rely on customer bookings through the Internet. The challenge for tourism sector SMEs is to be able to compete for their market shares and take advantage of emerging opportunities and associated benefits to enhance their profitability and viability in the global market-place.

7

Challenges and Strategies of Hospitality Industry

Competitiveness refers to-*the ability and willingness to compete* and two most important underlying criteria of competitiveness are-'Profitability' and 'Productivity', that is, increased competitiveness is reflected in sustained growth in productivity and profitability. Since 'productivity' and 'profitability' are vital for all organizations, industries, sectors and nations, it indicates that the concept of competitiveness is equally applicable to each of these entities, so it is a must that they appreciate the conceptual framework of competitiveness and the various forms that it takes, (commercial competitiveness, market competitiveness etc.) along with the fact that it is a complex ongoing process affected by a range of factors/inputs. Although, 'competitiveness' in parlance of business (and industries) is not a new phenomenon and is usually discussed in terms of – the decisions it makes, the resources it has, and the environmental factors which surrounds the business, but lately, the trend of categorizing and evaluating nations on basis of their competitiveness has become a norm among economists, policy makers, business executives and investors.

Liberalization, Privatization and Globalization (LPG) have worked together for reducing protection and creating a rapidly changing competitive environment resulting in fierce international competition 'in' and 'for' the world-market. With this, there has been a growing realization that avoiding the rigors of competition is not possible and developing strategies for enhancing sustainable competitiveness has emerged as a 'must do' exercise for all. However, the context of 'competitiveness' might vary for business, industries and nations, depending on their-objectives, form, nature and functions – that is-from completely social to hardcore commercial.

Competitiveness of Nations and the Service Sector-Most of the (developing) economies are in rapid transit towards becoming 'service economies" and therefore 'competitiveness of service sector' is emerging as a crucial factor influencing the overall competitiveness of a country, and India is no exception to this, where the share of services is increasingly getting higher in the total GDP, and also the growth rate of India's 'service exports' is higher then the world average, hence for India, out of the three pillars of competitiveness, one is certainly it's service sector (agriculture and manufacturing are the remaining two.) Variables of Competitiveness at country, industry and firm level-The paper deals with the issue of competitiveness at all the three levels (country, industry and firm) taking-'India' as the variable for 'country' and 'Indian Tourism and Hospitality Industry' as the variable for 'industry', and at the firm level, the paper identifies cases from many different organizations, rather then taking a particular organization as a variable, because a broader canvas is required to capture the diversity of businesses operating in this domain, and any one organization cannot symbolize the complete tourism and hospitality industry because this industry is formed by a combination of very different businesses. (Only infrastructure business, or only hotel business or only aviation business can not represent this industry alone, but all these businesses jointly do so).

Competitiveness Challenges of Indian Tourism and Hospitality Industry – as mentioned above, different diverse businesses jointly form this industry *(transportation, hotels, infrastructure, aviation etc.)*, and a balanced development of all these different businesses and high coordination amongst all the participants is a prerequisite for enhancing competitiveness of this industry and creating this 'fine blend' of such 'polar elements' is a tough challenge in itself.

This industry can be called as the "industry of big paradoxes", first, on one hand it has almost unbeatable competitive advantages, huge potential and high growth rates *(in terms of-generating foreign exchange, growth rates, & employment generation)*, and on the other hand, inspite of above mentioned positives, Indian Tourism and Hospitality Industry is still way behind even from its small neighbours in South-East Asia, not to mention the large counterparts like China.

Second paradox is that, on one hand, in order to be competitive, this industry needs the cooperation of both public and private sector players as both play a vital role in it, and on the other hand, cut throat competition also exists between the two in this industry itself.

Finally, the 'offering' of this industry is also paradoxical. For India, where 'history' is an important attraction for tourists, this industry has to offer 'history', but it can not loose sight of modernization either, in other words, Indian Tourism and Hospitality Industry has to be a 'historian' and a 'futurist' simultaneously.

Thus, in order to find a sustainable solution to the competitiveness issue of this industry, the paper suggest that it is important to identify the reasons behind its lack of competitiveness and then to search for 'breakthrough solutions' to face the unique challenges it offers, by undertaking a study of the innovative and best practices developed and adopted by players of this industry in the global arena which are applicable in Indian conditions and finally, redefining the role of government and private players to create a more competitive landscape might also be an effective part of the overall solution.

Case Study: Hongkong

The tourism industry has been a major source of revenue for Hong Kong. Along with the boom of tourism is the increase investment in hotel industry. Indeed, these two sectors have been indispensable that the subsequent decline in tourism following the economic crisis has impacted hotel operations significantly. The tourism and hotel industry in Hong Kong has been suffered major decline although it has manifested recovery during the previous years.

The factors contributing to the decline include high rates due to the high cost of living, the outbreak of SARS, deteriorating image of Hong Kong as shopper's paradise and the development of tourist attractions in other countries in the region. The following section will review the development of the tourism industry from its subsequent decline and its way to recovery.

Part A

Macro Analysis

The business environment is generally successful and attractive. The gross domestic product has grown consistently and became the envy of developed and developing systems. The unemployment rate has always been in a low rate while the demand for the employment remains to be buoyant. With this, there appeared to be an increase in the standard of living explaining the social stability in the country.

The government policy on the other hand has adopted a policy of positive non interventionism. In general, the business environment of the country is favourable for investors.

Hotel Industry

Hong Kong's hotel industry is a popular channel of investment along with the booming of the tourism industry. Tourism is a major revenue earner in Hong Kong. It has become the second largest source of foreign exchange. Hong Kong servcs as the travel gateway for the vast majority of business and recreational travels to China and as the primary travel hub for South East Asia. The hotel industry was geared to the tourist trade especially at the upper end (Gerzenberg, 1994).

In the years prior to the hand back to China, hotel room rates rose to high levels. Room rates may have been slashed and two for one flight promotions run but the image of Hong Kong as expensive destination has been fixed in the minds of potential tourist travellers.

Tourism and hotel industry has slumped badly during the Asian financial crisis. Despite the major rebound in the number of tourists coming during 1999-2000, the actual revenue received has declined. Explanations for the decline in revenue from tourists differed but include the high costs of living compare to other locations in the region. In addition to this, HK is no longer seen as a shopper's paradise. It has been characterized by the lack of initiatives to provide tourist attractions and above all the high level of pollution affects the territory.

In 1999, hotel prices in Asia rose again as the region recovered from the economic crisis of 1997-1998. Room rates in South Korea, Japan and Taiwan rose by 32%, 38% and 30% in euros. However, China and Hong Kong experienced continued fall in room rates by 31.5% though it stabilized slightly in 1999 and towards the end of that year. Yet the reality remains that hotels are property and properties are major investments and assets in Hong Kong. By 2000, room rates and occupancy are again at high levels (Joseph, 2005). One of the bright spot for Hong Kong hoteliers is the climbing of tourism.

By the end of last year, there were about 612 hotels and tourist guest houses in Hong Kong with 52, 512 rooms. The average occupancy rates in all hotel categories were 87% for the whole of 2006. This marked a one-percentage-growth as compared to 2005 regardless of the 7.4% increase in room supplies between December 2005 and December 2006. During 2006, about 62.75 of all visitors stayed one night and longer, a trend which reflects the importance of Hong Kong as a regional transport hub.

Today, the Hong Kong tourism and hotel industry is gambling its future as a tourist destination for Disneyland. The industry is expecting a boost from the increased number of tourists especially those coming from mainland China.

In 2003, Beijing has eased the travel rules for mainland tourist to Hong Kong which allowed people for Chinese cities to travel individually rather than in organized groups. It has also doubled the currency allowed for mainland tourists to take with them when traveling abroad. These new polices are part of the series of measures to help stimulate Hong Kong's' flagging tourism, lift property and share prices (Bezlova, 2004). As a result, China has become the major source of tourist arrivals in Hong Kong.

Competitor Analysis

The erosion of Hong Kong's price competitiveness resulting from regional currency turmoil and depreciation has made other destinations such as Thailand, Malaysia and Singapore to become more competitive. Thus, the industry must try harder to attract the foreign market by providing competitive packages, attractive tourism products and high quality services and satisfactory experiences. The need for such initiatives has been illustrated by the decreasing rate of hotel occupancy despite increase of visitor arrivals. There are increasing worries that the current tourism boom may fade in the years to come as wealthy mainland travellers set their destinations to Paris and London. Hong Kong is also competing with the nearby Macau.

For the next decade, it plans to create 60,000 new hotel rooms (Joseph, 2005). Macau is also planning to penetrate the untapped market of China by investing in the monopolized gaming industry. It is next to Hong Kong which is likely to benefit from the ease of travel rules from China. As Chinese people enjoy more and longer holidays, the urban rich are traveling in great numbers to Macau for gaming activities. The influx of mainland Chinese has already uplifted the economic growth of Macau which is highly dependent on tourism (Bezlova, 2004).

The local competition in the hotel industry is intense. The choices are vast and there are so many competitors. Few cities offer large numbers of first rate hotels and few places competes with the services that made the Hong Kong hotel industry legendary. Most of the hotels and guest houses are situated on Hong Kong Island and in Kowloon but there are also selections in the New Territories (including the outlying islands). The keen competition and the laws of supply and demand have ensured that these hotels maintain the highest standards.

Pestle Analysis

This analysis audits the impact on the market of large and usually long terms factors: political, economic, social, technological, legal and environmental changes going around the industry. These factors have dramatic impact on the working dynamics of the marketplace. Political factors such as government intervention distort the marketplace. Economic factors include the cycles of growth and decline that impact business. For instance, the increase or decrease in consumer spending impact the host of businesses from consumer goods. Social factors such as the increasing number of double income families impact the standard of living which may increase the purchasing power of consumers. Technological factors are changes in technology which created the need for people to upgrade their skills to remain employable and for businesses to engage in new technologies so that they are not left behind by their competitors. Legal factors involve general legislations that affect all organizations such as employment laws and other industry specific regulations. Lastly are the environmental factors such as pollution control and the spread of diseases such as SARS that has affected businesses in the Asian region.

Political Factors

- Government Policy of non Interventionism on Businesses
- Autonomy from People's Republic of China.

Economic Factors

- High Gross Domestic Product
- High Purchasing Power
- Low unemployment rate
- High Operating Costs.

Social Factors

- Social Stability
- Increase in the Standard of Living
- Lack of Skilled workers.

Technological Factors

- Use of Information and Communication Technology in the Hotel industry
- Technology transfer arrangements with foreign investors The use of Information Technology in various aspects of the industry.

Legal Factors

- Ease of Travel Rules from Mainland China
- Accommodations are subject for 3 percent government tax.

Environmental Factors

- High Levels of Pollution
- Fear of SARS outbreak.

Five Forces Analysis

This analysis discusses five competitive forces governing the tourism and hotel industry.

Force	*Strength*	*Trend*	*Comments*
Entry	High	Changing	Developers are seeing new hotel prospects at the South side of Hong Kong. This would mean new entrants in the industry. Also, 37 percent increase in hotel development is expected until 2008.
Suppliers	Low	Changing	Suppliers can negotiate prices and agreements based on the quantity of goods supplied.
Buyers	High	Increasing	The high purchasing power and increase in disposable income would mean that tourists are likely to spend more in exchange for satisfaction and best experience. This would require the hotels to improve their service standards if they are to remain competitive. Conversely, this may cause tourist to go other destinations such as Paris and London.
Substitutes		Low	Not Changing Hotels are not the only means for lodging. Hotels may also compete with lodging services such as tourists' guest houses and resorts.
Rivalry	High	Increasing	The competition for tourist with neighbouring countries is likely to increase. The development of tourist attractions such as casinos in Macau is likely to affect arrivals in Hong Kong. Also, the competitiveness of Thailand, Malaysia and Singapore in terms quality and price competitiveness is likely to impact the industry

Mobility Barriers

Ownership

Hostels and Guesthouses have minimal capital investment and are traditionally small hotels owned by an individual or family. The dependence of small hotels on individual and the type of security available for loan are among the factors that mitigates against the availability of external finance from lending institutions. While independently owned hotels may till be dominant in the industry, the growth of the industry has been greatly associated with the emergence of hotel groups. The increase in the size of hotel has resulted from these firms building or acquiring hotels in various locations under a central management. These hotels may be grouped in a restricted geographical area or distributed within the country or between countries. International hotels have essentially national companies with a head office in a particular country and engage to a greater extent of hotel operations in the country and other countries.

Marketing and Distribution Systems

Hostels and Guesthouses rely on personal recommendation and repeated visits rather than systematic promotion. On the other hand hotel groups have the marketing capability to promote its services. The international hotels are more advantageous in this aspect due to broad scope of the marketing activities in different countries. These last two groups have larger market and can formulate operations to meet market needs through employing promotion on a wider scale. Another barrier is in terms of the suppliers. Hotel groups has economies of buying because it can buy bulk and negotiate with advantageous prices and terms with suppliers of a wide range of goods. This is something which small hotels could not afford.

Part B

Future Scenarios for the Industry

Hotels in Hong Kong can be described as being capable of providing high levels of services and facilities. More than 20 million tourists are expected to visit the city every year mainly from mainland China. Developers are building up to nine new hotels in the remote industrial sectors on the south side of Hong Kong. Overall, the numbers of hotel rooms are expected to increase by 37 percent by mid 2008 to 56,816 rooms. Occupancy rates among the highest worldwide has already declined to 86 percent in 2005 from 88 percent in the previous year.

The introduction of the seven day free visa in 1993 and the five day work week in China had positive impacts in its outbound travel to Hong Kong. This implied that positive policies such as simplified visa application and extended visa-free status play an important role in attracting international tourists to Hong Kong. HK tourism authorities emphasized the importance of positive policies for the China outbound travel market and the top agenda is to make visas easier for Chinese tour groups. Further, the relaxation on the issue of travel document formalities boosts travel numbers. The tourism industry of Hong Kong has lobbied the Chinese government to increase daily quotas and this allowed additional 358 tourists into Hong Kong each day. With the increasing standard of living and further relaxation of the outbound travel, mainland Chinese travellers will continue to be the most important tourist market for Hong Kong in the future. Tourism related industry such as Hotels must strive to ensure that they provide the best experience and satisfaction possible. With the political and economic condition in China, outbound vacation travel will continue to expand and Hong Kong will be the first to benefit from this growing trend. In order to maximize and get fast return, Hong Kong must shift its emphasis to the China Market and design appropriate marketing strategies.

Conclusion

The tourism and hotel industry has been characterized by significant development, subsequent decline and recovery. This industry has been considered to be one of the major sources of revenues for the country. However, it has declined greatly following the economic crisis and the outbreak of epidemic in the country. This can also be attributed to the high cost of living and the lack of tourist attractions that will entice tourist to visit the country. The condition was even worsen by the intense competition with other international destinations such as Malaysia, Thailand and Singapore. All of which are offering relatively low prices with the quality services.

To date, the industry is recovering by developing attractions such as the Disneyland. While this will boost the industry, competition will also strengthen as other countries are developing their tourist attractions such as casinos in Macau. Indeed, the hotel industry must improve its competitive position by enhancing the experience of guests through quality services, innovation and affordable prices.

Recommendations

- Enhance Hong Kong's image as Asia's world city by leveraging endorsements in a wide audience reach. This would entail making use of traditional channels to communicate the essence of unique Hong Kong experiences to the targeted market segments.
- Introduce and develop major tourism attractions that will boost tourist's stay in Hong Kong. The construction of Disneyland has helped in promoting the country as a tourist destination. Also, Macau's concept of casino and gaming activities is a good example of tourist attraction.

- The importance of offering high quality experiences meaningful to the hotel guests is unquestionable. They should maximize the arrivals of visitors, length of stay, repeat visits and satisfaction through initiatives that will enhance visitor's experiences. Chinese mainland tourists are expected to be the most important market of the industry and hotels must ensure that they offer the best experience through quality service and modern facilities.
- Hoteliers must find a way of offering competitive prices that will suit the budget of travellers. The high costs of living has always been the problem of Hong Kong and this has led to the lost of potential tourist to other competitive locations in Asia.
- Offer promotional packages. A great example of this was the cooperation of HKTB and 53 Hong Kong Hotels in 2004 to offer discounted room rates to bona fide employees of airlines, tour operators, travel agents and tourist offices outside Hong Kong. The promotion showed the range of experiences Hong Kong offers so that these key influencers could in turn motivate and inform their customers about the city.
- Develop e-business. This will help hoteliers to better serve e-consumers by improving the quality of their online offers, expanding the quality of services and developing more competitive e-distribution channels.

The Importance of the Small Hotel

Boutique Hotel

Boutique hotel is a term popularised in North America and the United Kingdom to describe intimate, usually luxurious or quirky hotel environments. Boutique hotels differentiate themselves from larger chain/branded hotels and motels by providing personalized accommodation and services/facilities. Sometimes known as "design hotels" or "lifestyle hotels", boutique hotels began appearing in the 1980s in major cities like London, New York, and San Francisco.

Typically boutique hotels are furnished in a themed, stylish and/or aspirational manner. They usually are considerably smaller than mainstream hotels, often ranging from 3 to 50 guest rooms. Boutique hotels are always individual and are therefore extremely unlikely to be found amongst the homogeneity of large chain hotel groups. Guest rooms and suites may be fitted with telephony and Wi-Fi Internet, air-conditioning, honesty bars and often cable/pay TV, but equally may have none of these, focusing on quiet and comfort rather than gadgetry. Guest services are often attended to by 24-hour hotel staff. Many boutique hotels have on-site dining facilities, and the majority offer bars and lounges that may also be open to the general public.

Despite this definition, the popularity of the boutique term and concept has led to some confusion about the term. Boutique hotels have typically been unique properties operated by individuals or companies with a small collection. However, their successes have prompted multinational hotel companies to try to establish their own brands in order to capture a market share. The most notable example is Starwood Hotels and Resorts Worldwide's W Hotels, ranging from large boutique hotels, such as the W Union Square NY, to the W 'boutique resorts' in the Maldives, to true luxury boutique hotel collections, such as the Bulgari collection, Kimpton Hotels & Restaurants, SLS Hotels, Thompson Hotels, Joie De Vie hotels, The Keating Hotel, and O Hotel, among many others.

There is some overlap between the concept of a small boutique hotel and a bed and breakfast.

In the United States, New York remains the centre of the boutique hotel phenomenon, as the original Schrager-era boutique hotels remain relevant and are joined by scores of independent and small-chain competitors, mainly clustered about Midtown and downtown Manhattan.

The French Quarter and Garden District, New Orleans have several dozen boutique hotels, most of which are located in old homes or inns. These usually provide an ambience based on 19th-century antiques, artwork with New Orleans themes, vintage or reproduction furniture and decor and/or interesting historical associations. Miami and Miami Beach also have several boutique hotels, found mostly along the beachfront streets Ocean Drive and Collins Drive. Most of these are in buildings from the heyday of the Art Deco period. Their attractions include the Art Deco ambiance, beach access, nouvelle and Latin cuisines, and tropical-themed interior decor.

The concept of boutique or design hotels has spread throughout the world. Including European countries like Spain, and East Asian countries such as Thailand, where many boutique or design hotels are sprouting, especially in resort locations, such as Phuket and Hua Hin. Other Far Eastern cities in which boutique and design hotels are becoming increasingly popular include Bangkok, Singapore, and Hong Kong. Boutique hotels are even appearing in such places as Indonesia, mainland China, Iceland, Peru, and Turkey, demonstrating that the concept has penetrated beyond the typical design capitals of the world and is entering new markets.

Hotels and Other Accommodations

Significant Points

- Service occupations account for almost two-thirds of the industry's employment—by far the largest occupational group.
- Hotels employ many young workers and first-time job holders in part-time and seasonal jobs.
- Job opportunities should be good as low entry requirements for many jobs lead to high turnover and replacement needs.

Nature of the Industry

People travel for a variety of reasons, including for vacations, business, and visits to friends and relatives. For many of these travellers, hotels and other accommodations will be where they stay while out of town. For others, hotels may be more than just a place to stay; they are destinations in themselves. Resort hotels and casino hotels, for example, offer a variety of activities to keep travellers and families occupied for much of their stay.

Goods and services. Hotels and other accommodations are as different as the many family and business travellers they accommodate. The industry includes all types of lodging, from luxurious five-star hotels to youth hostels and RV (recreational vehicle) parks. While many provide simply a place to spend the night, others cater to longer stays by providing food service, recreational activities, and meeting rooms. In 2008, 64,300 establishments provided accommodations to suit many different needs and budgets.

Hotels and motels comprise the majority of establishments in this industry and are generally classified as offering either full-service or limited service. Full-service properties offer a variety of services for their guests, but they almost always include at least one or more restaurant and beverage service options other than self-service—from coffee bars and lunch counters to cocktail lounges and formal restaurants. They also usually provide room service. Larger full-service properties usually have a variety of retail shops on the premises, such as gift boutiques, newsstands, and drug and cosmetics counters, some of which may be geared to an exclusive clientele. Additionally, a number of full-service hotels offer guests access to laundry and valet services, swimming pools, beauty salons, and fitness centres or health spas. A small—but growing—number of luxury hotel chains also manage condominium units in combination with their transient rooms, providing both hotel guests and condominium owners with access to the same services and amenities.

The largest hotels often have banquet rooms, exhibit halls, and spacious ballrooms to accommodate conventions, business meetings, wedding receptions, and other social gatherings. Conventions and business meetings are major sources of revenue for these properties. Some commercial hotels are known as conference hotels—fully self-contained entities specifically designed for large-scale meetings. They provide physical fitness and recreational facilities for meeting attendees, in addition to state-of-the-art audiovisual and technical equipment, a business centre, and banquet services.

Limited-service hotels are free-standing properties that do not have on-site restaurants or most other amenities that must be provided by a staff other than the front desk or housekeeping. They usually offer continental breakfasts, vending machines or small packaged items, Internet access, and sometimes unattended game rooms or swimming pools in addition to daily housekeeping services. The numbers of limited-service properties have been growing. These properties are not as costly to build and maintain. They appeal to budget-conscious family vacationers and travellers who are willing to sacrifice amenities for lower room prices.

Hotels can also be categorized based on a distinguishing feature or service provided by the hotel. *Conference hotels* provide meeting and banquet rooms, and usually food service, to large groups of people. *Resort hotels* offer luxurious surroundings with a variety of recreational facilities, such as swimming pools, golf courses, tennis courts, game rooms, and health spas, as well as planned social activities and entertainment. Resorts typically are located in vacation destinations or near natural settings, such as mountains, seashores, theme parks, or other attractions. As a result, the business of many resorts fluctuates with the season. Some resort hotels and motels provide additional convention and conference facilities to encourage customers to combine business with pleasure. During the off season, many of these establishments solicit conventions, sales meetings, and incentive tours to fill their otherwise empty rooms; some resorts even close for the off-season.

Extended-stay hotels typically provide rooms or suites with fully equipped kitchens, entertainment systems, office space with computer and telephone lines, fitness centres, and other amenities. Typically, guests use these hotels for a minimum of 5 consecutive nights, often while on an extended work assignment or lengthy vacation or family visit. *All-suite hotels* offer a living room or sitting room in addition to a bedroom. *Casino hotels* combine both lodging and legalized gaming on the same premises. Along with the typical services provided by most full-service hotels, casino hotels also contain casinos where patrons can wager at table games, play slot machines, and make other bets. Some casino hotels also contain conference and convention facilities.

In addition to hotels, *bed-and-breakfast inns, RV parks, campgrounds,* and *rooming and boarding houses* provide lodging for overnight guests and are included in this industry. *Bed-and-breakfast inns* provide short-term lodging in private homes or small buildings converted for this purpose and are characterized by highly personalized service and inclusion of breakfast in the room rate. Their appeal is quaintness; they typically provide unusual service and unique decor.

RV parks and campgrounds cater to people who enjoy recreational camping at moderate prices. Some parks and campgrounds provide service stations, general stores, shower and toilet facilities, and coin-operated laundries. While some are designed for overnight travellers only, others are for vacationers who stay longer. Some camps provide accommodations, such as cabins and fixed campsites, and other amenities, such as food services, recreational facilities and equipment, and organized recreational activities. Examples of these overnight camps include children's camps, family vacation camps, hunting and fishing camps, and outdoor adventure retreats that offer trail riding, white-water rafting, hiking, fishing, game hunting, and similar activities.

Other short-term lodging facilities in this industry include *guesthouses*, or small cottages located on the same property as a main residence, and *youth hostels*—dormitory-style hotels with few frills, occupied mainly by students traveling on limited budgets. Also included are *rooming and boarding houses*, such as fraternity houses, sorority houses, off-campus dormitories, and workers' camps. These establishments provide temporary or longer term accommodations that may serve as a principal residence for the period of occupancy. These establishments also may provide services such as housekeeping, meals, and laundry services.

Industry organization. In recent years, the hotel industry has been dominated by a few large national hotel chains. To the traveller, familiar chain establishments represent dependability and quality at predictable rates. Many chains recognize the importance of brand loyalty to guests and have expanded the range of lodging options offered under one corporate name to include a full range of hotels from limited-service, economy-type hotels to luxury inns. While these national corporations own some of the hotels, many properties are independently owned but affiliated with a chain through a franchise agreement or management contract. Increasingly, hotel chains are moving away from owning properties to managing them. As part of a chain, individual hotels can participate in the company's national reservations service or incentive program, thereby appearing to belong to a larger enterprise. For those who prefer more personalized service and a unique experience, *boutique hotels* are becoming more popular. These smaller hotels are generally found in urban locations and provide patrons good service and more distinctive decor and food selection.

Although there are nationwide RV parks and campgrounds, most small lodging establishments are individually owned and operated by a single owner, who may employ a small staff to help operate the business.

Recent developments. The lodging industry is moving towards more limited-service properties mostly in suburban, residential, or commercial neighborhoods, often locating hotels near popular restaurants. Many full-service properties are limiting or quitting the food service business altogether, choosing to contract out their food service operations to third party restaurateurs, including long-term arrangements with chain restaurant operators. Urban business and entertainment districts are providing a greater mix of lodging options to appeal to a wider range of travellers.

Increased competition among establishments in this industry has spurred many independently owned and operated hotels and other lodging places to join national or international reservation systems. This allows travellers to make multiple reservations for lodging, airlines, and car rentals with one telephone call or Internet search. Nearly all hotel chains and many independent lodging facilities operate online reservation systems through the Internet or maintain Web sites that allow individuals to book rooms. Online marketing of properties is so popular with guests that many hotels promote themselves with elaborate Web sites and allow people to investigate availability and rates.

Working Conditions

Hours. Because hotels are open around the clock, employees frequently work varying shifts or variable schedules. Employees who work the late shift generally receive additional compensation. Many employees enjoy the opportunity to work part-time, nights or evenings, or other schedules that fit their availability for work and the hotel's needs.

Hotel managers and many department supervisors may work regularly assigned schedules, but they also routinely work longer hours than scheduled, especially during peak travel times or when multiple events are scheduled. Also, they may be called in to work on short notice in the event of an emergency or to cover a position. Those who are self-employed, often owner-operators of small inns, camp sites, or RV parks, tend to work long hours and often live at the establishment or nearby.

Office and administrative support workers generally work scheduled hours in an office setting, meeting with guests, clients, and hotel staff. Their work can become hectic—processing orders and invoices, dealing with demanding guests, or servicing requests that require a quick turnaround. Job hazards typically are limited to muscle and eye strain common to working with computers and office equipment.

Computer specialists, information technology technicians, and audiovisual technicians who are employed mostly by larger convention hotels typically maintain standard hours servicing the property's Web sites and computer and communications networks. However, they often work long hours setting up and testing equipment for events that require their services. Work environment. Work in hotels and other accommodations can be demanding and hectic. Hotel staffs provide a variety of services to guests and must do so efficiently, courteously, and accurately. They must maintain a pleasant demeanor even during times of stress or when dealing with an impatient or irate guest. Alternately, work at slower times, such as the off-season or overnight periods, can seem slow and tiresome. Still, hotel workers must be ready to provide guests and visitors with gracious customer service at any hour.

Food preparation and food service workers in hotels must withstand the strain of working during busy periods and being on their feet for many hours. Kitchen workers lift heavy pots and kettles and work near hot ovens and grills. Job hazards include slips and falls, cuts, and burns, but injuries are seldom serious. Food service workers often carry heavy trays of food, dishes, and glassware. Many of these workers work part time, including evenings, weekends, and holidays.

Employment

Hotels and other accommodations provided 1.9 million wage and salary jobs in 2008. Employment is concentrated in cities and resort areas. Compared with establishments in other industries, hotels and other accommodations tend to be small. About 74 percent employed fewer than 20 workers and 54 percent employed fewer than 10. As a result, lodging establishments offer opportunities for those who are interested in owning or running their own business. Although establishments tend to be small, the majority of jobs are in larger hotels—those with more than 100 employees.

Hotels and other lodging places often provide first jobs to many new entrants to the labour force. In 2008, about 19 percent of the workers were younger than age 25, compared with about 13 percent across all industries.

Occupations in the Industry

The vast majority of workers in this industry—83 percent in 2008—were employed in service and office and administrative support occupations. Workers in these occupations usually learn their skills on the job. Postsecondary education is not required for most entry-level positions; however, college training may be helpful for advancement in some of the occupations. For those in administrative support—mainly hotel desk clerks—and service occupations, positive personality traits and a customer-service orientation may be more important than formal schooling. The most important traits for success in the hotels and other accommodations industry are good communication skills; the ability to get along with people in stressful situations; a neat, clean appearance; and a pleasant manner.

Service occupations. Service workers are by far the largest occupational group in the industry, accounting for 65 percent of the industry's employment. Most service jobs are in housekeeping occupations, including *maids and housekeeping cleaners* and *janitors and cleaners*, and in food preparation and serving jobs, including *waiters and waitresses*, *bartenders*, *fast food and counter workers*, and various other kitchen and dining room workers. The industry also employs many *baggage porters and bellhops*, *gaming services workers*, and *grounds maintenance workers*.

Workers in cleaning and housekeeping occupations ensure that the lodging facility is clean and in good condition for the comfort and safety of guests. *Maids and housekeeping cleaners* clean lobbies, halls, guestrooms, and bathrooms. They make sure that guests not only have clean rooms, but have all the necessary furnishings and supplies. They change sheets and towels, vacuum carpets, dust furniture, empty wastebaskets, and mop bathroom floors. In larger hotels, the housekeeping staff may include assistant housekeepers, floor supervisors, housekeepers, and executive housekeepers. *Janitors* help with the cleaning of the public areas of the facility, empty trash, and perform minor maintenance work. Workers in the various *food preparation and serving* occupations deal with customers in the dining room or at a service counter. *Waiters and waitresses* take customers' orders, serve meals, and prepare checks. In smaller establishments, they often set tables, escort guests to their seats, accept payment, and clear tables. In larger restaurants, some of these tasks are assigned to other workers.

Bartenders fill beverage orders for customers seated at the bar or from waiters and waitresses who serve patrons at tables. *Dining room and cafeteria attendants* and *bartender helpers* assist waiters, waitresses, and bartenders by clearing, cleaning, and setting up tables, replenishing supplies at the bar, and keeping the serving areas stocked with linens, tableware, and other supplies. *Fast food and counter workers* take orders and serve food at fast-food counters and in coffee shops; they also may operate the cash register.

A variety of food preparation workers prepare food in the kitchen. Larger hotels employ *chefs and head cooks* who create menus, develop recipes, and oversee food preparation operations and personnel. *Food preparation and serving supervisors* direct workers and supervise specific tasks, such as overseeing banquet cooks or bartenders and servers at a private function, while the chef tends to other activities. *Restaurant cooks* specialize in the preparation of many different kinds of foods and menu items, generally cooking from scratch and typically only when ordered by diners. They may have titles such as salad chef, grill chef, or pastry chef. Individual chefs may oversee the day-to-day operations of different kitchens in a hotel, such as a full-service restaurant that specializes in fine-dining, a casual or counter-service establishment, or banquet operations. Chef positions generally are attained after years of experience and, sometimes, formal training, including apprenticeships. Larger establishments also employ *executive chefs* and *food and beverage directors* who plan menus, purchase food, and supervise kitchen personnel for all of the kitchens in the property. *Food preparation workers* shred lettuce for salads, cut up food for cooking, and perform simple cooking steps under the direction of the chef or head cook. Beginners may advance to more skilled food preparation jobs with experience or specialized culinary training. Many full-service hotels employ a uniformed staff to assist arriving and departing guests. *Baggage porters and bellhops* carry bags and escort guests to their rooms. *Concierges* arrange special or personal services for guests. They may take messages, arrange for babysitting, make restaurant reservations, provide directions, arrange for or give advice on entertainment and local attractions, and monitor requests for housekeeping and maintenance. *Doorkeepers* help guests into and out of their cars, summon taxis, and carry baggage into the hotel lobby.

Hotels also employ the largest percentage of *gaming services* workers because a large share of gaming takes place in casino hotels. Some gaming services positions are associated with oversight and direction—supervision, surveillance, and investigation—while others involve working with the games or patrons themselves, by tending the slot machines, handling money, writing and running tickets, dealing cards, and performing related duties.

The industry also employs a large number of *recreation and fitness workers*. At resort hotels and at vacation and recreational camps, recreation workers organize and conduct recreation activities for guests and campers. *Camp counselors* lead and instruct children and teenagers in outdoor-oriented forms of recreation, such as swimming, hiking, horseback riding, and camping. In addition, counselors at vacation and resident camps also provide guidance and supervise daily living and general socialization. Other types of campgrounds may employ trail guides for activities such as hiking, hunting, and fishing.

Office and administrative support occupations. These positions accounted for 19 percent of the jobs in hotels and other accommodations in 2008. Hotel desk clerks, bookkeeping and accounting clerks, and switchboard operators ensure that the front office operates smoothly. *Hotel, motel, and resort desk clerks* process reservations and guests' registrations and checkouts, monitor arrivals and departures, handle complaints, and receive and forward mail. The duties of hotel desk clerks depend on the size of the facility. In smaller lodging places, one clerk or a manager may do everything. In larger hotels, a larger staff divides the duties among several types of clerks. Management, business, and financial operations occupations. Hotels and other lodging places employ many different types of managers to direct and coordinate the activities of the front office, kitchen, dining room, and other departments, such as housekeeping, accounting, personnel, purchasing, publicity, sales, security, and maintenance.

Lodging managers, typically the general manager and assistant managers, make decisions that affect the general operations of the hotel, including setting room rates, establishing credit policy, and having ultimate responsibility for resolving problems. In smaller establishments, lodging managers also may perform many of the front-office administrative tasks. In the smallest establishments, the owners—sometimes a family team—do all the work necessary to operate the business. Other managers are responsible for different phases of hotel operations. For example, *food and beverage managers* oversee restaurants, lounges, and catering or banquet operations. *Rooms managers* look after reservations and occupancy levels to ensure proper room assignments and authorize discounts, special rates, or promotions. Large hotels, especially those with conference centres, use an executive committee structure to better facilitate departmental communications and coordinate activities. Other managers who may serve on a hotel's executive committee include *public relations* or *sales managers, human resource directors*, *executive housekeepers*, and *heads of hotel security*.

Other occupations. Hotels and other accommodations employ a variety of workers found in many other industries. *General maintenance and repair workers* fix leaky faucets, do some painting and carpentry, make sure that heating and air-conditioning equipment works properly, mow lawns, and exterminate pests. The industry also employs cashiers, accountants, personnel workers, and entertainers. As properties acquire and use more sophisticated computer systems, they employ more *computer specialists* to help maintain these systems as well as the hotel's Web site, and computer connections for guests. Also, many additional workers inside a hotel may work for other companies under contract to the hotel or may provide personal or retail services directly to hotel guests from space rented by the hotel. This group includes guards and security officers, barbers and cosmetologists, fitness trainers and aerobics instructors, valets, gardeners, and parking attendants.

Training and Advancement

Most large hotel properties employ persons in occupations that require a wide range of skills and experience. Most entry-level jobs require little or no previous training; basic tasks usually can be learned in a short time. Lodging managers and many department heads usually require some formal training, or years of hospitality industry experience, or both. All positions in this industry require employees to maintain a customer-service orientation. Almost all workers in the hotel and other accommodations industry undergo some on-the-job training provided under the supervision of an experienced employee or manager to acclimate new employees to any unique characteristics of the property or the local area. Hotel managers and owners recognize the importance of personal service and attention to guests, so they look for persons with positive personality traits and good communication skills when filling many guest services positions, such as desk clerk and host and hostess positions.

Many hotel managers place a greater emphasis on customer service skills while providing specialized training in other skill areas, such as computer technology and software. Vocational courses and apprenticeship programs in food preparation, catering, and hotel and restaurant management, offered through restaurant and lodging associations and trade unions, provide training opportunities. Programs range in length from a few months to several years.

Service workers. Most service workers need only a high school diploma or equivalent to get hired, but some can be hired with even less. Some entry-level jobs are filled by students looking for part-time or seasonal work. Most hotels, particularly the chain hotels, have some formal training sessions for new employees that may include video or online training. Advancement opportunities for service workers in the hotel industry vary widely. Some workers, such as housekeepers and janitors, generally have few opportunities for advancement. In large properties, some may advance to supervisory positions. Advancement opportunities for chefs and cooks are better than those for most other service occupations. Cooks often advance to chef or to supervisory and management positions, such as executive chef, restaurant manager, or food service manager. Hotel desk clerks sometimes advance to supervisory or managerial front-office positions.

Promotional opportunities often are greatest for those who are willing to take on a new assignment in a different department. Advancement for those who excel at customer service and demonstrate a willingness to learn front-office jobs can serve as a steppingstone to jobs in public relations, advertising, sales, and management.

Management, business, and financial operations occupations. Many hotels fill first-level manager positions by promoting staff from within—particularly those with good communication skills, a solid educational background, tact, loyalty, and a capacity to endure hard work and long hours. People with these qualities still advance to manager jobs, but, more recently, lodging chains have primarily been hiring persons with 4-year college degrees in the liberal arts or other fields and starting them in assistant manager or management trainee positions. Bachelor's and Master's degree programs in hotel, restaurant, and hospitality management provide the strongest background for a career as a hotel manager, with nearly 150 colleges and universities offering such programs. Graduates of these programs are highly sought by employers in this industry because of their familiarity with technical issues and their ability to learn related skills quickly. Eventually, they may advance to a top management position in a hotel or a corporate management position in a large chain operation.

Upper management positions, such as general manager, food service manager, or sales manager, generally require considerable formal training and job experience. Some department managers, executive housekeepers, and executive chefs, generally require some specialized training and extensive on-the-job experience. To advance to positions with more responsibilities, lodging managers frequently change employers or relocate within a chain to a property in another area. Office and administrative support occupations. For office and administrative support workers, advancement opportunities in the hotel industry vary widely. These occupations offer excellent entry-level job prospects and can serve as a steppingstone to jobs in hospitality, public relations, advertising, sales, and management.

Outlook

The hotels and other accommodations industry is expected grow by 5 percent over the 2008-18 period. The industry employs large numbers of part-time and younger workers who typically do not stay in these jobs for very long. The need to replace these workers will create job opportunities in an array of occupations and localities. Employment change. Wage and salary employment in hotels and other accommodations is expected to increase by 5 percent between 2008 and 2018, compared with 11 percent growth projected for all industries combined. Travel and tourism typically grows during expansion periods in the economy, which results in a greater need for transient rooms. The hotel market is expected to see increases in the number of rooms, but the greatest number of rooms is expected to open in limited service hotels that do not provide food service. Many of these newer hotels are being built in the suburbs where a growing population is increasingly based and a foundation of business establishments is being developed.

Employment outlook varies somewhat by service class of hotel and occupation. Growth of full-service hotels, casino hotels, and the smaller luxury hotel market that specializes in personal service will cause employment of lodging managers to grow more slowly than the average.

The accelerating trend among chain-affiliated hotels to establish regional management and staffing teams among several properties and across service classes should provide current assistant managers or department managers with opportunities to demonstrate their readiness for advancement, but may also limit the prospects for new manager positions. Opportunities should be more limited for self-employed managers or owners of small lodging places, such as bed-and-breakfast inns, because of the competition from long-established chains as they move into untapped markets that were once friendly to the quainter properties. Job opportunities at outdoor recreation and RV parks should grow as RVs and driving vacations gain popularity in the United States. Also, gaming services and gaming manager occupations should grow as more casino hotels are built. Employment of hotel, motel, and resort desk clerks is expected to grow faster than some other occupations in the industry in part because the growing numbers of limited-service hotels still require desk clerks. However, employment of dishwashers will decline within the industry—reflecting the increasing number of hotels and other accommodations that either do not offer full-service restaurants or contract them out to other food service establishments.

Job prospects. Although most of the hotels opening over the next decade will be limited-service hotels, most of the job openings will arise in full-service hotels, including convention, casino, and resort hotels, because they employ the most workers. Limited-service properties do not operate restaurants or lounges; therefore, these establishments offer a narrower range of employment opportunities. The streamlined organizational structure, however, offers a faster route to the general manager level for those more interested in running or owning their own hotel. Job opportunities will be concentrated in the largest hotel occupations, such as building cleaning workers and hotel, motel, and resort desk clerks. These workers are found in all types of hotels and accommodations, from the limited-service economy hotels to posh casino hotels. They also are important to the luxury hotel segment that emphasizes personal service. Some occupations in this industry have relatively high numbers of workers who leave their jobs and must be replaced. Many young people, and those looking only for seasonal or part-time work, take food service and administrative jobs that require little or no previous training. To attract and retain workers, the hotel and other accommodations industry is placing greater emphasis on training and retaining employees. Job opportunities in this industry should be good for first-time jobseekers, people with limited experience, and those interested in making a career in the lodging industry.

Earnings

Industry earnings. Earnings in hotels and other accommodations generally are much lower than the average for all industries. In 2008, average earnings for all nonsupervisory workers in this industry were $402 a week, compared with $608 a week for workers throughout private industry. Some workers in this industry earn the Federal minimum wage, which was $7.25 per hour as of July 2009. Some States have laws that establish a higher minimum wage.

Food and beverage service workers, as well as hosts and hostesses, maids and housekeeping cleaners, concierges, and baggage porters and bellhops, derive their earnings from a combination of hourly wages and customer tips. Waiters and waitresses often derive the majority of their earnings from tips, which vary greatly depending on menu prices and the volume of customers served. Many employers also provide free meals and furnish uniforms. Food service personnel may receive extra pay for working at banquets and on other special occasions.

The Chain Hotel Concept

Prior to examining the concept and the idea behind hotel chains and what exactly they are, it's important to have a peek at the interesting aspects of what a hotel is, what its mission supposed to be and how its operations are being carried out. With such an understanding, it's easier to see the value, purpose and the excitement behind hotel chains as opposed to a hotel.

As we all know, a hotel is regarded as an institution and or a service provider's establishment to offer paid lodging facilities to customers on limited time or short term basis. These facilities provided include, accommodation consisting of a room with a bed and other furniture (limited to the product bought), meals on room and board basis, attached bathrooms, air conditioning and climate control facilities, as well as, telephone facilities, cable television, internet connectivity and access plus the desirable mini bar. These are only some of the items included in a hotel room.

Apart from the facilities provided in the rooms of these hotels to the guests, there are many other additions and assortments available for a person staying in these hotels. They come in the form of, multi cuisine restaurants, swimming pools, fitness training centres, spas, conference and banquet halls and many others. Another aspect that anyone comes across with hotels is the classification. As a result of the tourism industry worldwide expanding at a rapid rate during recent decades, for purposes of comparability and standards, rating systems have been introduced. This rating system takes the form of one to five stars classification where the most stars bearing hotels provide the best product and the lower star hotels provide a mediocre or average product to their guests. 'Some consider this disadvantageous to smaller hotels whose quality of accommodation could fall into one class but the lack of an item such as an elevator would prevent it from reaching a higher categorization. In some countries, there is an official body with standard criteria for classifying hotels, but in many others there is none. There have been attempts at unifying the classification system so that it becomes an internationally recognized and reliable standard but large differences exist in the quality of the accommodation and the food within one category of hotel, sometimes even in the same country.

With a proper understanding of the concept, idea and the purpose behind a hotel, it is helpful now to look at the term hotel chain. The term hotel chain traits back its origins to the 1920s where a great trend began which shifted individual ownership of hotels to corporate ownership as a result of increasing costs of building and operating hotels.

As the corporate world took over the hotel business, they didn't believe in a single hotel at a single location but a chain of hotels at different locations with the same name but not necessarily with the same capacity and product range. Chain operations of 'hotels allows for efficient management through the use of mass purchasing, central reservations and billings, and extensive advertising and promotion campaigns. Today about 30 percent of all American hotels and motels are affiliated with chains or franchised groups.

Going International

In general, to be called a hotel, an establishment must have a minimum of six letting bedrooms, at least three of which must have attached (ensuite) private bathroom facilities. Although hotels are classified into 'Star' categories (1-Star to 5-Star), there is no standard method of assigning these ratings, and compliance with customary requirements is voluntary. A US hotel with a certain rating, for example, is may look very different from a European or Asian hotel with the same rating, and would provide a different level of amenities, range of facilities, and quality of service. Whereas hotel chains assure uniform standards throughout, non-chain hotels (even within the same country) may not agree on the same standards.

In Germany, for example, only about 30 percent of the hotels choose to comply with the provisions of the rules established by the German Hotels & Restaurants association. Although both WTO and ISO have been trying to persuade hotels to agree on some minimum requirements as worldwide norms, the entire membership of the Paris-based International Hotel & Restaurant (IH&RA) opposes any such move.

According to IH&RA, to harmonize hotel classification based on a single grading (which is uniform across national boundaries) would be an undesirable and impossible task.

As a rough guide: A 1-Star hotel provides a limited range of amenities and services, but adheres to a high standard of facility-wide cleanliness. A 2-Star hotel provides good accommodation and better equipped bedrooms, each with a telephone and attached private bathroom. A 3-Star hotel has more spacious rooms and adds high-class decorations and furnishings and colour TV. It also offers one or more bars or lounges. A 4-Star hotel is much more comfortable and larger, and provides excellent cuisine, room service, and other amenities.

A 5-Star hotel offers most luxurious premises, widest range of guest services, as well as swimming pool and sport and exercise facilities. The Official Hotel Guide (published in the US, and followed world wide) has its own classification scheme that ranks hotels in nine categories as (1) Moderate Tourist Class, (2) Tourist Class, (3) Superior Tourist Class, (4) Moderate First Class, (5) Limited Service First Class, (6) First Class, (7) Moderate Deluxe, (8) Deluxe, and (9) Superior Deluxe.

Marriott International

Marriott International, Inc. (NYSE: MAR) is a worldwide operator and franchisor of a broad portfolio of hotels and related lodging facilities. Founded by J. Willard Marriott, the company is now led by son J.W. (Bill) Marriott, Jr. Today, Marriott International has about 3,150 lodging properties located in the United States and 67 other countries and territories.

Marriott's operations are grouped into the following five business segments:

- Full-service lodging-65%
- Select-service lodging-11%
- Extended-stay lodging-5%
- Timeshare-15%
- Synthetic fuel-4% (primarily a tax shelter).

History

Marriott was founded by J. Willard Marriott 1927 when he and his wife opened a root beer stand in Washington D.C.. As a missionary in the sweltering, humid summers in Washington, Marriott was convinced that what the city needed was a such a place to get a cool drink. They later expanded their enterprises into a chain of restaurants and hotels.

The Key Bridge Marriott in Arlington, Virginia is Marriott International's longest operating hotel, and celebrated its 50th anniversary in 2009. Their son and current Chairman and Chief Executve Officer, J.W. (Bill) Marriott, Jr. has led the company to spectacular worldwide growth. Today, Marriott International has about 3,150 lodging properties located in the United States and 67 other countries and territories.

Marriott International was formed in 1992 when Marriott Corporation split into two companies, Marriott International and Host Marriott Corporation.

In 2002 Marriott International began a major restructuring by spinning off many Senior Living Services Communities (which is now part of Sunrise Senior Living) and Marriott Distribution Services, so that it could focus on hotel ownership and management. The changes were completed in 2003.

In April 1995, Marriott International acquired a 49% interest in the Ritz-Carlton Hotel Company LLC. Marriott International believed that it could increase sales and profit margins at the Ritz, a troubled chain with a significant number of properties either losing money or barely breaking even.

The cost of Marriott's initial investment was estimated to be about $200 million in cash and assumed debt. The next year, Marriott spent $331 million to take over the Ritz-Carlton Atlanta and buy a majority interest in two properties owned by William Johnson, a real estate developer who had purchased the Boston Ritz Carlton in 1983 and expanded his Ritz holdings over the next twenty years.

The Ritz began expansion into the lucrative timeshare market among other new initiatives made financially possible by the deep pockets of Marriott, which also lent its own in-house expertise in certain areas. There were other benefits for Ritz-Carlton flowing from its relationship with Marriott, such as being able to take advantage of the parent company's reservation system and buying power. The partnership was solidified in 1998 when Marriott boosted its interest in Ritz-Carlton to 99 percent. By 1999 revenues from the 35 hotels it operated around the world totaled about $1.4 billion. Marriott International owned Ramada International Hotels & Resorts until its sale on September 15, 2004 to Cendant. It is the first hotel chain to serve food that is completely free of trans fats at all of its North American properties.

In 2005, Marriott International and Marriott Vacation Club International comprised two of the 53 entities that contributed the maximum of $250,000 to the second inauguration of President George W. Bush.

On July 19, 2006, Marriott announced that all lodging buildings they operate in the United States and Canada would become non-smoking beginning September 2006. "The new policy includes all guest rooms, restaurants, lounges, meeting rooms, public space and employee work areas."

Terrorist Attacks

Several Marriott hotels around the world have been the target of bombings.

- 2001 Marriott world trade centre 9/11 atacks
- 2003 Marriott Hotel bombing
- 2008 Islamabad Marriott bombing
- 2009 Jakarta bombings.

Great America Parks

Marriott also developed three and ultimately opened two theme parks entitled Marriott's Great America from 1976 until 1984. The parks were located in Gurnee, Illinois, Santa Clara, California and a proposed but never-built location in the Washington, DC area, and were themed celebrating American history. The American-themed areas under Marriott's tenure of ownership included "Carousel Plaza" (the first section beyond the main gates); small-town-themed "Hometown Square"; "The Great Midwest Livestock Exposition At County Fair" with a Turn of the Century rural-fair theme; "Yankee Harbor", inspired by a 19th century New England port; "Yukon Territory," resembling a Canadian/Alaskan logging camp; and the French Quarter-modeled "Orleans Place". At opening, both parks were laid out nearly identically.

In 1984, Marriott disposed of its theme park division; both parks were sold and today are associated with national theme park chains.

The Gurnee location was sold to Six Flags Theme Parks where it operates today as Six Flags Great America. The Santa Clara location was sold to the City of Santa Clara, who retained the underlying property and sold the park to Kings Entertainment Company, renamed Paramount Parks in 1993. From 1993 to 2006, the Santa Clara location was known as Paramount's Great America. In 2006, Paramount Parks was acquired by Cedar Fair Entertainment Company; the Santa Clara park operates today as California's Great America. In the years after their sale, the layouts of the parks have diverged substantially.

Marriott Brands

Full Service Lodging

- Marriott Hotels & Resorts
- JW Marriott Hotels & Resorts
- Renaissance Hotels & Resorts
- Marriott Conference Centres
- Ritz-Carlton Hotels & Resorts
- BVLGARI Hotels & Resorts
- Edition Hotels & Resorts
- Autograph Collection Hotels & Resots.

Select Service Lodging

- Courtyard by Marriott
- Fairfield Inn by Marriott
- SpringHill Suites by Marriott.

Extended Stay Lodging

- Residence Inn by Marriott
- TownePlace Suites by Marriott
- Marriott ExecuStay
- Marriott Executive Apartments.

Timeshare

- Marriott Vacation Club International (MVCI)
- Marriott Grand Residence Club
- The Ritz-Carlton Club
- The Ritz-Carlton Destination Club.

Marriott Rewards

Marriott International also offers Marriott Rewards, a loyalty ("rewards") program that allows members to earn points or airline miles for their stays at participating Marriott brand hotels, in addition to other membership benefits.

Largest Hotel

The largest hotel in the world is the First World Hotel in Genting Highlands, Malaysia. This biggest hotel took the title from the MGM Grand Las Vegas in Las Vegas, Nevada. The First World Hotel hass 6,118 rooms with prices starting as low as $60.00 USD/night.

IHG (InterContinental Hotels Group)

Is the worlds largest and most global hotel chain. IHG's brands include: InterContinental Hotels, Crowne Plaza, Hotel Indigo, Holiday Inn, Holiday Inn Express, Staybridge Suites, and Candlewood Suites. As of March 2009 they had over 4,200 hotels in their portfolio representing over 621,000 Rooms.

Best Western uses the tag line "The Worlds Largest Hotel Chain"; however with a portfolio of just under 4,000 hotels representing 303,000 rooms. They come in number 7 behind IHG, Wyndham, Marriott, Hilton, Accor, and Choice Hotels.

Revenue Management Techniques in Hospitality Industry – A comparison with Reference to Star and Economy Hotels

The hospitality industry is part of a larger enterprise known as the travel and tourism industry. It is one of the oldest industries in the world. In early days, traders, explorers, missionaries and pilgrims needed a break in their journeys requiring food, shelter and rest.

People opened their homes and kitchens to these weary travellers, and an industry was born. Although accommodation today is varied and their services have changed and expanded over the ages, one thing about the hospitality industry has remained the same, guests are always welcome! From a friendly greeting at the door, room service, breakfast, to a host of facilities' the hospitality industry offers travellers a home away from home.

Hospitality is defined as "the friendly reception and treatment of strangers". For most people, hospitality means entertaining guests with courtesy and warmth. Hospitality is also an industry made up of businesses that provide lodging, food and other services to travellers.

The main components of this industry are hotels, motels, inns, resorts and Restaurants.

In a broad sense, the hospitality industry might refer to any group engaged in tourism, entertainment, transportation or lodging including cruise lines, airlines, railways, car rental companies and tour operators.

However the two main segments are the lodging industry also called the hotel industry, and the food and beverage industry, also called the restaurant industry. The lodging industry is made up of businesses providing temporary housing, and such a business is called a lodging establishment and the people who stay in it are called guests or clients.

What is Revenue Management?

Revenue Management is a technique to optimize the revenue earned from a fixed, perishable resource. The challenge is to sell the right resources to the right customer at the right time.

Revenue Management implements the basic principles of supply and demand economics in a tactical way to generate incremental revenues. There are three essential conditions for revenue management to be applicable:

- That there is a fixed amount of resources available for sale.
- That the resources sold are perishable. This means that there is a time limit to selling the resources, after which they cease to be of value.
- That different customers are willing to pay a different price for using the same amount of resources.

Revenue Management is of especially high relevance in cases where the constant costs are relatively high compared to the variable costs. The less variable costs there are, the more the additional revenue earned will contribute to the overall profit.

To illustate this, we can take the example of the luxury hotel which charges different prices for different customers. In India it is generally practiced in star hotels to maximise the revenues. The customer who is price sensitive and time conscious generally pays lesser tariffs than a customer who is willing to pay more and books the room one or two days before the stay.

Revenue Management in other words tries to maximise revenues by managing the tradeoff between a low occupancy and higher room rate senario (business customers) versus a high occupancy and lower room rate (vacation customers). Demand forecasting: Pricing and demand are inter-related and need to be coordinated. In the hospitality industry, demand for a room is cyclic in nature and follows a trend. Revenue management models help pinpoint demand by minimising uncertainity and producing the best possible forecast.

Allocation: the revenue management also puts light on the allocation of inventory (hotel rooms) among different segments. For example, if a hotel has two price categories of rooms, say Rs.4500 and Rs. 6000.

Since the pricing is different for the two rooms, these rooms are each targeted at a different customer set. Based on the historical preference pattern of customers in each segment, it would be possible to estimate the number of customers who would be willing to pabuy these rooms at a given price with a reasonable variance. For example, an average 50 customers may be willing to pay Rs. 6000 for some rooms, but it could also mean that the actual number of customers who turn up for Rs. 6000 could be 60 or even 40 with some probability, or 80 or 30 with a lesser probability. Overbooking: Overbooking is a practice of intentionally selling more rooms than available in order to offset the effect of cancellations. For example, suppose in the hotel industry, there are 180 rooms available, there is no certainity that all the rooms would be booed at a point of time. In the same way, during the season, there is a possibility of over booking.

Therefore if the booking is done 181 customers instead of 180, the hotel may end up with only 173 or less than 180 customers, since the probability of exactly 181 customers turning up is low, the revenue from that aditional customer generally compensates more than the expected cost.

Classification of Hotels

Hotels are classified into five main types:

- Economy/limited-service hotels
- Mid-market hotels
- All-suite hotels
- First class or executive hotels
- Luxury or deluxe hotels.

For the purpose of our research, Economy and Executive hotels are selected. Normally hotels have four rate categories: (1) Rack rates, (2) Group and tour rates, (3) Special and promotional rates and (4) package rates.

(1) Rack rates are normal room rates. It is based on the category of the room, type of bedding and occupancy. Unless specified, guests are quoted the rack rates and are charged for the same.

(2) Group and Tour rates are a discounted room rate for an organisation, which has blocked a large number of rooms. Most hotels have group rates that are lower than the rack rates. This rate is generally extended to a trade association or fraternal organisation that has scheduled a meeting, seminar or conference at the hotel. Discounts are also offered to a tour operator, in return for a commitment to purchase a minimum number of rooms over a given period of time.

(3) Special and promotional rates are offered to corporate travellers, traveling sales representatives, military personnel, airlines staff or other regular clients. Some times special rates are also offered along with an advertising campaign or to promote the hotel during lean periods.

(4) Package rates are offered to the public along with other services such as banquet or a ball, or recreational facilities or a special event. Such a package normally includes accommodation, tickets to the concerned event and transportation from hotel to the venue and back. Other popular packages offered by hotels are honeymoon, weekend, Christmas, New Year or any other sports activity. The package rate is normally lower than the combined component or rack rate.

A Case Study on Bentleys Hotel (Economy) and Hotel Godwin Hotel Bentleys, Colaba (Economy Hotel)

Bentley's is one of Mumbai's (formerly known as Bombay, India) best budget tourist hotels. It is highly rated in most Tourist/Traveller's Guides, including The Lonely Planet.

Ideally situated in South Mumbai, it is in the heart of the downtown area, close to the business, entertainment and shopping areas. The hotel has a clean, quiet, comfortable and homely atmosphere.

Victorian Ambiance

The hotel gets 95% of its customers as foreign tourists. The occupancy rate in this hostel is 110%. The rooms are occupied for the 365 days in this year. Demand is more than. Supply in this hotel. The customers are not provided with any food in this hotel. The hotel does not practice differential pricing for its customers. It charges single price for all of its customers irrespective of different nationality. Tourists generally would like to stay in this hotel for the wonderful service provided by the hotel. Generally the hotel gets repeated customers and the customer loyalty is very good over here. Marketing Strategies adopted by the hotel to attract more tourists:

- Reservation is done directly without the help of middleman like travel agents.
- Hotel provides prompt service to the enquiries of the customers mails. Usually the queries are answered within an hour.
- The services provided by the housekeepers are also very good. They are excellent in communication and they meet the customer demand promptly.
- Generally in this hotel, 80% of the customers are repeated which means there is customer loyalty to the maximum extent.
- Usually the hotels provide one room to one customer in a day. But Bentleys uses its perishable capacity 3 times a day for the purpose of maximizing the revenue.

Hotel Godwin, Colaba (Three Star Hotel)

The hotel has been accredited as a 3 star hotel and is situated in colaba. They find most of their customers from Gulf. Hotel Godwin, a 3 Star Hotel with 52 rooms has been serving the travellers and business community for well over 30 years and from the testimonials of its patrons, both Indian and Foreign, it is considered a real home away from home. hotel godwin occupies an ideal location from the point of view of businessmen and tourists. Adjacent to Colaba Causeway, the fashionable shopping centre in South Mumbai, it is close to the tourists attractions like the Gateway of India; Museum, the business centres of Flora Fountain, Churchgate Reclamation and Nariman Point, Offices of National & International Airlines, and headquarters of both the main Railway line close by. Prominent Clubs, Cinemas & Restaurants are near by.

- They get the customers through travel agents in Mumbai and the other parts of India.
- The average occupancy rate is 60%
- Most of the customers are tourists.
- They charge different tariff to different customers.
- Usually they get repeated customers.
- They do overbook the rooms to maximize the revenues.
- There are 65 employees in the hotel.

Revenue Management Strategies Adopted by the Hotels Findings

- It is believed that the hotels, which are functioning at the large scale, are good in revenue management and they apply most advanced techniques to manage their revenues. But through this research on star and economy hotels, it can be said that the star hotels provide the state of the art facilities and services to the customers and very hygiene food to the customers. But when it comes to the occupancy rates measure in terms of foreign tourists, the economy hotels are exceedingly doing well.
- Economy Hotels give importance to the cultural values of the country.
- The concept of overbooking is followed in both kinds of hotels.
- The market segmentation is not there in case of economy hotels. But it is practiced in star hotels.
- Rooms are booked directly through internet by the customers in case of economy hotels and indirectly through the travel agents in case of star hotels.
- Economy hotels do not practice revenue management techniques neither through its differential pricing nor through market segmentation. They just manage their revenues by applying the concept of logical booking.

8

Concept of Effective Tourism Marketing

Introduction

Tourism is one of many activities in a community or region that requires planning and coordination. This bulletin provides a simple structure and basic guidelines for comprehensive tourism planning at a community or regional level. Planning is the process of identifying objectives and defining and evaluating methods of achieving them. By comprehensive planning we mean planning which considers all of the tourism resources, organizations, markets, and programs within a region. Comprehensive planning also considers economic, environmental, social, and institutional aspects of tourism development.

Two Sides of Tourism Planning

Tourism planning has evolved from two related but distinct sets of planning philosophies and methods. On the one hand, tourism is one of many activities in an area that must be considered as part of physical, environmental, social, and economic planning. Therefore, it is common to find tourism addressed, at least partially, in a regional land use, transportation, recreation, economic development, or comprehensive plan. The degree to which tourism is addressed in such plans depends upon the relative importance of tourism to the community or region and how sensitive the planning authority is to tourism activities.

Tourism may also be viewed as a business in which a community or region chooses to engage. Individual tourism businesses conduct a variety of planning activities including feasibility, marketing, product development, promotion, forecasting, and strategic planning. If tourism is a significant component of an area's economy or development plans, regional or community-wide marketing plans are needed to coordinate the development and marketing activities of different tourism interests in the community. A comprehensive approach integrates a strategic marketing plan with more traditional public planning activities. This ensures a balance between serving the needs and wants of the tourists versus the needs and wants of local residents. A formal tourism plan provides a vehicle for the various interests within a community to coordinate their activities and work toward common goals. It also is a means of coordinating tourism with other community activities.

Steps in the Planning Process

Like any planning, tourism planning is goal-oriented, striving to achieve certain objectives by matching available resources and programs with the needs and wants of people. Comprehensive planning requires a systematic approach, usually involving a series of steps. The process is best viewed as an iterative and nagging one, with each step subject to modification and refinement at any stage of the planning process. There are six steps in the planning process:

1. Define goals and objectives.
2. Identify the tourism system.
    (a) Resources.
    (b) Organizations.
    (c) Markets.
3. Generate alternatives.
4. Evaluate alternatives.
5. Select and implement.
6. Monitor and evaluate.

***Step One*:** Defining Goals and objectives. Obtaining clear statements of goals and objectives is difficult, but important. Ideally, tourism development goals should flow from more general community goals and objectives. It is important to understand how a tourism plan serves these broader purposes. Is the community seeking a broader tax base, increased employment opportunities, expanded recreation facilities, better educational programs, a higher quality of life? How can tourism contribute to these objectives?

If tourism is identified as a means of serving broader community goals, it makes sense to develop plans with more specific tourism development objectives. These are generally defined through a continuing process in which various groups and organizations in a community work together toward common goals. A local planning authority, chamber of commerce, visitors bureau, or similar group should assume a leadership role to develop an initial plan and obtain broad involvement of tourism interests in the community. Public support for the planning process and plan is also important. Having a good understanding of tourism and the tourism system in your community is the first step toward defining goals and objectives for tourism development. The types of goals that are appropriate and the precision with which you are able to define them will depend upon how long your community has been involved in tourism and tourism planning. In the early stages of tourism development, goals may involve establishing organizational structures and collecting information to better identify the tourism system in the community. Later, more precise objectives can be formulated and more specific development and marketing strategies evaluated.

***Step Two*:** Identifying Your Tourism System When planning for any type of activity, it is important to first define its scope and characteristics. Be clear about exactly what your plan encompasses. A good initial question is, "What do you mean by tourism?" Tourism is defined in many ways. Generally, tourism involves people travelling outside of their community for pleasure. Definitions differ on the specifics of how far people must travel, whether or not they must stay overnight, for how long, and what exactly is included under travelling for "pleasure". Do you want your tourism plan to include day visitors, conventioneers, business travellers, people visiting friends and relatives, people passing through, or seasonal residents?

Which community resources and organizations serve tourists or could serve tourists? Generally, tourists share community resources with local residents and businesses. Many organizations serve both tourists and locals. This complicates tourism planning and argues for a clear idea of what your tourism plan entails. You can begin to clarify the tourism system by breaking it down into three subsystems:

(1) tourism resources,

(2) tourism organizations, and

(3) tourism markets.

An initial task in developing a tourism plan is to identify, inventory, and classify the objects within each of these subsystems.

Tourism Resources are any (1) natural, (2) cultural, (3) human, or (4) capital resources that either are used or can be used to attract or serve tourists. A tourism resource inventory identifies and classifies the resources available that provide opportunities for tourism development. Conduct an objective and realistic assessment of the quality and quantity of resources you have to work with.

Tourism Organizations combine resources in various proportions to provide products and services for the tourist. It is important to recognize the diverse array of public and private organizations involved with tourism.

The most difficult part of tourism planning is to get these groups to work toward common goals.

You should develop a list of these organizations within your own community and obtain their input and cooperation in your tourism planning efforts. Setting up appropriate communication systems and institutional arrangements is a key part of community tourism planning.

Natural Resources

* Climate-seasons.
* Water resources-lakes, streams, waterfalls.
* Flora-forests, flowers, shrubs, wild edibles.
* Fauna-fish & wildlife.
* Geological resources-topography, soils, sand dunes, beaches, caves, rocks & minerals, fossils.
* Scenery-combinations of all of the above.

Cultural Resources

* Historic buildings, sites.
* Monuments, shrines.
* Cuisine.
* Ethnic cultures.
* Industry, government, religion, etc.
* Anthropological resources.
* Local celebrities.

Human Resources

* Hospitality skills.
* Management skills.

* Seasonal labour force.
* Performing artists-music, drama, art, storytellers.
* Craftsman and artisans.
* Other labour skills from chefs to lawyers to researchers.
* Local populations.

Capital

* Availability of capital, financing.
* Infrastructure-transportation roads, airports, railroads, harbours & marinas, trails & walkways.
* Infrastructure: utilities water, power, waste treatment, communications.

Tourism Management Organizations and Services

Off-Site: Coordination, planning, technical assistance, research, regulation:

* Federal & state departments of commerce, transportation, & natural resources.
* Federal, state, regional, & local tourism associations.
* Educational organizations & consultants, e.g., Travel & Tourism Research Association; U.S. Travel Data Centre; Travel Reference Centre, Univ. of Colorado, Boulder; Travel, Tourism, & Recreation Resource Centre, Michigan State University.
* Travel information & reservation services On-Site: development, promotion and management, of tourism resources:
    - Federal agencies, NB. departments of commerce, transportation, & land management agencies.
    - State agencies, NB. departments of commerce, transportation, & land/facility management agencies.
    - Local government organizations, e.g., visitor information, chamber of commerce, convention & visitor's bureaus, parks.
* Businesses: Accommodations: Hotels, motels, Lodges, resorts, bed & breakfast cabins & cottages, Condominiums, second homes, Campgrounds-Food & Beverage: Restaurants, Grocery, Bars, nightclubs.

Fast Food, Catering Services

- Transportation: Air, rail, bus; Local transportation: taxi, limo, Auto, bicycle, boat rental; Local tour services.

- Information: Travel agencies, Information and reservation services, Automobile clubs.
- Recreation Facilities & Services: Winter sports: ski, skating, snow mobile areas; Golf courses, miniature golf; Swimming pools, water slides, beaches; tennis, handball, racquetball courts, bowling alleys; Athletic clubs, health spas; Marinas, boat rentals and charters; hunting & fishing guides; Horseback enterprises; Sporting goods sales & rentals.
- Entertainment: Nightclubs, amusement parks, spectator sport facilities; Gambling facilities: casinos, horse racing, bingo; video arcades; art galleries and studios, craft shops, studios, demonstrations; performing arts: theatre, dance, music, film; historic & prehistoric sites; museums: art, history, science, technology; arboreta, zoos, nature centres.
- Special festivals and events-Support services: Auto repair, gasoline service stations; boat & recreation vehicle dealers and service; retail shops: sporting goods, specialties, souvenirs, clothing; health services: hospitals, clinics, pharmacies; laundry and dry cleaning; beauty & barber shops; baby-sitting services; pet care; communications: newspaper, telephone; banking and financial services.

Tourism Markets: Tourists make-up the third, and perhaps most important subsystem. Successful tourism programs require a strong market orientation.

The needs and wants of the tourists you choose to attract and serve must be the focus of much of your marketing and development activity.

Therefore, it is important to clearly understand which tourism market segments you wish to attract and serve. Tourists fall into a very diverse set of categories with quite distinct needs and wants. You should identify the different types of tourists, or market segments that you presently serve or would like to serve.

This may involve one or more tourism market surveys. A visitor survey identifies the size and nature of the existing market and asks the following questions:

* What are the primary market segments you presently attract?
* Where do they come from?
* What local businesses and facilities do they use?
* What attracted them to the community?

* How did they find out about your community?
* How satisfied are they with your offerings?

A market survey (usually a telephone survey) also can be conducted among households in regions from which you wish to attract tourists. This type of study helps identify potential markets, and means of attracting tourists to your area.

Tourism Market Segments

In a general tourism plan, some clear target tourism market segments should be identified. You might begin by defining the market area from which you will draw most of your visitors. The size of your market area depends upon the uniqueness and quality of your "product", transportation systems, tastes and preferences of surrounding populations, and your competition.

Identifying the market area will help target information and promotion and define transportation routes and modes, competition, and characteristics of your market. Next, divide your travel market into the following trip length categories:

* day trips from a 50 mile radius,
* day trips from 50 to 200 miles away,
* pass-through travellers,
* overnight trips of 1 or 2 nights (most likely weekends), and
* extended overnight vacation trips.

After you have an idea of your market area and kinds of trips you will be serving, begin defining more specific market segments like vehicle campers, downhill skiers, sightseers, family vacationers, single weekenders, and the like. These segments can be more clearly tied to particular resources, businesses, and facilities in your community.

What kinds of products and services are likely to attract each of these groups? Tourist needs as well as their impact on the local community are quite different for day tourists versus overnight tourists. Areas catering primarily to weekend traffic will experience large fluctuations in use. In deciding the relative importance of these different segments, communities need to assess both their ability to provide required services (do you have enough rooms?), as well as the demand for different types of trips relative to the supply and your competition.

The Environment: A tourism plan is significantly affected by many factors in the broader environment. Indeed, one of the complexities of tourism planning is the number of variables that are outside of the control of an individual tourism business or community. These include such things as tourism offerings and prices at competing destinations, federal and state policy and legislation, currency exchange rates, the state of the economy, and weather. These factors are discussed more fully in Extension bulletin E-1959 as part of the market environment analysis.

Local populations also must be considered in tourism planning. As they compete with tourists for resources, they can be significantly affected by tourism activity, and they are an important source of support in getting tourism plans implemented. A survey of local residents can be conducted to assess community attitudes toward tourism development, identify impacts of tourism on the community, and obtain local input into tourism plans.

Public hearings, workshops, and advisory boards are other ways to obtain public involvement in tourism planning.

Local support and cooperation is important to the success of tourism programs and should not be overlooked.

I. Geographic market areas.

II. Trip categories.

Day Trips:

* short-within 50 miles.
* long-up to 200 miles.

Pass through traffic:

* day visitors.
* overnight stays.

Overnight Trips:

* weekend.
* vacation.

III. Activity or trip purpose Outdoor Recreation:

* Water-based Activity:
    - Boating: sail, power, cruise, row, canoe, water ski.
    - Swimming: pool, beach, sunbathing, scuba.
    - Fishing: charter, sport, from pier, boat, shore, ice.
* Land-based Activity:
    - Camping: back packing, primitive, developed.
    - Hiking: climbing, beachcombing, spelunking.

- Hunting.
- Skiing: downhill, cross country.
- Snowmobiling.
- Bicycling.
- Horseback riding.
- Picnicking.

* Air-based Activity:
  - Aeroplane rides, hang gliding, ballooning, parachuting.
* General:
  - Nature study.
  - Photography or landscape painting.
  - Viewing natural scenery.

Sightseeing & Entertainment:

* Visiting particular sites or areas:
  - historic or prehistoric.
  - cultural.
  - amusements.
  - scenic.
* Attending particular events, shows, or demonstrations:
  - ethnic festivals.
  - sporting events.
  - performances.
  - agricultural fair or festival.
  - boat show.
  - shopping.

Other Primary Purpose for Trip:

* Visiting Friends & Relatives.
* Convention & Business/Pleasure.

***Step Three*:** Generating Alternatives. Generating alternative development and marketing options to meet your goals requires some creative thinking and brainstorming. The errors made at this stage are usually thinking too narrowly or screening out alternatives prematurely. It is wise to solicit a wide range of options from a diverse group of people. If tourism expertise is lacking in your community, seek help and advice outside the community. Tourism planning involves a wide range of interrelated development and marketing decisions. The following development questions will get you started:

* How much importance should be assigned to tourism within a community or region?
* Which general community goals is tourism development designed to serve?
* Which organization(s) will provide the leadership and coordination necessary for community tourism planning?

What are the relative roles of public and private sectors? Tourism marketing decision questions include:

* *Segments:* Which market segments should be pursued; geographic markets, trip types, activity or demographic subgroups?
* *Product:* What kinds of tourism products and services should be provided? Who should provide what?
* *Place:* Where should tourism facilities be located?
* Promotion: What kinds of promotion should be used, by whom, in which media, how much, when? What community tourism theme or image should be established?
* *Price:* What prices should be charged for which products and services. Who should capture the revenue?

***Step Four*:** Evaluating Alternatives. Tourism development and marketing options are evaluated by assessing the degree to which each option will be able to meet the stated goals and objectives. There are usually two parts to a systematic evaluation of tourism development and marketing alternatives: (1) Feasibility analysis, and (2) Impact assessment.

These two tasks are interrelated, but think of them as trying to answer two basic questions: (1) Can it be done?, and (2) What are the consequences? A decision to take a specific action must be based both on feasibility and desirability.

***Feasibility Analysis*:** First, screen alternatives and eliminate those that are not feasible due to economic, environmental, political, legal, or other factors. Evaluate the remaining set of alternatives in more detail, paying particular attention to the market potential and financial plan. Make a realistic assessment of your community's ability to attract and serve a market segment or segments. This requires a clear understanding of the tourism market in your area and how this market is changing. Also carefully identify your competition and evaluate your advantages and disadvantages compared to the competition.

Plan toward the future because it takes time to implement decisions and for your actions to take effect. Therefore, look at the likely market and competition for several years to come. Review forecasts for the travel market in your area, if available. Careful tracking of tourism trends in your own community can help identify changes in the market that you will have to adapt to.

***Impact Assessment*:** When evaluating alternative development and marketing strategies it is important to understand the impacts, both positive and negative, of proposed actions. A classification of economic, environmental, and social impacts associated with tourism development. The types of impacts and their importance vary across different communities and proposed actions. Generally, the size, extent, and nature of tourism impacts depend upon:

- volume of tourist activity relative to local activity.
- length and nature of tourist contacts with the community.
- degree of concentration/dispersal of tourist activity in the area.
- similarities or differences between local populations and tourists.
- stability/sensitivity of local economy, environment, and social structure.
- how well tourism is planned, controlled, and managed.

Look at both the benefits and costs of any proposed actions. While tourism development can increase income, revenues, and employment, it also involves costs. Evaluate benefits and costs of tourism development from the perspectives of local government, businesses, and residents.

Impacts of Tourism

Economic Impacts:

- Sales, revenue, and income.
- Employment.
- Fiscal impact-taxes, infrastructure costs.
- Prices.
- Economic base & structure.

Environmental Impacts:

- Lands.
- Waters.
- Air.
- Infrastructure.
- Flora & fauna.

Social Impacts:

- Population structure & distribution.
- Values & attitudes.
- Education.
- Occupations.
- Safety & security.
- Congestion & crowding.
- Community spirit & cohesion.
- Quality of life.

Impacts on Local Government Local government provides most of the infrastructure and many of the services essential to tourism development, including highways, public parks, law enforcement, water and sewer, garbage collection and disposal. Evaluate tourism decisions with a clear understanding of the capacity of the local infrastructure and services relative to anticipated needs, and take into account both the needs of local populations and tourists. A fiscal impact analysis evaluates the impact of tourism on the community's tax base and local government costs. It entails predicting the additional infrastructure and service requirements of tourism development, estimating their costs, deciding who will pay for/provide them, and how. Will tourism generate increased local government revenue through fees and charges, local sales or use taxes, increased property values or property tax rates, or larger local shares of federal and state tax revenues? Impacts on Business and Industry Businesses that are directly serving tourists benefit from sales to tourists. Through secondary impacts, tourism activity also benefits a wide range of businesses in a community. For example, a local textile industry may sell to a linen supply firm that serves hotels and motels catering primarily to tourists. A local forest products industry sells to a lumberyard where local woodcarvers or furniture makers buy their supplies. They in turn sell to tourists through various retail outlets. All of these businesses benefit from tourism. If most products and services for tourists are bought outside of the local area, much of the tourist spending "leaks" out of the local economy. The more a community is "self-sufficient" in serving tourists, the larger the local impact.

Impacts on Residents

Local residents may experience a broad range of both positive and negative impacts from tourism development.

Tourism development may provide increased employment and income for the community. Although tourism jobs are primarily in the service sectors and are often seasonal, part time, and low-paying, these characteristics, are neither universal nor always undesirable. Residents may value opportunities for part time and seasonal work. In particular, employment opportunities and work experiences for students or retirees may be desired. Residents may also benefit from local services that otherwise would not be available. Tourism development may mean a wider variety of retailers and restaurants, or a better community library. It may also mean more traffic, higher prices, and increases in property values and local taxes. The general quality of the environment and life in the community may go up or down due to tourism development. This depends on the nature of tourism development, the preferences and desires of local residents, and how well tourism is planned and managed.

Steps Five and Six

Implementation, and Monitoring and Evaluation. We will not attempt a complete discussion of decisionmaking, plan implementation, and monitoring, but these are critical steps in the success of a tourism plan. A set of specific actions should be prescribed with clearly defined responsibilities and timetables. Monitor progress in implementing the plan and evaluate the success of the plan in meeting its goals and objectives on a regular basis. Plans generally need to be adjusted over time due to changing goals, changing market conditions, and unanticipated impacts. It is a good idea to build monitoring and evaluation systems into your planning efforts.

9

Recent Trends in Tourism Sector

Promotion of Barrier-free Tourism for People with Disabilities in the Asian and Pacific Region

Tourism is a rapidly growing industry in the Asian and Pacific region. Following the trauma of the recent Asian financial crisis, the region has regained its status as one of the world's fastest growing destinations. As reported by the World Tourism Organization (WTO), the Asian and Pacific region, after two years of decreasing tourist arrivals, registered in 1999 a growth rate of 7.5 percent reaching a new record of more than 94 million international tourists. It is also expected that such a positive trend will continue into the early years of the new millennium.

Tourists, today are not content with staying within the confines of a resort hotel compound, being bussed to individual sites and entertained in places that mainly cater to tourists. Instead, tourists are increasingly interested in experiencing diversity of holiday environment in all aspects, including its people, culture, nature, architecture and way of life. This trend will be even more marked as consumers become better informed about options and entitlements, as well as more sophisticated and less willing to accept poor quality facilities and services that entail discomfort and stress. Tourists want access to everything that a city or a country has to offer. In view of the changing consumer demand, tourism for all is an increasingly important sales argument in a competitive market. At the same time, it can serve as an effective tool in furthering the human rights of people with disabilities in the destination communities. People with disabilities and older persons are becoming a growing group of consumers of travel, sports, and other leisure-oriented products and services. Furthermore, with regard to physical access, families with young children, who are also becoming part of this increasing tourist market, have similar needs to persons with disabilities and older persons. Thus large numbers of people require tourism to be made barrier-free.

Although the number of tourists who would benefit from accessible facilities and services is on the increase, most tourism services providers in the Asia-Pacific region have still not yet recognized the importance of taking action on this issue. Most hotels, transportation facilities and tourist sites are not physically accessible for many people with disabilities and older persons. Their staff members have not been trained to provide disabled person-friendly services. This is associated with an absence of explicit government policies and strategies for promotion of accessible tourism, lack of training for tourism service personnel on means of meeting the access needs of tourists with disabilities, and shortage of tourism programmes that address such needs.

Disability and Access

Present policies and programmes suffer from a dearth of disability data and inadequacy of existing data. In the majority of the countries and areas of the Asia-Pacific region, it is difficult to estimate the number of people with disabilities. There is a wide variation in the estimated disability rates reported by the developed and developing countries. The variation depends, to a large extent, on the definitions of disability used. The types of disability range from hearing, vision, and mobility impairment to intellectual impairment and psychiatric disorders.

For example, Australia's 1993 survey indicated that persons with a disability comprise 18 percent of its population. New Zealand's first national household survey (1996) yielded a disability rate of 19.1. In 1994, the United States Census Bureau estimated that some 54 million Americans were covered under the Americans with Disability Act (ADA) of 1990, constituting nearly 21 percent of the United States population. In contrast, China's (1987) and Pakistan's (1984-85) sample surveys both indicated a 4.9 percent disability rate. The 1991 National Sample Survey of India, covering four disabilities — visual, hearing, speech and locomotor — yielded a prevalence rate of 1.9 percent.

The share of the older people in the populations of developed countries is already rising dramatically. The same phenomenon is occurring in developing countries. According to United Nations projections, by the year 2025, about 14 percent of the Asia-Pacific region's total population will be 60 years or older, and the region will be home to 56 percent of the world's older persons. Among older persons, a significant percentage presents some type of disability. For example, in Western Australia over 50 percent of people over 60 years of age have a disability.

It is now widely recognized from many quarters that people with disabilities, together with carers, friends and relatives, and older persons constitute a large potential consumer market segment for the tourism and hospitality industry.

However, to take advantage of this potential niche market will depend on how the tourism sector as a whole and the tourism industry in particular will address the issue of tourism accessibility for people with disabilities. Indeed good access will benefit not only people with disabilities, but also many other members of the community, especially senior citizens. Access varies depending on disability and goes well beyond the physical type alone. Darcy (1998) 3 has characterized access from three main dimensions:

(a) Physical access which involves people with physical disabilities requiring the use of wheelchairs or walking aids and requires the provision of, for example, handrails, ramps, lifts and lowered counters.

(b) Sensory access which involves people with hearing or sight impairments requiring the provision of, for example, tactile markings, signs, labels, hearing augmentation-listening systems and audio cues for lifts and lights.

(c) Communication access, which involves those people who have difficulty with the written word, vision, speech, and hearing impairment of persons from other culture.

In one way or another, all travellers who move out of their familiar surroundings are handicapped by new environments, the exciting aspects notwithstanding. Thus, the degree of sensitivity, clarity, safety and convenience required in designing tourism facilities from the perspective of disabled travellers will benefit everyone else.

Main Constraints of Disabled Travellers

People with disabilities have a right to, and do want to enjoy travel and leisure experiences. Tourism is a means of broadening horizons and developing friendships for a social group, which increasingly is less willing to remain segregated from mainstream society. Furthermore, as more people acquire disabilities or survive with disabilities, they too wish to enjoy travel, just like everyone else. However, their travel experiences are still characterized by transportation constraints, inaccessible accommodation and tourism sites, and inadequate customer services.

Transportation

While air travel in general has become easier and airlines increasingly provide friendly services to the average travellers, still some problems arise from time to time, such as misplaced luggage or delays in flight schedules. However, these mishaps might seriously inconvenience travellers with disability. For example, an issue among some travellers with disabilities is the damage to and loss of wheelchairs on airplanes. Indeed, being without one's wheelchair is much more distressing than having the misfortune of lost or delayed luggage for the average travellers. Other constraints facing wheelchair-travellers include the difficulty of boarding and disembarking the aircraft, changing flights and the inaccessibility of airplane restrooms. For blind people, identifying and retrieving luggage becomes another additional obstacle in the course of their already difficult journey. The pain of long-haul travel in air economy class seat for someone with stiff limbs or arthritis, the sheer size of modern airports for those with mobility problems and endless forward planning for all are some of the challenges still facing travellers with disabilities.

Most travellers negotiate structural constraints associated with air travel by using other modes of transportation – car, bus or train. Private automobiles equipped with customized features have the advantage of providing schedule flexibility if used for pleasure travel. However, only a small group of affluent people with disability can afford such cars.

Modern technology greatly facilitates bus travel by people with disabilities. People with physical disabilities can now journey in buses equipped with hydraulic lifts, which help them to board easily. So-called "low-floor" buses are gradually becoming the standard for intra-urban public transportation in a growing number of countries. These buses have the floor some 50 cm above street level. They feature a hydraulic "kneeling" function, which reduces the step to some 25 cm. However, in most developing countries the availability of such specially designed buses remains limited. While trains could better accommodate disabled persons travel needs, often the gap between car doors and the platform are too wide; access to toilets and compartments remains a constraint, especially for people with physical disabilities and wheelchair users.

Accommodations

Reasonable accommodations for people with disabilities constitute still another set of challenges. For example, very few hotels offer accessible disabled person-friendly rooms with wider entrances; low-level switches, hand dryers, towels racks and beds; chair lifts and room information written in simple and concise language for people with cognitive disabilities. Of the rooms available, few have ground floor access Access throughout hotels is also problematic. Few hotels have lifts to all floors on slow timers, access to reception, pool and bar areas, clear signage, visual alarms and clear access through the entire building. While the majority of hotels provide special parking areas, often these are uncovered and quite distant from the main hotel entrances, requiring that steps be negotiated in order to access the buildings.

Another issue relating to accommodation facilities and amenities concerns the different types of disability to be provided for. Indeed the needs for people with vision or hearing impairment or intellectual disability are quite different from those with physical disability. Most of the hotels provide facilities and amenities responding more to the special needs of people with physical disabilities and specifically those in wheelchairs. For example, among hotels that offer wheelchair access, few provide information available in Braille or in audiovisual format.

Many travellers with disabilities find facilities at eating and drinking establishments within tourist destination areas to be difficult to access. Some others encounter problems when making hotel reservations. It was observed that in some hotels, specific accessible rooms even when available, could not be reserved by an individual. In some other instances, some room accommodations, which were promoted as accessible rooms, actually appeared to be inaccessible to people with disabilities. For example, showers with handrails may well accommodate some people, but for many wheelchair users, bathtubs present a major barrier.

Tourism Sites

Attractions are the elements of a tourism destination that stimulate the purpose of a journey and visit. They may be of a leisure-type, such as visiting theme parks or participating in sport events; nature-based, such as seaside tourism or mountain trekking; historical, such as visiting museums or antique shopping; or socio-cultural, such as festivals or visiting friends or relatives. Most of the constraints encountered by tourists with disabilities in the course of these activities focus on site inaccessibility. For example, beaches are often not equipped to accommodate wheelchair users. Similarly, poor access to museums, historical monuments or shopping areas restricts people with disabilities from enjoying the opportunity of participating in these activities.

Travel Planning

For people with disabilities, planning a vacation can be somewhat more complicated. Depending on the type of disability, the would-be travellers need to ensure that during the envisaged vacation due attention will be given to their special needs such as special lifts for coaches and adapted hotel rooms. Such arrangements cannot be made without the assistance of travel agencies that cater to those special needs. As for several years accessible tourism shows promising sign of expansion, tour operators have started to appreciate the potential of a market that has traditionally been poorly served. However, tailoring packages to people with various disabilities requires labour intensive work, making therefore a low-margin business. Yet specialized agents, especially in Europe, are joining forces through transnational association to exchange information, set up data banks, launch joint marketing campaigns and lobby for better services. At the same time, specialized European travel agents and non-profit organizations have been cooperating by pooling what they have learned about the availability of special facilities in various countries.

Conditions to Promote Barrier-free Tourism for people with Disabilities

People with disabilities are being acknowledged as a consumer group of travel, sports, and other leisure-oriented products and services. If professionals of the tourism industry are to succeed in accessing this potential new market, they must understand the needs involved and learn how to respond to these challenges for the benefit of both parties.

Legislation Framework

One crucial element in meeting this goal is the existence of a legal framework, which ensures that people with disabilities have the right to access to tourism facilities and services and to encourage tourism professionals to adopt related measures. Several governments in the region have passed comprehensive legislation to protect the rights of persons with disabilities. Others are in various stages of adoption, formulation and planning such legislation. Those countries, which have already adopted such legislation, enacted additional laws and regulations or amended existing one to further protect the rights of persons with disabilities in specific areas crucial to the equalization of opportunities.

For example, in Australia the Commonwealth Disability Discrimination Act 1992 (DDA) and the Disability Service Act 1993, plus various other State legislation, require departments, public authorities and the tourism industry to ensure that people with disabilities have the same fundamental rights as the rest of the community. Furthermore, the 1993 Act specifically relates to access to appropriate accommodation and services and allows people with disabilities the opportunity to make decisions, which affect their life. Tourism providers are subject to all requirements of both acts, which means that all premises, good and services used by the public must be accessible to people with disabilities. Failure to provide equal access is illegal, unless it is proved to cause unjustifiable difficulties such as excessive cost.

Legislation on access should also apply to a variety of public areas and services — including information services – such as travel agents, cafes, restaurants, libraries, transport, shops, theatres and other places of entertainment. Accordingly, related information needs to be provided to people with disabilities. Lack of proper physical access to transport, buildings and sites will not only exclude people with disabilities from participating in community life but also affect tourism and leisure providers. In this connection, the appropriate legislation would indeed help to design an air travel transportation system able to remove barriers to travel for people with disabilities. In Australia, the Air Carrier Access Act (1986) ensures that no air carrier might discriminate against disabled persons in the provision of air transportation. This Act represents a major advance towards a comprehensive adaptive air travel system for people with disabilities.

One great challenge regarding legislation implementation is the provision of information to tourism professionals, such as for instance hospitality providers, of the key relevant legislation relating to people with disabilities and their obligations under the legislation. According to the findings of a recent survey, the majority of the hospitality providers interviewed in Western Australia stated that they were not aware of any specific legislation regarding issues of access for people with disabilities. This was further supported by representatives from disability agencies who said that there was a general lack of awareness on those issues. There is also evidence that most of the laws enacted lack of any credible legislative power, due to low enforcement.

Tourism Services Providers

To fully harness the potential of barrier-free tourism, it is essential that the tourism industry improve its services to people with disabilities. This includes improved access of hotel facilities within all areas of the property to the entire disabled community, including those with physical, sensory and communication disabilities. For example, particular attention should be given to providing people with physical disabilities with a clear accessible route to the main entrance of an establishment and then to the reception desk. Similarly, persons with sight or hearing impairments need to be provided for with adequate facilities to facilitate their free mobility within the premises. Accessible rooms should also be made available and designed with features, which can accommodate wheelchair users as well as people with sight and hearing impairments.

In the area of transportation, efforts need to be pursued to upgrade and improve the level of facilities for people with disabilities. Accessible transportation features, such as toilets in aircrafts, are fundamental requirements for barrier-free travel. Airport authorities should ensure that basic accessible infrastructure adjustments for people with disabilities are included in the design of new and/or renovated airports, such as the introduction of greater areas of level access as well as the provision of easy access to toilets.

Travel operators that specialize in services for, and provide tailoring packages to, people with disabilities are instrumental in assisting them with their vacation planning.

They are able to provide them with the information regarding the availability of accessible facilities suited to their needs. People with disabilities are more likely to rely on tourism professionals, such as specific travel agents and hotels that best serve their needs. It is therefore imperative that specific barrier-free tourism promotional activities be undertaken by travel agents in close cooperation with other professionals of the tourism industry such as hospitality providers.

Disability organizations may also contribute to these promotional efforts by drawing the attention of the tourism industry to the needs and desires of the people with disabilities, especially with regard to flexibility in travel options.

Training and Education

Training and education is one of the major challenges facing the tourism industry in relation to meeting the needs of people with disabilities. Sensitive and willing staff with the right attitude and strong interpersonal skills can overcome many of the barriers that persons with disabilities face and turn what may be perceived as an inaccessible property into a accessible one. It is essential for the tourism industry to strengthen its customer services training in order to serve those with disabilities. Indeed, regardless of how well an establishment has been designed to accommodate people with disabilities or how well policies have been formulated to cater to the needs of disabled travellers, it will be of little value if the staff employed are uncomfortable and ill-prepared serving guests with disabilities.

Comprehensive programmes should include policy setters and managers as well as front-line staff and should be extended at all educational levels, especially within tertiary level hospitality management programmes.

The availability of specialized tour guides is another important factor for people with disabilities, especially those with sight and hearing impairments to enable them to enjoy tourism activities. Efforts should be made to develop and strengthen appropriate specialized tour-guiding courses in training curricula on tourism management and related tourism services.

Priority Areas for Promotion of Barrier-free Tourism

Notwithstanding the number of initiatives already pursued by countries in the region to make tourism barrier-free for people with disabilities, there are three key issues that require immediate attention.

One key area is the formulation and implementation of related legislation in order to protect the right of persons with disabilities to accessible facilities and environment.

Countries should be encouraged to continue developing such legislation as well as introduce new amendments in keeping with changes in the tourism sector, including travel conditions, and the specific situations of different disability groups. While it is essential that legislation needs to be reviewed in a continuous manner, it is imperative that members of the tourism industry be informed of their obligations and operational implications in order to protect not only their interest, but also the interests of the people with disabilities. Of equal importance is the role of the various disability bodies and organizations, which must begin to work closely with the tourism industry to improve existing practices. The organizations are well acquainted with and knowledgeable about various disability issues.

They should assist the tourism industry in introducing the necessary changes required under the legislation and to assist in the organization of related staff training programmes. Education and training on awareness and sensitivity to disability issues is another top priority area in the promotion of accessible tourism. The education sector should be encouraged to include in their training curricula on tourism management and related tourism services courses on "disabled persons' right to access" as well as "customer services to, and relations with, people with disabilities". Here again, the close collaboration between the disability organizations and the tourism industry along with the education sector would facilitate the development of required training programmes. It would also help in the publication of training material, such as facilitative guide, student handbook and audiovisual training support, for wider distribution amongst the tourism industry.

Provision of accessible facilities is by far the most important area of concern for achieving a barrier-free tourism for people with disabilities. Taking into consideration that it is highly unrealistic to presume that the situation would change overnight, owing to cost and time limitations, what is required in the short-term is that the tourism sector strives to achieve a reasonable level of accessibility, which balances disabled users' needs, the constraints of existing conditions and the resource available for such adjustments. In many cases, this relates to the issue of physical access, such as main hotel entrance access, appropriate access ramp, reception counters, disability friendly rooms, access to and location to all public areas. In the long-term, the approach will be to encourage major restructuring and/or refurbishment of hospitality establishments and tourism sites.

Attracting Tourism and Hospitality Industries

The Indian tourism and hospitality industry is on a roll, driven by the huge surge in both business and leisure travel by domestic and foreign tourists. The country's travel and tourism industry is expected to generate approximately US$ 100 billion in 2008, rising to Rs. 15 US$ 275.5 billion by 2018 over the next ten years, as per the latest Tourism Satellite Accounting (TSA) research released by the World Travel and Tourism Council (WTTC) and its strategic partner Accenture.

The growth of tourist inflow into India was well above world average, leading to a rise of India's share in World arrivals from 0.37 percent in 2001 to 0.53 percent in 2006. Also, as noted by UN World Tourism Organisation (UNWTO), the growth of Indian tourism industry was instrumental in the 'emergence' of South-Asia as a tourist destination.

Further, tourism is an important industry in Indian economy contributing around 6.8 percent of the Gross Domestic Product and providing employment to over 41 million persons. According to a research University of New South Wales (UNSW), Australian School of Business (ASB), India and China will be the new global players competing for a huge chunk of tourists, transforming the geopolitical landscape.

Inbound Tourists

The flow of foreign tourist arrivals has been recording phenomenal growth rates. The number of arrivals has increased from 3.9 million in 2005 to 4.4 million in 2006 and 4.95 million in 2007, recording a growth rate of 13.5 percent in 2006 (over 2005) and 11.9 percent in 2007 (over 2006).

Alongside, there has been a concomitant rise in the foreign exchange earnings. Total earnings from foreign tourists has shown an annual growth rate of 19.2 per in 2006 and 33.8 percent in 2007 to garner US$ 7.49 billion in 2005, US$ 8.93 in 2006 and US$ 11.96 billion in 2007.

Continuing the foreign tourists' interest in the country, the first four months of 2008 recorded a growth rate of 11.9 percent (in tourist arrivals) over the corresponding period in 2007, receiving 2.02 million in foreign tourist arrivals. Simultaneously, foreign exchange earnings grew by a much faster rate at 28.9 percent in 2008, against 20 percent during corresponding period in 2007. Total foreign exchange earnings totalled US$ 4.84 billion, against US$ 3.76 billion in 2007.

Significantly, while India's share in world arrivals was about 0.5 percent, its share in revenue generated from tourism worldwide was over 1 percent.

India, with its diverse landscape, offers huge scope for various theme-based travel like Medical Tourism, Adventure tourism, Heritage tourism, Wellness tourism, Pilgrimage tourism, Golf tourism, Ecotourism, Wildlife tourism among others. India's growing reputation as a major medical tourism destination is attracting more and more foreign visitors. In fact, Indian hospitals are fast becoming the first choice for foreign patients owing to easy access to visa facilities coupled with the best emerging medical infrastructure which will help India earn to an extent of US$ 1.86 billion in foreign exchange by 2012.

Currently India's earnings through medical tourism annually is an estimated US$ 821.40 million. In fact, according to the World Travel and Trade Council, Indian tourism demand will continue to grow at a rapid pace. It estimates the demand to grow at an average of 8.8 percent between 2004 and 2013, making India the world's third fastest growing tourist market. The boom in the Indian tourism industry has cascaded to the rural areas as well. India continues to attract tourists owing to its splendid historical architecture and rich culture along with beautiful beaches, rural tourism or what now is called 'responsible tourism' is also fast gaining popularity with travellers flocking to discover the best in rural arts and heritage.

Outbound Tourists

With the economy growing consistently at over 9 percent, increasing disposable incomes, a change in the spending habits, liberalization of exchange controls, increasing affordability due to numerous holiday packages and cheaper air fares, outbound tourist traffic has been growing at a rapid pace. Outbound tourist market has been growing at an annual average growth of around 25 percent. In 2007, an estimated 8 million Indian tourists ventured abroad. Moving ahead, the United Nations World Tourism Organisation (UNWTO) estimates the figure to reach about 50 million by 2020.

Along with the rise in the number of Indians travelling abroad, both the total and per capita expenditure spent abroad has been increasing. For example, according to the European Travel Commission, average spend per trip of Indian outbound tourists has increased from US$ 611 in 2000 to US$ 822 in 2006. Similarly, Euromonitor International estimates the outgoing tourism expenditure from India to grow to US$ 21 million by 2011, representing a growth rate of over 25.7 percent between 2006 and 2011.

Hospitality

The booming tourism industry has had a cascading effect on the hospitality sector with an increase in the occupancy ratios and average room rates. While occupancy ratio is around 75-80 percent, the average increase in room rates has been hovering around 22-25 percent.

And with the continuing surge in tourist inflow, this sector is likely to offer tremendous opportunity for investors. For example, while the estimated number of required hotel rooms is around 240,000, the current availability is just 90,000 rooms-leaving a shortfall of 150,000 rooms to be provided.

With such a huge potential available in this segment, several global hotel chains like the Hilton, Accor, Marriott International, Berggruen Hotels, Cabana Hotels, Premier Travel Inn (PTI), Inter Continental Hotels group and Hampshire among others have all announced major investment plans for the country.

The Government's move to declare hotel and tourism industry as a high priority sector with a provision for 100 percent foreign direct investment (FDI) has also provided a further impetus in attracting investments in to this industry.

It is estimated that the hospitality sector is likely to see US$ 11.41 billion in the next two years, with around 40 international hotel brands making their presence in the country by 2011. Simultaneously, international hotel asset management companies are also likely to enter India. Already, US-based HVS International has firmed up plans to enter India, and industry players believe others like Ashford Hospitality Trust and IFA Hotels & Resorts among others are likely to follow suit.

Government Initiatives

To unlock the huge potential in this sector, the Government has taken various initiatives for the development of this sector.

- Launch of Incredible India campaign to promote tourism both in domestic and international markets.
- Recognition of spare rooms available with various house owners by classifying these facilities as "Incredible India Bed and Break fast Establishments"', under 'Gold' or 'Silver' category.
- A new category of visa, "Medical Visa" ('M'-Visa), has been introduced which can be given for specific purpose to foreign tourists coming into India.
- Guidelines have been formulated by Department of AYUSH prescribing minimum requirements for Ayurveda and Panchkarma Centres.
- Ministry of tourism has tied up with United Nations Development Programme (UNDP) to promote rural tourism.

International Recognition

Along with the growth of this industry, international accolades have been pouring in, rising India's appeal as a leading global tourist destination.

- India has been elected to head the UN World Tourism Organisation (UNWTO), the highest policy making world tourism body represented by 150 countries.

- The world's leading travel and tourism journal, "Conde Nast Traveller", ranked India as the numero uno travel destination in the world.
- The Association of British Travel Agents (ABTA) has ranked India as No.1 amongst the top 50 places for 2006.
- The "Incredible India" campaign has been ranked as the Highest Recall Advertisement worldwide by "Travel and Leisure".
- India was adjudged Asia's leading destination at the regional World Travel Awards (WTA).
- India's Taj Mahal continues to figure in the seven wonders of the world.
- Bangalore-based Leela Palace Kempinski has been rated as the favourite business hotel in the world in a Readers' Choice Awards by Conde Nast Traveller.

The Travel Channels: Tourism and Hospitality Industries are Changing to Meet the Demands of Experience-Hungry Travellers

Consumers today are in constant pursuit of new experiences. They want an escape from a busy, demanding life, to be moved and inspired emotionally and spiritually. They respond to messages that evoke feelings and fantasy rather than those that outline a function. In short, they are dream chasers.

In the travel, tourism and hospitality industry in particular, companies that want to stay competitive must therefore define their unique value proposition—the "experience" only they can provide. The experience must be authentic, not contrived, and built on strong values. This means building an emotional connection with consumers, something that's never been so easy and so difficult at the same time.

Says Iris Brouwer, founder of Barcelona, Spain-based Silk Marketing: "Customers are more informed, more travelled and experienced than in the past. Not only have they become independent, demanding and self-sufficient, they are also more savvy. They know how to enjoy life; they are looking for experiences, feelings, pampering—and they know where to find it. Innovation in communication is key to keeping up with the market. This means working with the latest and most effective media." One example of packaging a feeling is a new campaign for tourism in Slovenia, which is actively promoting itself as a hot new destination. Seizing on opportunities offered by its entry into the European Union and its position as EU chair from January to

June 2008, it launched a new marketing campaign called "I Feel Slovenia." The campaign invites travellers to "feel" and experience the many wonders of the country.

"We are proud that our country has the word love in its name, and we can use this to communicate stories, a love story, about Slovenia, our unique cultural heritage and the pristine nature of our country," says Rok Klancnik, director of the Slovenia Tourist Office based in Brussels, Belgium.

Yet Slovenia is realistic and doesn't try to compete on the level of mature destinations such as France and Spain (respectively the world's top destinations in terms of international tourist arrivals, according to the U.N. World Tourism Organization's "Tourism Highlights, 2007 Edition"). Instead, Slovenia is committed to being the "best-kept secret in Europe" and to preserving the authenticity of the experience.

Says Klancnik: "Slovenia should and will stay on the path of sustainable tourism development. If we ruin the beauty of our nature, old traditions and culture, we'll lose tourism as well, not only our national identity. It's not about quantity [of tourists]. Tourism of tomorrow is about quality and emotions, both for visitors and for the locals who work and live in tourism."

Delivering on the Promise

"Travelling today is not always easy, between security checks and long waits in transit," says Marco Ferrari, vice president and director of external communication at Starwood Hotels & Resorts for Europe, Africa and Middle East. "When guests arrive at their destination, we must deliver on our promise. We are lucky enough to sell dreams, experiences, emotions and sensations. We must represent the dream, and we must surpass expectations and stand for the promise of our brands."

Starwood Hotels & Resorts has been creative in using a mix of offline and online communication tools to engage with their guests before, during and after their experience. For example, Starwood Preferred Guest TV (SPG TV) is a "new means of communicating directly with guests in 300-plus hotels in Europe, Middle East and Africa," Ferrari explains. It features compelling reports of off-the-beaten-track experiences, such as the best restaurants, secret discoveries, romantic rendezvous, art exhibits and secluded beaches. Produced entirely by Starwood, SPG TV also features interviews with guests, who share their personal stories and tips. "SPG TV has now obtained 86 percent viewership of guests," says Ferrari.

The Customer as Storyteller

While the message focuses on "fantasy" and "experiences," the means to deliver that message is changing rapidly. In travel, Trip Advisor has led the way by giving customers the chance to post reviews and recommendations of their travel experiences and hotel stays, and its success was immediate: Trip Advisor claims that "85 percent of consumers trust recommendations from other consumers" over brand web sites and advertising.

This trend is being watched carefully by hotels that seek to be the first source for customer information and sales. So far, hotels have offered pull techniques on their web sites such as "best rate guarantees" and benefit-loaded customer loyalty programs. How can hotels use new social media tools to their advantage? According to a September 2007 report from Hospitality Sales & Marketing Association International, "This new consumer behavior applies as much to travel as it does to industries as different as electronics, books, automobiles and financial planning.... According to a recent TIA/Ypartnership Travel Horizons study, two-thirds of online adult leisure travellers consume online video and audio clips; four in 10 read blogs, share photos and take virtual tours; and one in four posts responses to blogs and participates in social networks."

Emotional Connections

Marriott International is another hospitality industry leader when it comes to embracing social media tools.

Chairman and CEO Bill Marriott launched his blog, "Marriott on the Move," on 16 January 2007. "Blogging will allow me to do what I've been doing for years—on a global scale," Marriott wrote. "Talking to the customer comes easily to me. I visit 250 hotels around the world every year."

According to Marriott, the blog fulfills several goals:

* To be a part of the growing conversation online and to speak more directly with customers without a filter.
* To embrace innovative communications and be an early adopter among non-tech companies.
* To communicate to a new generation of travellers the way they prefer to communicate.

Every couple of days, Bill Marriott posts a blog entry and a recorded voice message with a new story or anecdote—everything from the latest

Marriott hotel opening to his recommendations for great books or films. Whether personal or professional musings, each "Marriott on the Move" conveys the values of the company as personified by Bill Marriott himself. "Our guests are very loyal to our brand, and this blog builds on that loyalty and gives customers a better insight into our company and its values, such as community service and saving the environment, as represented by Mr. Marriott," says Marriott International's John Wolf, senior director of public relations.

By focusing on the experience-sharing stories and promising fantasy and unique experiences—all tourism suppliers can make an emotional connection with their guests. Says Iris Brouwer: "Through the story, a destination transforms itself from an asset, 'a place to stay,' into 'a place to experience,' with a value proposition that no other destination can possibly match." The same holds true for any industry and any business looking to capture the hearts and minds of its stakeholders.

Related Article: The Middle East 'Experience': Close-up on Dubai

Tourism in the Middle East is growing fast, particularly in the Gulf States, and especially in Dubai, United Arab Emirates. Dubai already offers an astounding array of "experiences," with more resorts and attractions under construction. The builders of "Dubailand," a 3 billion-square-foot development, claim it is "the world's most ambitious tourism, leisure and entertainment project, designed to catalyse the position of Dubai as an international hub of family tourism."

Universal Studios is set to run a large theme park in Dubailand, while Jumeirah, the Dubai-based luxury hospitality group, plans to build a waterpark complete with a hotel in the shape of a ship.

According to Hotels magazine's February 2007 feature "EMEA's Next Generation," "No Middle East market can outshine Dubai, but Oman and Qatar are carving out a niche of the tourism pie." Dubai's neighbor Abu Dhabi, the capital of the United Arab Emirates, has set a target of more than doubling annual visitor numbers from 1.35 million in 2006 to more than 3 million by 2215.

Like the Eiffel Tower in Paris, Jumeirah's iconic Burj Al Arab Hotel has become the symbol of Dubai. This hotel is a spectacular edifice built in the shape of a ship's sail and is known by a collection of superlatives: "the world's tallest hotel," "the most luxurious hotel in the world" and "the world's only seven-star hotel." The Burj Al Arab Hotel is part of Jumeirah's collection of properties that "are regarded as among the most luxurious and innovative in the world."

Jumeirah is also a master at offering a different experience, with a promise to guests that at Jumeirah they will "Stay Different." Among the innovative communication tools that support the "Stay Different" promise is JCast, a podcast service launched in May 20o6 to deliver to guests all around the world the latest news and property videos of Jumeirah.

"JCasts can be accessed at the user's convenience, to deliver a virtual, personal ized experience of Jumeirah," explains Kristie Willmott Coshow, group director for Jumeirah e-business and consumer development. "These technologies can transform the value we deliver to our guests and make our properties more accessible. Our goal is to enhance our guests' overall experience and engagement with us." Jumeirah produces new podcasts every two weeks and features news on its individual properties and amenities.

The initiative is a hit with guests, many of whom use iPods. It allows them to share their Jumeirah experiences with friends and family worldwide, thereby growing Jumeirah brand awareness while building customer loyalty and attracting new guests Consumers today are in constant pursuit of new experiences. They want an escape from a busy, demanding life, to be moved and inspired emotionally and spiritually. They respond to messages that evoke feelings and fantasy rather than those that outline a function. In short, they are dream chasers.

In the travel, tourism and hospitality industry in particular, companies that want to stay competitive must therefore define their unique value proposition—the "experience" only they can provide. The experience must be authentic, not contrived, and built on strong values. This means building an emotional connection with consumers, something that's never been so easy and so difficult at the same time.

Says Iris Brouwer, founder of Barcelona, Spain-based Silk Marketing: "Customers are more informed, more traveled and experienced than in the past. Not only have they become independent, demanding and self-sufficient, they are also more savvy. They know how to enjoy life; they are looking for experiences, feelings, pampering—and they know where to find it. Innovation in communication is key to keeping up with the market. This means working with the latest and most effective media." One example of packaging a feeling is a new campaign for tourism in Slovenia, which is actively promoting itself as a hot new destination. Seizing on opportunities offered by its entry into the European Union and its position as EU chair from January to

June 2008, it launched a new marketing campaign called "I Feel sLOVEnia." The campaign invites travellers to "feel" and experience the many wonders of the country.

"We are proud that our country has the word love in its name, and we can use this to communicate stories, a love story, about Slovenia, our unique cultural heritage and the pristine nature of our country," says Rok Klancnik, director of the Slovenia Tourist Office based in Brussels, Belgium.

Yet Slovenia is realistic and doesn't try to compete on the level of mature destinations such as France and Spain (respectively the world's top destinations in terms of international tourist arrivals, according to the U.N. World Tourism Organization's "Tourism Highlights, 2007 Edition"). Instead, Slovenia is committed to being the "best-kept secret in Europe" and to preserving the authenticity of the experience. Says Klancnik: "Slovenia should and will stay on the path of sustainable tourism development. If we ruin the beauty of our nature, old traditions and culture, we'll lose tourism as well, not only our national identity. It's not about quantity [of tourists]. Tourism of tomorrow is about quality and emotions, both for visitors and for the locals who work and live in tourism."

Trend Watch

"Most travel suppliers have invested substantial sums in the development and promotion of their web sites. And for good reason: The Internet is now cited as the exclusive source of information when planning both business and leisure travel by over two-thirds of all active travellers."

At Eurocomm

The IABC 2008 EuroComm Conference will be held 4-5 February in Barcelona, Spain, with Silk Marketing's Iris Brouwer speaking on social media in tourism.

Popular Destination

"In the Middle East, international tourist arrivals have risen by 9 percent... in fact most of the destinations in the region continue to report remarkably good results."

Based in France, native Californian Summer Jauneaud is a communication and marketing consultant specializing in the international tourism and hospitality industry.

10

Programmes and Policies of Hospitality Sector

National Tourism Policy of India

Tourism emerged as the largest global industry of the 20th century and is projected to grow even faster in the 21st century. India has immense possibilities of growth in the tourism sector with vast cultural and religious heritage, varied natural attractions, but a comparatively small role in the world tourism scene. A New Tourism Policy, which builds on the strength of the national Tourism Policy of 1982, but which envisages new initiatives towards making tourism the catalyst in employment generation, environmental re-generation, development of remote areas and development of women and other disadvantaged groups in the country, besides promoting social integration is, therefore, vital to our economy. It would lead to larger foreign exchange earnings and create conditions for more Foreign Direct Investment.

The Mission

To promote sustainable tourism as a means of economic growth and social integration and to promote the image of India abroad as a country with a glorious past, a vibrant present and a bright future. Policies to achieve this will be evolved around six broad areas such as Welcome (Swagat), Information (Suchana), Facilitation (Suvidha), Safety (Suraksha), Cooperation (Sahyog) and Infrastructure Development (Samrachana). Conservation of heritage, natural environments, etc. and development and promotion of tourist products would also be given importance.

Objectives

The objectives of tourism development are to foster understanding between people, to create employment opportunities and bring about socioeconomic benefits to the community, particularly in the interior and remote areas and to strive towards balanced and sustainable development and preserve, enrich and promote India's cultural heritage. One of the major objectives is the preservation and protection of natural resources and environment to achieve sustainable development.

Given the low cost of employment creation in the tourism sector and the low level of exploitation of India's tourism potential, the new tourism policy seeks to expand foreign tourist arrivals and facilitate domestic tourism in a manner that is sustainable by ensuring that possible adverse effects such as cultural pollution and degradation of environment are minimised.

The New Tourism Policy also aims at making the stay of foreign tourists in India, a memorable and pleasant one with reliable services at predictable costs, so that they are encouraged to undertake repeated visits to India, as friends. This would be in tune with India's traditional philosophy of giving the highest honour to a guest (Atithi debo bhava).

Tourism A Multi-Dimensional Activity

(a) The Government will aim to achieve necessary linkages and synergies in the policies and programs of all concerned Departments/agencies by establishing effective coordination mechanisms at Central, State and District levels. The focus of national policy, therefore, will also be to develop tourism as a common endeavour of all the agencies vitally concerned with it at the Central and State levels, public sector undertakings and the private sector.

(b) It will be the policy of government to encourage people's participation in tourism development including Panchayati Raj institutions, local bodies, Co-operatives, non-governmental organisations and enterprising local youth to create public awareness and to achieve a wider spread of tourist facilities. However, focused attention will be given for the integrated development of identified centres with well directed public participation.

(c) Public and Private Sector Partnership: A constructive and mutually beneficial partnership between the public and the private sectors through all feasible means is an absolute necessity for the sustained growth of tourism. It is, therefore, the policy of the Government to encourage emergence of such a partnership. This will be achieved by creating a Tourism Development Authority consisting of senior officials of the Government and tourism experts and professionals from the private sector.

(d) Role of the Government: Tourism is a multi-sectoral activity and the industry is affected by many other sectors of the national economy. The State has to, therefore, ensure intergovernmental linkages and coordination. It also has to play a pivotal role in tourism management and promotion. The specific role of the Government will be to :

i. Provide basic infrastructural facilities including local planning and zoning arrangements.

ii. Plan tourism development as a part of the over all area development strategy.

iii. Create nucleus infrastructure in the initial stages of development to demonstrate the potential of the area.

iv. Provide the required support facilities and incentives to both domestic and foreign investors to encourage private investment in the tourism sector.

v. Rationalise taxation and land policies in the tourism sector in all the States and Union Territories and in respect of land owned by Government agencies like Railways.

vi. Introduce regulatory measures to ensure social, cultural and environmental sustainability as well as safety and security of tourists.

vii. Ensure that the type and scale of tourism development is compatible with the environment and socio-cultural milieu of the area.

viii. Ensure that the local community is fully involved and the benefits of tourism accrue to them.

ix. Facilitate availability of trained manpower particularly from amongst the local population jointly with the industry.

x. Undertake research, prepare master plans, and facilitate formulation of marketing strategies.

xi. Organise overseas promotion and marketing jointly with the industry.

xii. Initiate specific measures to ensure safety and security of tourists and efficient facilitation services.

xiii. Facilitate the growth of a dynamic tourism sector.

(e) Role of Private Sector : Tourism has emerged as the largest export industry globally and all over the globe private sector has played the lead role in this growth. The private sector has to consider investment in tourism from a long term perspective and create the required facilities including accommodation, time share, restaurants, entertainment facilities, shopping complexes, etc. in areas identified for tourism development. Non-core activities in all airports, major stations and interstate bus terminus such as cleanliness and maintenance, luggage transportation, vehicles parking facilities, etc. should be opened up to private operators to increase efficiency and profitability.

The specific role of the Private Sector will be to :

i. Build and manage the required tourist facilities in all places of tourist interest.

ii. Assume collective responsibility for laying down industry standards, ethics and fair practices.

iii. Ensure preservation and protection of tourist attractions and give lead in green practices.

iv. Sponsor maintenance of monuments, museums and parks and provision of public conveniences and facilities.

v. Involve the local community in tourism projects and ensure that the benefits of tourism accrue to them in right measure.

vi. Undertake industry training and man-power development to achieve excellence in quality of services.

vii. Participate in the preparation of investment guidelines and marketing strategies and assist in database creation and research.

viii. Facilitate safety and security of tourists

ix. Endeavour to promote tourism on a sustained and long term perspective.

x. Collaborate with Govt. in the promotion and marketing of destinations.

Role of voluntary efforts: Voluntary agencies and volunteers have to contribute their expertise and understanding of local ethos to supplement the efforts of other sectors to provide the human touch to tourism and foster local initiatives. All such efforts shall be encouraged.

Tourism Development Fund and Resources for Development

It would be the policy of the Government to facilitate larger flow of funds to tourism infrastructure and to create a Tourism Development Fund to bridge critical infrastructural gaps.

Priority would be given for development of tourist infrastructure in selected areas of tourist importance and for those products which are considered to be in demand in the existing and future markets so that limited resources are put to the best use.

Foreign Investments and Incentives and Rationalization of Taxes

In order to off-set the specific constraints of tourism industry and to put in place the required infrastructure as quickly as possible, particularly in less developed areas, appropriate incentive schemes would be considered. It would also be the endeavour of the Government to persuade the State/UT Governments to rationalise taxes, to put a cap of 20% on all taxes taken together on the accommodation and hospitality units, to allocate suitable land for tourism purposes at reasonable prices, harmonize movement of tourist transport across State borders, etc.

Adoption of New Technologies

Efforts will be made to adopt the technological advances in the tourism sector to provide better facilities to tourists and to market the tourism product, to the benefit of all concerned.

Information technology shall be given the pride of place in the efforts to promote Indian tourism. Evey endeavour in this regard would increasingly rely on optimising the use of e-commerce/m-commerce, use of internet for disemination of tourism related information, increasing use of portals as gateway to accessibility to tourism information, development of Handy Audio Reach Kit (HARK) Tourist Guidance System at important monuments and heritage sites, networking of States, setting of tourist information Kiosks, encouoragement to information technology and eco-friendly practices by the private industries and above all keeping abreast with the global technologies for promoting and facilitating tourism.

It shall be ensured that Information Technology(IT) and Indian Tourism(IT) become synonymous.

The Central Government will set up a Paryatan Bhawan in New Delhi as a modern Tourist Interpretation Centre to cater to various needs of travellers, foreign as well as domestic and to offer facilities for air and train reservation, money changing counters and information about all tourist centres in the country. The Centre will be equipped with e-connectivity and networking facility to all state tourist offices. Efforts will be made to have similar state level Paryatan Bhawans in state Capitals.

The economic and social benefits of tourism and its importance as an instrument of economic growth have to be fully recognised by all sections of the society. It would, therefore, be the endeavour of the Government to bridge the information gap through proper statistical documentation of the impact of tourism and its wide publicity to create awareness so that the economic and social significance of tourism is well recognised and tourism is given due attention and national priority

Safety and Security

The safety and security of tourists are of primary importance both from the point of view of tourism development and the national pride. It will be, therefore, given high priority in the national strategy for tourism development. Central Government will take up with the State Government to enact suitable legislation on travel trade/ tourist police for protection and security of tourists and for providing institutional mechanism to deal with complaints received from tourists and the industry so as to create a better security perception amongst actual and potential visitors.

Facilitation Services

Tourists have to pass through several Government agencies so as to meet the requirements under various laws. These include obtaining visas, undergoing immigration checks, obtaining permits to visit certain areas, payment of fees for certain facilities, etc. The endeavour of the Government would be to improve efficiency in providing such facilitation services and make travel to and within India a pleasant experience. Introduction of issue of Visa on arrival at least for 15 days at all the airports, computerisation of the system of issue of Visa, streamlining of luggage handling system at airports improving tourist facilitation services at the airports by adopting technological solutions are some of the important facilitation services proposed in this regard.

Tourism Economic Zone, Tourist Circuits, Special Tourism Area and Areas of Special Interests

Tourism Economic Zones will be created with private participation based on the intrinsic attractions, potential for development and availability of resources in these zones. Air, road and rail connectivity to these areas will be established to facilitate direct and easy access to these zones from international and domestic destinations. Adequate backward and forward linkages will also be established to ensure flow of benefits to the local community. The development of such zones will be guided by well conceived Master Plans and executed by specific Tourism Development Authorities which will be created by the Government involving senior officers from the Department of Tourism, and other relevant Ministries/Departments of the Govt. of India, professionals from tourism industry and representatives of Industry & Trade Associations.

India with vast cultural and religious heritage and varied natural attractions has immensed potential of growth in the tourism sector. 25 travel circuits and destinations have already been identified for development through joint efforts of the Central Govt., the State Governments and the private sector. State Governments of Kerala, Tamil Nadu, Orissa and Maharashtra and Union Territory Administration of Daman & Diu have also declared Bekal Beach, Puri-Konark, Sindhudurg, Muttakadu-Mamallapuram and Diu as Special Tourism Area for integrated development. Steps will be taken to work towards the integrated development of all the tourist circuits of the country with the involvement of all the infrastructural departments, State Governments and the private sector.

Areas of Special Interest: Government would initiate and support special programmes and schemes for the development of tourism in North Eastern States, Himalayan region and island States/U.Ts with a view to achieve overall economic development of the regions, and as part of the strategy for removing regional imbalances.

Sustainable Development and Perspective Plans

The principle of sustainable development stipulates that the level of development does not exceed the carrying capacity of the area. It will be governments' policy to ensure adherence to such limits through appropriate planning instruments, guidelines and enabling regulations and their enforcement. Efforts will be made to diversify the tourism products in such a way that it supplements the main stream of cultural tourism. Comprehensive perspective plans for developing sustainable tourism by assessing the existing tourism scenario in each State/Union Territory with respect to availability of natural resources, heritage and other socio-cultural assets, quantitative/demographic factors like population, employment, occupation, income levels etc., services and infrastructure will be developed by initiating immediate action in this direction.

Conservation and Development

Tourism development needs to be properly guided and regulated to avoid adverse impact on the natural environment and cultural heritage which constitute the tourist attraction. A judicious balance needs to be maintained between conservation and development. Government will continue its policy of trying to maintain balance through planning restrictions and by educating the people in appreciating their rich heritage and by eliciting their cooperation in preserving and protecting it.

Promotion and Marketing

Promotion and marketing is an important component of tourism development and needs to be undertaken along with product development in conformity with consumer profiles and product characteristics. The policy of the Government therefore will be to develop and implement cost effective marketing strategies based on market research and segmentation analysis in each of the tourist generating countries.

International Cooperation

Tourism is a global industry requiring inputs from various international agencies and collaborations with other countries. The policy of the Government therefore will be to foster positive win – win partnership with all the international agencies and other countries.

Professional Excellence

Tourism being a service industry it is necessary to enhance its service efficiency. The new policy will strive towards excellence by introducing professionalism through training and re-training of human resources and providing memorable visitor experience to both domestic and international tourists.

Placing Tourism in the Concurrent List of the Constitution of India

Tourism as a separate subject does not find a place in the Seventh Schedule of the Constitution of India even though a number of its components are either in the Union List or in the State List or in the Concurrent List. Under the new Policy, Tourism will be placed in the Concurrent List as such a step will provide a Constitutional recognition to the tourism sector and help in channelising development of tourism in a systematic manner by enabling the Central Government to bring in legislation governing the activities of various service providers in the tourism sector.

Action Programme

The following is a list of action points emerging from the National Tourism Policy indicating the Ministries/Departments/Agencies responsible for implementing these actions.

Action Points Relating to Suvidha (Facilities)

Paryatan Bhawan in Delhi and at State Capitals: Setting up of Paryatan Bhawan in Delhi as one stop tourist reception centre to cater to various needs of travellers, foreign as well as domestic and offer air and train reservations, money changing counters and information about all tourist centres with e-connectivity and networking facilities to all State tourist offices. Construction of similar State level Paryatan Bhawans at State Capitals.

Augmentation of International Air Seat Capacity:-

- Assessing sector wise and season wise air seat capacity, and load factors and augmentation of capacity in the critical sectors either by the National Airlines or by encouraging Foreign Airlines.
- Improvement of accessibility in States and regions of tourist interest. Special interest would be given to areas having important tourist centres which are not connected by trains/ buses. Promoting arrivals in destination of interest by creating hub and spoke operations. Giving impetus to Heli Tourism and Helicoper services to areas not serviceable by fixed wing Aircraft.

Construction of airports on Built-Operate-Transfer (BOT) through private sector participation.

Rail Services:-

- Increasing the number of tourist trains. Special funds need to be earmarked for this purpose.
- Improving hygienic conditions, environment and passenger facilities in and around Railway Stations serving important tourist centres.
- Construction of budget hotels at important railway nodes.

Road Network:-

- Providing wayside amenities along with filling stations or otherwise at a distance of about 100 kilometres on all the highways connecting important tourist centres.

Providing standard signages on all roads leading to tourist spots.

- Ensuring uninterrupted inter-state movement of tourist coaches and vehicles through rationalisation and single point collection of taxes.

Maintenance of Heritage Sites and Improvement of Tourist Facilities:-

- Ensuring proper maintenance and professional site management of important tourist attractions/monuments under the control of Archaeological Survey of India/State Archaeology Departments.
- Involving local authorities, trusts, etc. in the restoration/ preservation of tourist attractions and maintenance of the surroundings.
- Providing world class tourist facilities, amenities and land scaping of area around important monuments in a phased manner.
- Identification, documentation and video publishing of all the monuments which are great tourist attractions.

General Improvement of Tourist Facilities

- Computerisation of the system of issue of visas by the Embassies/High Commissions.
- Introduction of issue of visas on arrival atleast for 15 days at all the airports.
- Distribution of tourist information brochures through Indian Emabssies/High Commissions.
- Streamlining of luggage handling systems at the airports to ensure that the luggage is transported and cleared within about 30 minutes after the arrival of the flights.
- Improving tourist facilitation services at the airports by adopting technological solutions and imparting training to functionaries at the cutting edge level like customs and immigration officials, taxi drivers, guides, etc.
- Introduction of airconditioned taxis with electronic fare metres in all the international airports.
- Provision of special taxi and coach enclosures extending from arrival halls in all the international airports and controlled by security staff so that passengers can queue up easily and pick-up taxis and coaches without hassles.

- Mounting Video-Cameras in strategic places inside and outside arrival areas to prevent corruption.
- Providing direct access to airport hotels and railway platforms in all the international airports.
- Augmenting information services at the airports.
- Removal of RAP/PAP restrictions from most parts of the country.
- Provision of money changing facility in all the tourist centres.
- Providing international standard signages at tourist centres, airports, railway stations, bus stands, etc.

Action Points Relating to Soochana (Information)

- Setting-up a chain of exclusive souvenir shops stocking specially manufactured and beautifully packed information books and other souvenir items at all the nationally important tourist places in a professional manner.
- Introduction of audio-guides at the important tourist places on a commercial basis.
- There have been revolutionary changes in the computer and communication technologies and other relevant sectors, which are still changing. Such technologies have helped sharing of information globally to the advantage of all. Information Technology for improving visitor information and facilitation should be effectively used. Setting up of Touch Screen Information Kiosks , development of Tourism Portals with links to all tourism related web sites, production of CD-ROMs, creation and maintenance of websites, introduction of computer based information and reservation systems, use of virtual reality systems and video-conferencing for tourism promotion, etc. are the activities proposed in this regard.

Action Points Relating to Safety and Security (Suraksha)

- Launching of campaigns through local bodies, non-governmental organisations, youth centres, etc. to create awareness about the traditions of Indian hospitality and the importance of providing an assurance of safety and security to tourists so as to control touting, extortion and harrasment to tourists.
- Providing a legal framework for the protection of tourists and their belongings.

- Providing an institutional mechanism to deal with the complaints received from tourists and the industry so as to create a better security perception amongst actual and potential visitors.
- Introducing tourist police at important tourist centres through the respective State Governments.
- Strict prohibition of soliciting and enticing of tourists both within the airport premises and in its immediate neighbourhood by unethical operators and traders and keeping both the airports and its vicinity tout free.
- Central Government to take up with the State Governments to enact suitable legislations on travel trade/tourist police for protection and security of tourists. Model guidelines to be circulated to the State Governments.

Action Point relating to Infrastructure Development

- In order to off-set the specific constraints of tourism industry and to put in place the required infrastructure as quickly as possible, particularly in less developed areas, appropriate incentive schemes would be considered. It would also be the endeavour of the Government to persuade the State/UT Governments to rationalise taxes and to allocate suitable land for tourism purposes at reasonable prices, harmonize movement of tourist transport across State borders, etc.
- Efforts will be made to prepare Master Plan for land use in each tourist destination/urban centre for infrastructure purposes. Ministry of Tourism & Culture will also be the agency to effect any changes in the master plan relating to land use for tourism infrastructure.
- It will be the endeavour of the Govt to provide single window clearance facilities in the areas like allotment of lands, environment, electricity, water, sewerage, etc. in order to facilitate speedy implementation of tourism projects.
- Tourism being an area where generally strategic issues are not involved, maximum impetus and incentives need to be given to FDI and involvement of NRIs, PIOs and OCBs to evolve appropriate means to facilitate FDIs such as Special Purpose Vehicles (SPVs). At present NRIs & PIOs are allowed 100 percent investment in tourism projects.
- Development of tourism to the extent desired would involve heavy investments in infrastructure. The resources for such

investments have to come mostly from private investors, financial institutions and external borrowing. Financial viability and commercial returns are the guiding factors in such investments. Very often, it would depend on investments to bridge certain critical gaps in infrastructure which by itself may not be commercially remunerative. Special funds have to be therefore, created for such investments. The Institutions like Tourism Finance Corporation of India (TFCI) will be strengthened and a special fund namely Tourism Development Fund will be set up for development of Tourist Infrastructure.

Action Point Relating to Cooperation

- Encouraging Panchayati Raj Institutions, local bodies, religious trusts, co-operatives, and other community level institutions to take up tourism promotion activities through the general rural development and employment generation programmes and specific rural tourism development schemes.
- Encouragement of non-governmental organisations to create and manage tourist facilities.
- Involvement of non-governmental organisations to create environmental awareness on Eco-tourism, national parks, coastal tourism and urban/rural hygiene in tourist centres.
- Involvement of local community in the formulation and implementation of tourism development plans through District Tourism Promotion Councils, etc.

Action Point Relating to Product Development and Promotion

- Giving guidance and financial assistance to State/Union Territory Governments for preparing tourism Master Plans and perspective plans identifying tourism resources, prioritising development circuits and projects and specifying the most suitable forms of tourism.
- Implementing integrated/intensive development of tourist destinations after assessing the carrying capacity, local aspirations and the benefits likely to accrue to the community.
- Involving the town and country planning agencies of Central and State Governments and integration of spatio-economic development plans with tourism development.
- Focussing on the development of Eco-tourism.

- Developing the places of pilgrimage by providing the requisite infrastructural facilities with a view to promote domestic and international pilgrim tourism.
- Develop a clear identity/theme around some important existing attractions and package them to offer an attractive product e.g. Varanasi as the present living city with roots into deep ancient civilisation on similar lines as Jericho/Rome/Bethlehem;
- Expand "Events Tourism" through organisation of international events such as sports, conferences etc.; also market existing cultural and religious festivals as tourist attractions.
- Expand "Shopping Tourism" through good value for money with the exquisite range of hand-crafted products made in the country.
- Expand "Cruise Tourism", in view of the huge coastlines and large number of ports.
- Developing heritage and village tourism as a package by identifying and developing villages around heritage properties, which have already been restored.
- Diversifying the tourism product to make India a unique multi-attraction tourism destination which can meet the needs of all forms of tourism particularly rural tourism, spiritual tourism, eco tourism, adventure tourism, incentive tourism, conference and convention tourism, etc.
- Developing natural health resorts of Yoga, Ayurveda, etc. as unique tourism products of India.
- Developing seamless inter-modal transfers by improving linkages.
- Involvement of NRIs and PIOs in product development.
- Amusement parks promote tourism by attracting both international and domestic tourists, generate demand in the transport, accommodation and service sectors and create employment opportunities. The Government will prepare appropriate guidelines to encourage private sector to invest in development of amusement parks.
- Peoples Participation in Development of Tourism : - Tourism policy 1982 envisaged a selective approach based on travel circuit concept in the provision of tourism infrastructure to achieve intensive development of selected centres. The National Action Plan for Tourism 1992 also reiterated the need for such

a policy to achieve significant impact on infrastructural development with the limited resources available. These policies, however, did not succeed in view of persistent demands for several small projects to meet the needs of domestic tourists in almost every place of tourist interest. Even the Government of India essentially followed a scheme approach instead of area approach in providing financial assistance for the development of tourism infrastructure. The approach for the future development of tourism has to, therefore, take into account both the needs for selective development and the demands of a wide cross section of domestic tourists. The activities in this regard would include:

- Creating public awareness about economic and social benefits of tourism amongst administrators, planners and the masses through seminars, workshops, presentations, etc.
- Launching entrepreneurship development and self employment programmes to involve the educated youth in providing various tourist facilities and services and thereby creating employment opportunities.
- Integrated development of special tourism areas and selected circuits.
- *Integrated Development of Tourist destinations: Int*ernational tourist traffic to the country is largely confined to certain selected centres and destinations at present. There is also a fair level of seasonality in the international tourist arrivals. As a result there is a good deal of congestion and scarcity of facilities in some of these centres during peak seasons. The tourist traffic to some of the centres have even exceeded the carrying capacity with the attendant problems of environmental degradation. It has, therefore, become necessary to go beyond the beaten tracks and to facilitate direct visit of tourists to new destinations. However, the choice of such new destinations for development will have to be based on their intrinsic attractions, potential for development and the carrying capacity as well as availability of resources. Such development will be guided by well conceived master plans, and executed by specific Tourism Development Authorities. Adequate backward and forward linkages will also be established to ensure adequate flow of benefits to the local community.
- Creation of Tourism Economic Zones

- Constitution of Tourism Development Authorities
- *Diversification of Tourism Products:* - The main strength of Indian tourism at present is its cultural attractions, particularly, the large number of monuments and archaeological remains scattered through out the country, its art and artefacts and colourful fairs and festivals. The country is also endowed with a number of other tourist attractions and options including beach tourism; forests, wild life and land scapes for eco-tourism; snow, river and mountain peaks for adventure tourism; technological parks and science museums for science tourism; centres of pilgrimage for spiritual tourism; heritage trains and hotels for heritage tourism; etc. The tradition of Indian system of medicine and its curative and preventive effect are well known the world over. Yoga, Ayurveda and other forms of natural health resorts have thus become unique tourist attractions of the country. There are also facilities for conference and convention tourism, cruise tourism and shopping tours. The development of natural health resorts of Yoga, Ayurveda etc. along with rural tourism, spiritual tourism and eco-tourism will be given adequate attention.
- *Sustainable Development of Tourism:* - Assessment of carrying capacity and Environment Impact Assessment studies would be insisted while developing tourism in ecologically fragile areas and all developmental activities will be guided by such studies. The other activities in this regard would include:
    i. Providing a legal frame work through appropriate legislation for ensuring social, cultural and environmental sustainability of tourism development and protecting the tourists.
    ii. Evolving specific policies and guidelines for the development of specific forms of tourism like ecotourism, adventure tourism, etc.

Action Point relating to Conservation

- Formulation and publication of appropriate policies and guidelines, creation of public awareness about such guidelines, etc. are the activities envisaged in this regard apart from providing the requisite legal frame work for ensuring social, cultural and environmental sustainability.
- Despoilation of natural environment, archaeological monuments, beaches, mountains and places of natural beauty; disruption in

the eco-system of environmentally sensitive regions; destruction of traditions in the culturally sensitive areas; clandestine selling of antiques and vandalism are some of the possible adverse effects of unimaginative and unregulated development of tourism.

Action Points Relating to Promotion and Marketing

- Achieving effective coordination and synergy with other Departments, agencies and the private sector in tourism promotion and marketing.
- Fully utilising the Indian missions abroad for tourism promotion and related activities.
- Identifying potential tourism markets and segments and adopting focussed marketing strategies based on research to make promotional and marketing efforts cost effective.
- Enhancing the image of India as a fascinating multi-attraction and multi-activity destination with rich cultural heritage and a vibrant society.
- Observing 1999-2000 as Millennium/Explore India Year.
- Developing a Millennium Yatra Package and Youth packages.
- Organising Bauddha Mahotsav with international seminars and exhibitions at Sarnath/Bodhgaya.
- Organising photo exhibitions and creation of a photo library.
- Launching of a multi-media CD-ROM and creating an integrated website on Indian tourism.
- Developing a clear identity of Indian tourism product by promoting selected theme based tourist attractions.

Action Points Relating to International Cooperation

- Ensuring active participation in the activities of international agencies like United Nations Development Programme (UNDP), Economic and Social Commission for Asia and Pacific (ESCAP), World Tourism Organisation (WTO), Pacific Asia Travel Association(PATA), Indian Ocean Tourism Organisation (IOTO).
- Enhancing multilateral cooperation in tourism with different groups of countries like Association of South-East Asian Nations (ASEAN), Bangaldesh-India-Myanmar-Sri Lanka- Thailand-Economic Cooperation (BIMSTEC), South Asian Association for Regional Cooperation (SAARC), etc.

- Strengthening tourism promotion and investment through multilateral and bilateral agreements.

Action Points Relating to Areas of Special Interest

The seven States of the North East with beautiful landscapes, lush green forests, exotic wildlife, unique forms of art and culture and affable tribal societies have hitherto remained backward due to various reasons including poor infrastructure. These States alone offer enormous potential for the development of eco-tourism. At least ten percent of Plan funds of the Ministry will be used for the promotion of tourism in North East apart from taking up special projects and schemes for the development of the area. Other Special Tourism areas such as Himalayan areas, Islands and coastal areas which are identified will also be developed.

Action Points Relating to the Economic and Social Benefits

- Standardisation of statistical definitions and methods of data collection, tabulation and dissemination.
- Strengthening of statistical machinery and improvement of statistical systems on tourism both at the Central and State levels.
- Development of Tourism Satellite Accounts in association with the Department of Statistics to estimate the economic benefits of tourism precisely and regularly.
- Undertaking tourism impact assessment studies and case studies.
- Launching of tourism awareness campaigns at all levels of society.

The Action Points Relating to Professional Excellence

- Strengthening the institutional set-up for human resource development including the setting-up of an Advanced Institute of Hotel Management and a Culinary Institute.
- Qualitative improvement and modernisation of existing training institutions.
- Setting-up atleast one Food Craft Institute in each State, particularly in North Eastern States.
- Improving the standards of training in private institutes through accredition and quality control.
- Setting up a National Tourism Documentation Centre equipped with modern technology systems to function as a repository of research findings and publications on tourism.

- Involving the tourism industry in human resource development activities and encouraging them to set-up independent training facilities.
- Streamlining and strengthening of guide training and training of other grass root level workers.
- Introduction of optional courses in tourism related topics at Graduate and under Graduate levels in order to meet requirement of trained personnel in this sector.

11

Emerging Patterns of Travel and Tourism

The Philippines is an archipelago consisting of about 7,100 islands. The country is divided into three major island groups: Luzon, Visayas and Mindanao. It is bounded on the north by the Bashi Channel, on the west by the South China Sea, on the South by the Sulu and Celebes Seas, and on the east by the Pacific Ocean.

Its northernmost islands, the Batanes, are approximately 240 kilometers south of Taiwan, while the southernmost islands, the Sulu group, lie approximately 24 kilometers from the Borneo coast. Situated between the Pacific and Indian Oceans, and between Australia and mainland Asia, the Philippines is at the crossroads of international travel routes.

Land Area. The total land area is approximately 300,000 square kilometers. The archipelago stretches out for about 1,800 kilometers from north to south, and for about 1,050 kilometers from east to west.

Topography. The Philippines has an irregular configuration of extensive coastline, vast extent of mountainous country lying close to the sea, narrow and interrupted coastal plains, and a generally north-south trend of inland water bodies. Population. As of 1995, the population was estimated at 70 million with persons 15 years old and above considered the productive segment of the economy, comprising 63 per cent. The population density is about 234 persons per square kilometer of land.

Updates on the Philippine Economy

The economic turn around that began in 1992 continued to gain momentum in 1995 with the real growth in gross national product

(GNP) accelerating at 5.7 per cent, an improvement on the previous year's 5.3 per cent. On the production side, industry and services expanded significantly, accounting for about 96 per cent of increase in aggregate domestic production during the year which offset the weak showing of agriculture which was hit by typhoons and other natural disasters. Meanwhile, strong exports and personal consumption expenditures accounted for growth in the demand side, the highest so far since 1992. Inflation was at single digit levels as of end 1995 and is expected to attain the same level by year end 1996.

The bright economic picture can be attributed to a number of factors, foremost of which were measures to maintain a stable macroeconomic environment and reforms to create a liberalized environment for business. Furthermore, the necessary conditions for growth such as political unity, peace and order, and infrastructure support were attended to by the government. The government recognized that physical infrastructure development must keep in step with economic growth.

The huge cost to the economy of under-investment in infrastructure was witnessed in 1992-1993, at the height of the power crisis. Cognizant of the huge investment requirement in infrastructure and the insufficiency of public funds to bridge this investment gap, the government instituted policies that encouraged private sector participation. The decision to mobilize private sector involvement in power generation proved to be fruitful as the crisis was resolved in 1994.

The government has adopted reforms and initiatives towards easing the entry of foreign and local investors into industries. Industries whose growth were previously hampered by government regulations like telecommunications and inter-island shipping were deregulated. The efficiency gains are visible. In telecommunications, for example, waiting time for a telephone connection has been drastically reduced while charges for overseas calls declined. As a result, markets are getting integrated both domestically and internationally, and mutually beneficial transactions are being realized in the process. The liberalization of the shipping industry, on the other hand, opened up domestic routes to other firms.

The noteworthy performance of the economy over the period 1993-95 is no reason to be complacent. The development strategy that has been embraced has opened up the economy to global competition. This means that policies supportive of long-term growth must continue.

Raising agricultural productivity, in particular, is a major challenge, given the inclusion of trade in agriculture in the World Trade Organization (WTO). To the extent that majority of poor families are dependent on traditional subsistence agriculture, success in raising agricultural productivity begets success in poverty alleviation.

The government recognizes that public policies based on privatization, liberalization, deregulation, and decentralization provide incentives for efficiency and growth. They expand the economic opportunities of people, enabling them to raise their standards of living. The Ramos Administration is committed to pursue, and to accelerate where possible, these structural policy reforms, all of which have contributed to the sound economic performance from 1993 to 1995 and have provided a foundation for meeting any economic and social challenges in the future.

Long-term Objectives for Infrastructure Development

As the backbone of development of any economy, the provision of infrastructure is a prerequisite towards attaining economic growth and improving the country's productive capacity. The anticipated growth of the economy is expected to exert more pressure on infrastructure support facilities.

There are two major objectives for the infrastructure sector in the long-term: (1) to provide adequate, convenient, fast and safe facilities and competitively priced services to meet the primary needs of the population and; (2) to provide support facilities for the productive sectors and act as catalyst of development in desired areas.

Strategies for Infrastructure Development to Support National Objectives

The government has to design the proper policies and corresponding strategies for infrastructure development to ensure that the appropriate infrastructures will be provided in the right places at the right time. The following are the general policies and strategies to be pursued in the next three years in support of the sector's development under the Medium-Term Philippine Development Plan. (MTPDP):

1. Further encourage increased and broad-based private sector investments in the provision, operation and maintenance of infrastructure facilities through but not limited to the Build-Operate-Transfer (BOT) scheme;
2. Improve coordination among national government agencies, local government units (LGUs), the private sector and affected

communities in the formulation and implementation of infrastructure plans and projects;

3. Ensure provision of adequate funds for required capital investment and operations and maintenance (O & M) with priority on the latter;
4. Strictly implement and upgrade maintenance and rehabilitation programs and standards;
5. Enhance integration of environmental and socio-cultural concerns in the planning and implementation of infrastructure projects;
6. Strengthen infrastructure support to socially depressed areas and to growth centres and areas with the highest growth potentials;
7. Promote, where feasible, labour-based technology in infrastructure activities;
8. Promote research, development and use of innovative construction materials and environment-friendly technology for energy-efficient structures and costefficient construction design;
9. Adjust fees and charges to approximate real costs incurred in the provision of infrastructure services;
10. Adopt the integrated area development approach in the planning, programming and implementation of complementary support infrastructure for regional growth centres, tourism areas, and identified poverty areas;
11. Give priority to appropriate sanitation infrastructure facilities (e.g. toilets, water supply and sewerage) in Metro Manila and other urban centres, especially in depressed areas; and
12. Strengthen local technical and financial capacity for project implementation and service management through broad-based training programs and organizational and fiscal reforms.

Subsectoral Objectives, Policies Strategies and Priority Subsector Activities

Going down to the different subsector of infrastructure, the objectives and specific policies and strategies adopted for each and the corresponding priority activities are as follows:

Energy

The objectives of the energy subsector on ensuring the availability and security of market-based energy supply; promoting the judicious and efficient use of energy resources; and averting negative impacts of energy activities to health, safety and environmental quality in the design and operation of energy projects will be supported by the following policies and strategies.

To ensure energy availability and security:

1. Diversify sources and types of local and imported energy;
   - i. utilization of natural gas for power generation or other competitive uses;
   - ii. explore and develop oil and geothermal resource potential;
   - iii. mine-mouth coal power plant operations for low-grade coal deposits;
   - iv. large-scale utilization of new and renewable sources of energy including small-and mini-hydro resources, solar, wind and biomass-based resources;
   - v. promote the use of decentralized energy systems for areas outside electricity grids; and
   - vi. rationalize expansion of petroleum distribution networks.
2. Expand coverage of electrification for the energy needs of countryside development;
3. Secure existing and future sites of power and energy resource development projects;
4. Enhance private sector participation in energy projects; and
5. Promote competition and long-term efficiency in the energy industry.

To promote judicious and efficient use of energy:

1. Pursue least-cost options;
2. Restructure electricity tariffs to reflect cost of provision;
3. Strictly implement comprehensive O & M and rehabilitation programs;
4. Enforce standards of efficiency and reliability in power generation and distribution utilities;
5. Promote energy conservation, energy efficient technologies, and energy R & D;
6. Move towards the deregulation of downstream oil industry to promote efficiency, e.g. petroleum product pricing and distribution.

To avert negative impacts of energy activities to health, safety and environmental *quality*:

1. Promote adoption of clean technologies for utilization of coal and other hydrocarbons;
2. Integrate environmental and socio cultural concerns in the planning and implementation of energy programs and projects, e.g., environmental management and community relations activities in energy project sites.

Priority Subsector Activities

1. Maintenance, rehabilitation and construction of power plants, transmission lines and substations in the Luzon, Visayas and Mindanao grids;
2. Exploration and development of indigenous energy resources including downstream activities;
3. Expansion of electrification coverage and improvement in the efficiency of distribution through the construction, rehabilitation, upgrading and maintenance of facilities; and
4. Implementation of research and development, institutional strengthening and energy conservation programs.

Transportation

As the economy expands toward the countryside and aims at global markets, the transport objective on strengthening interregional and urban-rural linkages to ensure people's mobility and continuous flow of goods; ensuring the safety and efficiency of transport services to meet the needs of an increasing population and dynamic market demands; and developing international gateways to optimum standards to enhance the country's global competitiveness; will be supported by the following policies and strategies:

1. Identify and provide basic transport infrastructure to ensure access and allow the integration of depressed communities;
2. Maintain existing transportation facilities properly to prolong their use;
3. Continuously upgrade transport facilities and service standards to make sure that their quality and quantity are responsive to traffic growth;
4. Promote multimodal transport to facilitate trade;
5. Develop the arterial road network consisting of a north-south backbone, east-west laterals, and other strategic roads;
6. Establish specialized handling facilities for grains and bulk cargo in selected ports and construct additional fishing ports;

7. Provide the transport facility requirements of agriculture, fishing, and agrarian reform areas, regional industrial centres, and tourism areas;
8. Proceed with the development of feeder ports under the Nationwide Feeder Ports program in preparation for the devolution of their O & M to LGUs;
9. Implement urban transport management measures and develop alternative modes of transport in coordination with LGU's to alleviate traffic. Expand existing mass transit systems to provide affordable means of transport, and pursue new projects, including expressways and tollways;
10. Intensify transport safety programs to minimize accident risks and protect lives through the implementation of relevant recommendations of the Civil Aviation Master Plan, Maritime SafetyMaster Plan, and the Road Safety Program;
11. Strictly enforce environmental protection measures controlling vehicle emissions, water pollution, and noise pollution to safeguard the health of the population;
12. Strengthen institutional and inter-agency coordination of planning and project implementation to ensure effective and efficient intermodal linkage and reduce disruption of services;
13. Promote private sector participation in transport development, e.g., construction, maintenance, and operation of roads, expressways, mass transit systems, ports, railways, and terminals;
14. Enhance the capability of LGUs in administering, implementing and developing infrastructure facilities, i.e., local roads, municipal ports, as embodied in the Local Government Code;
15. Pursue efficiency-and competition-enhancing measures such as deregulation, decentralization, appropriate pricing mechanisms, and rationalization of user charges;
16. Adjust truck load limits along with road design standards to achieve a proper balance between trucking and infrastructure costs, and strictly enforce load limits;
17. Rehabilitate the PNR Mainline South, study the rehabilitation and possible extension of the northern line in Luzon and explore the feasibility of adopting rail as means of transportation in other areas of the country; and
18. Upgrade the NAIA and explore the use of the reverted baselands for its relocation or as a site for transport-related industrial complexes;

Priority Subsector Activities

1. Upgrading of national arterial and secondary roads to all-weather roads, and conversion of all bridges along these roads into permanent structures;
2. Construction and improvement of airport facilities including aircraft movement areas, terminal buildings, fire stations, etc.;
3. Upgrading and modernization of air navigation and communication facilities, and crash-fire-rescue vehicles;
4. Development and improvement of national ports and port facilities, feeder, fishing, and municipal ports, and river landings;
5. Acquisition and upgrading of aids to maritime navigation, search and rescue vehicles, hydrographic fire-fighting vessels, marine pollution control vessels, and other vessels;
6. Expansion and development of urban rail transit in Metro Manila, including the rehabilitation of LRT Line 1, the construction of new LRT lines, and the rehabilitation of PNR's Commuter Line South; and
7. Completion and the rehabilitation of PNR's Main Line South and study of viability of adopting rail transport in various areas of the country.

Communication

Increased globalization of production and finance requires that the Philippines keep pace with the latest advancements in the area of communications. In this connection, the sector will strive to interconnect all local telephone exchanges into the main backbone; strengthen the regulatory and management capability of government to enable the private sector to meet the growing demand for telephone and other value-added services, and to achieve and maintain a high quality of telecommunications service; and expand postal service to far-flung/unserved areas and improve delivery efficiency in those areas covered. To attain these objectives; the following policies and strategies will be pursued:

1. Privatize all government telecommunications assets by 1998 as mandated by Republic Act 7925; allow more open entry of private firms to promote greater competition and efficiency in telecommunications services;
2. Phase out unnecessary taxes and fees that divert resources away from rapid growth of the sector, wean government away from

the ownership, provision and direct operation of telecommunication services and privatize the postal service;

3. Adopt clear and simpler rules for interconnecting all public networks; encourage toll revenue sharing schemes that will ensure the financial viability of the local exchanges; and establish rules and regulations for a more rationalized delivery of broad band and personal communication services;
4. Reorient the regulatory system, initially towards forward arbitration of the issues arising from interconnection, revenue-sharing, rates restructuring based on cost radio spectrum usage, and complex technical options under a multi-operator business environment;
5. Increase telephone density and widen coverage consistent with the developmental stage of the various localities and the needs of the business, by private entities in concert with government investing their respective resources to anticipate and build capacities accordingly;
6. Upgrade the quality of postal communication service to internationally accepted standards; establish postal circuits in barangays not effectively covered by existing post offices and postal stations;
7. Introduce value-added services and initiate advanced users on the business and professional opportunities arising from the convergence of computers and communications; and
8. Modify the legal framework to permit and promote more electronic-based transactions, aside from phasing in deregulation measures as the sector achieves maturity.

Priority Subsector Activities

1. Installation of telephone main stations and public calling office (PCOs) throughout the country;
2. Construction of postal offices buildings and improvement of mail distribution service;
3. Improvement of the quality of telecommunications service; and
4. Establishment of telecommunication facilities to improve weather forecasting, enhance safety and improve information exchange.

Water Resources

In support to the objectives of increasing the provision of irrigation, safe and adequate water supply, sanitation services and appropriate flood control and drainage mechanisms are the following policies and strategies:

1. Pursue a decentralized, coordinated and efficient management of water resources; adopt an integrated planning and development strategy for an area-wide development schemes combining irrigation, power, flood control, and domestic and industrial water supply;
2. Determine investments in water resources and sanitation development would be based on demand and local initiative;
3. Encourage/facilitate participation of LGUs, NGOs, and private groups in sector development;
4. Integrate quality and quantity concerns in resource management and introduce appropriate environmental charges to protect public health and ensure environmental sustainability;
5. Implement cost-efficient water resources development projects for increased productivity and employment opportunities;
6. Integrate the provision of improved sewage and sanitation services in all water development programs and projects;
7. Determine the allocation of water among users where the primary bases shall be the socio-eocnomic consideration/greater beneficial use.

Priority Subsector Activities

1. Construction, rehabilitation and maintenance of national and communal irrigation facilities nationwide;
2. Construction and upgrading of water supply and sewerage/ sanitation facilities nationwide; and
3. Construction and implementation of flood control and drainage projects in the 12 major river systems in the country including Metro Manila.

Strategies for Supporting Regional Infrastructure Development

In support of programs for regional cooperation in infrastructure development, the following strategies shall be pursued in the sector:

1. Rapid expansion and integration of the network/facilities across urban and rural areas;
2. Active involvement of the private sector under the Local Government Code in local governance to ensure delivery of basic infrastructure facilities/services;

3. Integrate infrastructure planning with urban and regional planning, land use, environment, industry, agriculture, tourism and other sectors of the economy; and
4. In telecommunications, exploit the opportunities created by the overlaps of broadcasting and telecommunications through the production of cultural and entertainment programs geared for the Asia-Pacific market.

Scope and Priorities of Infrastructure Programs and Projects

Under the MTPDP, we have also identified specific programs and projects to implement such policies with corresponding key measurable targets. These targets will enable our government to monitor the implementation of programs and projects on infrastructure. They are the following:

Energy

1. More than 2,000 megawatts of new power-generating capacity to be put on stream up to the year 1998 to meet the projected 11.7 per cent yearly growth in power demand;
2. Integrate the three major island groups of the Philippines into a single grid in the next five years to strengthen system reliability and to allow the flexible shifting of power from areas with excess supply to deficient ones;
3. Dependence on imported energy to be reduced to 57 per cent of the total energy consumption of 258 million barrels of fuel oil equivalent by year 1998 from 67 per cent in 1995;
4. Expand rural electrification coverage to benefit an additional 1.1 million households under the government assisted electric cooperatives to 63 per cent by 1998 from 55 per cent in 1995;
5. Convert Clark Air Base into a freeport zone and investment haven just like Subic Bay Freeport Zone;
6. Rehabilitate and improve 100 per cent of national arterial roads and 95 per cent of national secondary roads into all-weather roads;
7. Improve major ports and airports and upgrade to international standards the Mactan, Davao and Zamboanga airports;
8. Construct new light rail transit lines in Metro Manila;
9. Install 4.2 million telephone lines to improve telephone density to 7.37 lines per 100 population from 2.01 in 1995;
10. Install public calling offices in all 1,565 municipalities;

11. Increase the proportion of the population served with potable water to 79 per cent from 72 per cent in 1995; and
12. Provide an additional 106,011 hectares with irrigation facilities.

Tourism Development

The overall objective for the development of the tourism sector hinges on the promotion of the Philippines as an attractive tourist destination not only for foreigners but also for Filipinos as well.

In support, the following policies and strategies will be aggressively pursued:

1. Promotion of destination clusters for major island groups, i.e., corresponding to the Luzon, Visayas and Mindanao island groups, where each cluster will be supported by at least one major international gateway and tourism estates/zones connected to a variety of satellite destinations;
2. Promotion of history, culture and arts;
3. Promotion of a mix of destinations and products for various tourist segments;
4. Conduct policy review in response to changing trends;
5. Establish and strengthen linkages and networking to ensure the provision of adequate infrastructure facilities and services in tourism areas, as well as the development, enhancement and promotion of existing and potential tourist attractions.

Priority Subsector Activities

1. Formulation of tourism master plans for all regions and detailed physical plans for priority tourism areas or 'must-see' destinations identified in the regional development framework;
2. Preparation of a Cluster Development Plan for Luzon, Visayas and Mindanao including the development of an integrated tourism infrastructure plan along the lines of conserving the socio-cultural heritage and preserving the environment;
3. Conduct of market research programs to identify target segment, product offerings, pricing, etc.;
4. Promotion of investments by both local and foreign developers in tourism priority areas;
5. Establishment of regional tourism training centres including the formulation of training modules at crafts/skills level and mobile training units in the regions;

6. Establishment of cultural and heritage centres in areas identified in the TMP and regional master plans including the restoration of national parks, historical sites and shrines, e.g., Rizal Park, Intramuros, Vigan, Taal and Nayong Pilipino.
7. Conceptualization and packaging of "freedom trail tours" in line with the Philippine Freedom Centennial Celebration;
8. Pursuit of aggressive marketing campaigns focusing on the thematic campaign "Islands Philippines" during the Plan period culminating in the holding of a "Philippine Visit Year" Campaign in 1998.

Administrative Structure for Policy-making and for the Implementation of Infrastructure Programs and Projects

In explaining the administrative structure for the approval and implementation of infrastructure projects in the Philippines, discussions will be limited to BOT projects for brevity. The main actors in the BOT approval/implementation process are as follows:

Infrastructure Committee (INFRACOM) of the NEDA Board

The INFRACOM is a policy-level committee of the NEDA Board composed of the Secretaries of NEDA, DPWH, DOTC, DBM, DOF, DOE, and the Executive Secretary from the Office of the President. NEDA acts as the Secretariat to the Committee. In addition to its regular functions, it is tasked to coordinate the discussion/resolution/reformation of policies an issues pertinent to the implementation of the Build-Operate-Transfer Schemes. Investment Coordination Committee (ICC) of the NEDA Board The Investment Coordination Committee (ICC) is another cabinet committee of the NEDA Board composed of the Secretaries of DOF, NEDA, DBM, DTI, DA, BASP, DOE, CCPAP and the Executive Secretary from the Office of the President. Its basic mandate is to coordinate the utilization of fiscal resources for the public investment program, approve the implementation of major projects and monitor the same thereof.

With respect to BOT projects, ICC shall approve national projects costing up to 300 million and local projects costing more than 200 million pesos. ICC shall recommend the approval of national projects costing more than 300 million pesos to the National Economic Development Authority (NEDA) Board and all Build-Operate and Own projects to the President.

Implementing Agency

The implementing agencies for infrastructure development, such as the Department of Public Works and Highways, the Department of Transportation and Communications and the National Power Corporation, perform the following functions:

1. Identify and recommend particular projects for BOT;
2. Undertake at least the pre-feasibility studies for the projects;
3. Ensure that projects are part of its development program;
4. Secure ICC approval of the project before bidding;
5. Responsible for leading the project through bidding, negotiation and approval; and
6. In the absence of an appropriate regulatory body, issue a franchise to operate.

Local Government Unit (LGU)

The LGU identifies and recommends projects for BOT. It then secures project confirmation of the local development council or regional development council or the Metropolitan Manila Development Authority (for Metro Manila projects) prior to bidding. It is likewise responsible for leading the project though bidding, negotiation and approval. Finally, the LGU or appropriate regulatory body may issue a franchise to operate, as provided by existing laws.

Coordinating Council of the Philippine Assistance Program

The Coordinating Council of the Philippine Assistance Program (CCPAP) has been tasked to handle the promotion of the BOT scheme and projects. It provides training/information to lead actors for BOT implementation, technical assistance for a prefeasibility study to assess if a project is suitable for BOT implementation, and support for tender document preparation, marketing and contract compliance.

Private Sponsors

The private sector agent is responsible for leading the project through packaging, negotiation and approval of the security package. It assembles the needed financial commitments for the project. There are also other actors that have important roles to play in the BOT approval process. These are:

- o *Local Development Council*
  - Evaluates/approves/integrates the project into a larger development plan

- o *Local Sanggunian or Council*
  - Approves the project prior to call for bids
- o *Board of Investments (BOI)*
  - Decides if a project is eligible for investment incentives
- o *Department of Environment and Natural Resources (DENR)*
  - Reviews compliance with environmental laws
  - Issues the Environmental Compliance Certificate
- o *Regulatory Agencies*
  - Ensures that tolls and fees are just

Market Preparations for Private Sector Investment

As in any country in the world, the Philippines' economic growth cannot be sustained and further improved without continuously adopting measures to enhance the infrastructure system. To realize this, a broad policy framework has been adopted by the government to encourage private sector to participate in economic development, e.g. financing, operation and construction of vital infrastructure facilities.

Current Laws Affecting Infrastructure Development

In the formulation of policies and programs for infrastructure development and in the course of implementation of such projects, we are bound by certain laws, foremost among which are the Build-Operate-Transfer (BOT) Law, the Public Service Law and other regulations.

BOT Law

Although provision of infrastructure facilities and services is mainly the responsibility of government because of its "public goods" aspect, severe fiscal constraints in the case of the Philippines, has resulted in the decline of public investment in infrastructure development. In consonance with the new era of low public sector deficits which the government aims to impose to contain inflation within manageable levels and ensure sustainable long-term growth, we are constrained to restrict our expenditure program. This means putting a limit to public investments in infrastructure projects. On the other hand this forces our government to seek other sources of financing such as Official Development Assistance (ODA) and private investments, either domestic or foreign. This kind of scenario opens a great number of opportunities for the BOT scheme.

Republic Act (RA) No. 6957 enacted on July 9, 1990 institutionalized the BOT/BT concept in the Philippines and this served as an avenue for the Philippine Government to address the following national concerns:

1. To encourage private sector participation in the financing, construction, operation and maintenance of infrastructure and power projects, the lack of which is considered one of the overriding barriers to economic growth in the Philippines;
2. To reduce the fiscal burden on the part of the Government of the Philippines (GOP) by making the private sector an effective partner and/or participant in infrastructure building; and
3. To effectively encourage the inflow of foreign capital financing, technology and expertise, especially in the operation of major and capital-intensive infrastructure projects.

Recognizing the need to put in place an environment conducive to private sector's entrepreneurial initiatives RA 6957 was enacted. RA 6957 initially sought to provide the necessary policy framework and clear-cut implementation of BOT/BT projects. In the course of its implementation, it became evident that further changes in some provisions were necessary in order to further stimulate private sector participation. In line with the government's commitment to a liberal and facilitative socioeconomic environment, amendments to the Law were introduced through RA 7718 which was enacted on 05 May 1994. The amended BOT Law allows more types of infrastructure projects to be implemented by the private sector. In addition to traditional projects like power plants, highways, ports, airports and similar projects, new ones have been added. These are solid waste management, information technology networks and database infrastructure, education and health facilities, tourism projects, government buildings, and other projects that may be approved by the President of the Philippines.

The scope of the amended BOT Law has also been liberalized and widened. Nine variations of contractual arrangements that go beyond building, owning, operating and transferring are now allowed. These new features include leasing, contracting, adding, rehabilitating, developing adjacent areas, etc.

Unsolicited project proposals may be accepted on a negotiated basis subject to certain conditions. Furthermore, direct negotiation shall be resorted to when there is only one complying bidder. This was not allowed before.

The amended BOT Law likewise now allows government appropriation and/or access to ODA of up to 50 per cent of project cost for projects with difficulty in sourcing funds. The Implementing Rules and Regulations of the amended BOT Law also requires that the economic viability indicators of the project shall be evaluated against a hurdle rate of 15 per cent.

Rate setting will be deregulated for projects which are bid out. On the other hand, the appropriate regulatory agencies will approve the rates for negotiated contracts. In the case of negotiated contracts for public utility projects which are monopolies, the rate of return base will not exceed 12 per cent.

Investment incentives contained in the Omnibus Investment Code as well as direct cost-sharing and credit enhancements may be extended to projects as necessary. Considering the overwhelmingly favourable reactions to the new BOT law, we are very optimistic that more private investors will signify their interest to invest in infrastructure projects in our country.

Public Service Law of 1936

The Public Service Law defines "public utilities" as including:

1. Roads and thoroughfares
2. Railways and Urban Rail Mass Transit
3. Distribution (not production) of Electricity and Gas
4. Water Distribution and Sewerage Systems
5. Telephone Systems
6. Wireless Broadcast Stations
7. Any common carrier, either for freight or passenger.

Proposed amendments to the Public Service Law are now pending in Congress which seek to remove the following activities from being classified as "public utilities":

1. Domestic messenger and parcel delivery services
2. Shipyards, marine railways, marine repair shops, wharves or docks
3. Ice plants and ice-refrigeration plants
4. Irrigation systems
5. Warehouses
6. Airships within the Philippines;

- The Foreign Investments Act of 1991;
- The Omnibus Investments Code of 1987 and
- The Investment Priorities Plan.

The Foreign Investments Act identifies the areas where foreign investors can enter while the Omnibus investments Code identifies the kind of fiscal incentives that may be availed of by investors under certain conditions. The Investment Priorities Plan identifies the areas in which these incentives can be availed of. It is drawn up annually.

There are pending proposals in Congress to amend the Foreign Investments Act and the Omnibus Investments Code to further liberalize the entry of foreign investments into the country, including national treatment of equity investments put in by multilateral financing agencies.

The General Banking Code

Sections 111 and 112 of the General Banking Code establishes a single-borrower's limit of 15 per cent for Philippine banking institutions. This means that a Philippine bank cannot lend out more than 15 per cent of its capital base to any single entity.

This could have the effect of restricting domestic term loans to large BOT infrastructure projects. However, these projects would have to be very large, as the single borrower limit for the top five commercial banks is between five hundred million and one billion pesos per bank.

Executive Order No. 215

Executive Order No. 215 is the legal basis for tapping private sector power generation prior to the more expansive BOT Law. It is noteworthy for two reasons:

1. It allowed the private sector to participate in the generation of power.
2. It gave the National Power Corporation the authority to develop the implementing rules and regulations. In particular, NPC was given the leeway to determine (a) process of bidding and awarding of projects, thus allowing them to avoid-to some degree-the lengthy approval process for BOT projects, and (b) credit enhancements it could give in order to make the project more attractive to the private sector.

Local Government Code

The Local Government Code encourages the participation of the private sector in local governance, particularly in the delivery of basic services, to ensure the viability of local autonomy as an alternative strategy for sustainable development.

Government Commitment, Support and Riskmanagement

The critical challenge facing the government is to constantly monitor, improve, and refine policy measures and general guidelines when and where required. This is necessary to motivate and enable interested parties to take a more competitive form under a global climate of rapid change.

To encourage further private sector participation, the government has maintained its open-mindedness and receptiveness to suggestions on how to improve the process, e.g. possible amendment of the IRR of the amended BOT law to remove sources of irritants and bottlenecks and to resolve conflicts with other laws. In this regard, there is an inter-agency goverment committee that can be convened anytime there is a need to review or revise the IRR.

The country has come a long way since the path of liberalization was taken in developing the infrastructure crucial to the country's industrialization. Having put in place institutional measures to open up the sector to competition, coupled with a market demand projected to increase in size in the future, the government has succeeded in stimulating significant investment in the sector.

Since the adoption of policies geared towards a more liberal business environment, many foreign and local industry observers agree that the Philippine market is increasingly competitive, e.g. in telecommunications, power, transportation. These are on top of what the country now offers, e.g. political stability, an investor-friendly legal framework, free market for foreign exchange and guaranteed repatriation rights.

Bidding Procedures

In line with its effort to achieve economy and efficiency in the implementation of public infrastructure projects, the government formulated in 1978 and in 1987 a standard set of rules and regulations for civil works and consultancy contracts, respectively, with the aim of: a) minimizing project cost through the adoption of sound practices in contract management; b) promote a healthy partnership between the government and the private sector in furthering national development; and c) enhance the growth of the local construction and consulting industries.

The government's bidding procedure generally advocates for an open competitive selection process. However, it also allows negotiated contracts under exceptional circumstances such as in times of emergencies or where there is lack of qualified bidders.

Foreign contractors/consultants may participate in the bidding of projects provided that they comply with the documentary requirements stipulated in the rules and regulations. In cases of consultancy contracts, foreign consultants are required to associate themselves with Filipino consultants in the interest of bringing about the transfer and introduction of new technologies into the country.

The government's bidding process is similar to that of foreign lending institutions like the World Bank, ADB and OECF except for some extra features/provisions which are basically designed to address unique local conditions.

Following hereunder are the steps in the procurement of consulting services for government infrastructure projects. A flowchart of the process is presented in Annex 4.

1. Announcement of the project. The requirements for consulting services is announced for at least two (2) times within a period of not more than two (2) weeks in at least two (2) newspapers of general circulation. Copies of the announcement are also posted in any conspicuous place in the agency concerned.
2. Issuance of qualification statements to interested consultants. Only those consultants who express their desire to offer their services for the work contemplated are included in the long list and requested to submit prequalification statements.
3. Preparation of the short-list of consultants. The pre-qualification statements are evaluated by the agency concerned to determine the short list of consultants. The following are considered in drawing-up the short list of consultants: applicable experience of the consultant, qualification of personnel to be assign to the project, and current work load relative to capacity.
4. Issuance of invitations to the short-listed consultants to submit proposals. The invitation generally includes the Terms of Reference, information required to be submitted by the consultants such as its experience and capability/current work assignments, criteria and system of rating the consultants, etc.
5. Evaluation of technical proposals. As a general rule, the two envelope-two stage procedure is adopted whereby the short-listed

consultants are requested to submit their technical and financial proposals in two (2) separate sealed envelopes. The first stage involves the evaluation and ranking of the consultants' technical proposals vis-à-vis certain predetermined criteria. Once the rankings of the consultants' technical proposals have been established and approved by the appropriate authority, the first-ranked firm is then invited for negotiation and their financial proposal opened in their presence (second stage). The first-ranked firm's financial proposal shall be the basis upon which negotiations shall be conducted to arrive at a fair and reasonable contract amount. Should negotiations with the first-ranked consultant fail, the financial proposal of the second-ranked consultant shall then be opened and negotiations conducted, and so on until an acceptable agreement with a consultant is reached.

6. Preparation of Agreement/Contract. The Agreement/Contract is prepared after negotiations with the selected consultant had been finalized. The contract includes, among others, the scope and cost of services, method of payment, obligations of the consultant and agency concerned, and the list personnel to be involved in the project.
7. Approval of Agreement/Award of Contract. The Head of the agency shall approve the contract. In case of foreign-assisted projects, the agreement is submitted to the financial institution for concurrence.
8. Issuance of notice to proceed. After the contract had been approved, the agency concerned issue the notice to proceed to the selected consultant.

For civil works contracts, following hereunder are the procedures adopted by the government. A flowchart of the process is presented in Annex 5.

1. Announcement of the project. The project is advertised for at least three (3) times within a period of not less than two (2) weeks in at least two (2) newspapers of general circulation. Copies of the announcement are also posted at any conspicuous place in the agency concerned.
2. Issuance of qualification statements to prospective bidders. The agency concerned provides the prospective bidders with the notice to pre-qualification to guide them in evaluating their capabilities and decide whether or not to participate in the bidding.

3. Pre-qualification of contractors. In the evaluation of the qualification statements, both the technical capability and financial capacity of the contractor is considered. The technical capability of the contractor is gauged by the extent of his relevant experience, suitability of available construction equipment and adequacy of his proposed organization and personnel. The financial capacity of the contractor, on the other hand, is based on his ability to obtain a credit line statement from a reputable bank or financing institution licensed by the Central Bank of the Philippines.
4. Issuance of plans, specifications, proposal book forms and draft contract to pre-qualified bidders. The agency concerned issue the tender documents to the prospective bidders in accordance with the schedules stated in the rules and regulations. For projects costing less than P= 1.0 million, for example, the tender documents are issued to the bidders 15 days before the date of bidding. For projects costing more than P= 100.0 million, the tender documents are issued 90 days before the date of bidding.
5. Submission, opening and abstracting of bids. Bids are submitted in two (2) sealed envelopes. The first envelope contains, among others, the manpower schedule, construction schedule, equipment utilization schedule, and construction methods. The second envelope contains the bid prices, detailed estimates and cash flow by quarter.
6. Evaluation of bids. A bid which does not comply with the conditions of the bid documents is rejected by the agency. At the time of the opening of bids, there should be at least two (2) competing bidders. In case there is only one bidder, the agency can either consider the lone bid for award provided it does not exceed the approved agency estimate (AAE), or return the lone bid unopened and conduct a rebidding thru sealed canvass of at least five (5) qualified contractors.
7. Award/Approval of contract. No award of contract is made to a bidder whose bid price is higher than the allowable government estimate (AGE) or the AAE, whichever is higher, or lower than 70 per cent of the AGE. The AGE is equal to one half the sum of the AAE and the average of all responsive bids. Responsive bids pertain those bids not higher than 120 per cent of the AAE or lower than 60 per cent of the AAE. The head of the agency shall approve the contract.

12

Tourism Cooperation

More on Cooperation in Tourism

Statistical support is one of the major tools needed for a better understanding of the tourism sector. The finalisation of a new Statistical Regulation in the field of tourism is in an advanced state and it is expected to enter in force in 2010. At the same time, the Commission, together with Member States and in collaboration with OECD and the World Tourism Organisation, is promoting the introduction of TSA (Tourism Satellite Account) in Member States. TSA is a statistical accounting framework in the field of tourism to measure the goods and services according to international standards of concepts, classifications and definitions, which allow valid comparisons from country to country in a consistent manner. A complete TSA contains detailed production accounts of the tourism industry and their linkages to other industries, employment, capital formation and additional nonmonetary information on tourism.

Enhancing the visibility of European tourism is another of our main goals. To draw attention to the value, diversity and shared characteristics of European tourist destinations, and to promote destinations where the economic growth objective is pursued in such a way as to ensure the social, cultural and environmental sustainability of tourism, the European Commission is running the European Destinations of Excellence (EDEN) preparatory action. Some of the main aims of such a preparatory action are enhancing visibility of the emerging European tourist destinations of excellence, especially the lesser known, and creating awareness of Europe's tourist diversity and quality. The Commission also intends highlighting the richness and diversity of European tourism through its Calypso programme, which seeks to facilitate tourism exchanges in Europe.

Finally, again in the direction of cooperation with other actors of the tourism sector, and with the aim of strengthening European tourism, the Commission proposed an operational framework through the organisation of a number of events. Such events are deemed important in order to improve the interface between European tourism stakeholders. One of the measures provided are an annual European Tourism Forum, which normally brings together more than 300 leading representatives from the tourism industry, civil society, European Institutions, national and regional authorities dealing with tourism, and international organisations to discuss the challenges of the sector. Every year the Forum focuses on specific themes of interest.

E-Collaboration: A Universal Key to Solve Fierce Competition in Tourism Industry?

The development of Internet technology and the dramatic spread of its use throughout the world in the past decade brought business into a new stage, a stage known 'e-time'.

Before 'e' time, tourism industry players mainly maintained workable vertical relationships with its suppliers and their sales force (Appleman & Go 2002). The walls of each company's office were not just physical bricks; they were also the spiritual boundaries isolating the company from its horizontal neighbours who do similar business. While drivers in the business environment such as globalization, regionalization, information technology and e-commerce decreased barrier effect of brick walls (Timothy 2003). Consumers are becoming more experienced. Competition between organisations by throwing bricks to each other can no longer lead to success (Stern & Hicks 2000). This article starts with relevant definitions of e-collaboration and the description of the change in the business environment and then analyses these motivations, advantages and the problems of e-collaboration in the tourism industry. Multinatinational enterprise (MNE) and small business/tourism organisations are tending to adapt e-collaborative strategies. Gartner (2001) predicts that 70% of firms will have a coherent e-business strategy within a year. However, this is not a universal key if being used improperly. Addressing the theories of collaboration and e-business in other industries and trying to find a way of applying them to today's tourism industry players to create and guide thriving e-collaboration strategies is the main aim of this article.

E-collaboration bridges national borders and continents. E-collaboration and collaborative systems bring geographically dispersed teams together, supporting communication, coordination and cooperation. Indeed, it has become a cornerstone of global competition (Doz & Hamel 1998; Timothy 2003). It is a logical and timely response to the quick change in the economic and IT world and split organizations into two competition divisions: one for the global market, one for the future development.

Relevant Definitions

E-Business

This field of activity is relatively young and evolving rapidly, and as such no single definition of the term has become accepted as the universal norm (Clegg *et al* 2001). E-business was initially limited to the financial transactions online. It was coined with a meaning of conducting business on the Internet by IBM back in 1997 as part of an advertising campaign. For the purposes of this essay, both business-to-business (B2B) and business-to-consumer (B2C) transactions and relationships are considered. Thus, e-business here is defined as the transaction of commercial activities on global open networks between an ever-increasing number of corporate and individual participants (Richmond *et al.* 1998).

Collaboration

According to Cambridge Advanced Learner's Dictionary (2003), collaboration means working jointly with others or together for some purpose or achieve the same thing. Words like strategic alliance, collaborative partnership, collaborative form, collaboration, partnership, and coalition are interchangeable utilized . E-collaboration is an extension from the old collaboration type in e-age. It is Internet-based cooperation/collaboration with exchange of information, materials, or cash among entities .

The Changing of the Business Environment

Information is the "lifeblood" of tourism. Since the tourism products can not be pre-tested, the access to accurate, timely and relevant information is therefore essential to consumers. Before the spread of Internet, telephone, fax, letter and face-to-face meeting were the main communication channels between suppliers and buyers. The generation, gathering, processing, application and communication of information was time consuming (O'Connor *et al* 2002).

Consumers almost completely relied on representation and description to make an appropriate choice (Go and Pine 1995). Intermediaries played a very important role between disciplines and end-customers. Collaborations between horizontal tourism players were very rare.

While technology can act as a 'creator, enhancer, focal point and/or destroyer of the tourism experience' as O'Connor (2002 p332) indicated, the development of IT brought the business world a revolution of electronic. Business-related "dotcom" Web sites emerged all over the virtual world. A matching between buyer and seller was set up. Andy Grove, the chairman of Intel, predicted in 1999 that, within five years, all companies will be Internet companies or they will not exist.

As web-based technologies expanded, core back-office processes, including order management, procurement, logistics, financial management, and supply chain planning was incorporated (Gould 2004). The barriers and distance competitors were reduced. Information flows among the client, intermediaries and each of the suppliers involved in serving the client's needs. New relationships with customers, new relationships between competitors and suppliers and buyers, new business process, new information and communications technologies came into being and empowered employees are required.

Motivations for Collaboration

Globalization and regionalisation are emerging worldwide. This macro environment stimulates the development of IT; and the development of IT enhances the integration inversely. Hastings (1993) states that the need for 'quality, as well as the high costs and complexity of servicing global markets' is forcing organisations into collaborating with their clients, their suppliers and with their competitors in many new ways.

The power of IT allows information to be managed more effectively, and transported worldwide almost instantly (Frew and Pringle 1995). The physical boundaries between brick walls or territories can't block the information flow. Smaller countries, organisations, in particular, can benefit by gaining access to a much larger market than that in their own territories; large economic regions become available to them for sale of their goods and services (Timothy 2003).

From horizontal view, market is limited, the more ratio one company occupies, the less other companies occupies. But competitors in well-matched strength always exist. It's time for antagonists to begin to use the bricks to build something useful instead of throwing bricks at one another . Collaboration offers a way to pursue business development, revenue increase, cost reductions in promotions and marketing and enhance market image and reputation (Fyall & Spyriadis 2003). A partnership of collaboration is a tailored business relationship based on mutual trust, openness, shared risk and shared rewards that yields a competitive advantage, resulting in business performance greater than would be achieved by the firms individually.

In an executive report, META pointed that by 2001/02, high-performing enterprises will recognize the value of business collaboration to achieve flexibility, speed, and agility. By 2004, more than 30% of G2000 companies will have developed a collaborative competency and will use collaborative tools to extract superior value from their collaborative efforts (Passori 2000).

Types of Collaboration

There are three types of collaboration: vertical relationships, horizontal relationships and diagonal relationships. This is a classifying according to the different structure of collaboration and could suit *International Business Research* October 2008

Vertical Relationship

Vertical relationship is the collaboration between suppliers and buyers e.g. travel operator and travel agency, travel agency and hotel. There is growing emphasis in modern supply chain literature on the importance of forming collaborative strategic partnerships with select trading partners . The official site of Scotland's tourism board is one example. The links to travel agencies which sales its products can be found in this website. It offers you the service of journey booking while not owning a travel agency itself.

Horizontal Relationship

Horizontal relationship is the collaboration between competing companies selling similar products or services, e.g. hotel and hotel . In tourism industry, horizontal collaboration happens more often than other two types with the spread of IT. This collaboration can be either inter-organisational which refers to licensing, franchising, sub-contracting and etc under one brand or alliance between different brands. Whichever horizontal collaboration the tourism industry players join, they are separated organisations by law. Orbitz.com, for instance, was initially started by five airlines-American, Continental, Delta, Northwest and United to serve customers better and only sell flight tickets of these five owners. To gain more "click", it encourages other airlines to sell their tickets through its website. At the same time, other airlines are seeking for multi-distribution channels to explore market. Now Orbitz's inventory has hundreds of choices of airlines for customers.

Marriott International has just signed a deal with Hotels.com. As part of the agreement, Marriott will have a direct link to the websites from its own central reservation systems. It will make its inventory of hotel rooms available to the sites.

Diagonal Relationship

Diagonal relationship is the relation where companies in different industries and sectors are working jointly. It's a dynamic structure and is growing follow closely to the other two types of e-collaboration (Brenner 2004).

Grandheritage.com can illustrate this type of collaboration. Grandheritage.com is an online hotel booking website, but it has collaboration with Currency Converter, BBC Weather, Multi Map, British Tourist Authority (a site for events & general information), British Airports Authority, London Transport, UK Genealogy (a site for tracing UK ancestry), Festivals.com (festivals and events in Europe), BITOA (The British Incoming Tour Operators Association), (suppliers of water to hotels), and (low cost car hire). The collaboration is not just limited to the vertical supplier and buyer's relationship and horizontal relationship with competitors, but extends to other industries.

The Influence of E-Collaboration

Advantages

Wider market and better competitive position. Collaborative partners share common reservation system and customer databases. In this way tourism destinations, hotels, travel agencies and etc. can access to worldwide markets despite of the territory boundaries (Fyall & Spyriadis 2003). The collaborated members can market as a whole sometimes (Teye 2000). Hospitality industry is witnessing the growth of technology-based collaboration best. An example of this is the Hilton International (UK based unit of Ladbroke Plc.) and Hilton Hotel Corporation (US based) alliance.

These companies have entered into a relationship that involves sharing customer databases throughout the world. According to Hilton, the objective of this collaboration is to grow the brand to be able to compete on a global basis. Hotels.com is another good example for global market. It is one of the fastest growing hotel booking sites on the Internet. It offers savings of up to 70% off regular hotel rates in some of the world's most popular and expensive cities.

What's more, the collaboration of the hotels guarantees traveller a room when cities are sold out. As Bruce Wolff, Marriott's senior vice president of sales and e-commerce strategy, said on Marriott's collaboration with expedia and hotel.com:' We want to ensure the travelers have access to Marriott properties no matter how they prefer to plan and book travel.'

This advantage is especially helpful to small and medium size tourism industry players. Collaboration through Internet enables them to source components and raw materials so as to widen their market and reputation (Gani 2001). E-collaboration offers the opportunity for companies to increase the numbers of potential suppliers, and for smaller companies to reach a larger trans-national client base (Leadbetter 1999) 'Through a close collaboration between hotels, restaurants, tourism and commerce, we can cater for anyone who wants to arrange their meeting or conference in Kristianstad or the surrounding area,' says Gunnel Ahlbeck of Turism Kristianstad (2003). When cross-border collaboration and cooperation in tourism promotion are formed, the global competitive advantage is likely to increase (Timothy 2003).

Value Creation

Collaboration between competing firms may create favourable conditions for "inter-partner" learning (Dussage *et al.* 1999), allowing one firm to acquire capabilities that they lack from a partner, particularly when partners from different geographic region. Each partner will bring its product markets, technology, and experience to the collaborated group. A high-speed search and accurate results can be offered to customers with the sharing resources contributed by collaborators (O'Connor *et al* 2002). This caters for the increasing business-to-business or business-to-consumer demands for products and services with a wider resource of combination of each partner's limited resource.

What's more, value creation and its role in business network relationships is becoming an area of increasing interest (Blankenburg-Holm *et al.* 1998 in Bernal 2002) and enables firms to focus on combining internal and external resources in innovative ways.

Inventories Reduction

The closer, long-term, collaborative buyer-supplier relationships, i.e. partnerships, are enabled through seamless integration and transfer of information up and down the chain (Kolluru & Meredith 2001). Strategic SCM can lower inventory risks and costs, improve customer service and satisfaction, increase customer retention and more effective marketing. (Horvath 2000) As distributors enter the same web, data on sales and inventories are received; forecasts are much easier to be made. With the forecasting and planning ability's improvement, collaborators will get benefit to know what to do next clearly. For example, Depkon's Hilton properties use a software application called Birch Street that manages the procurement and inventory at the property level. It allows the properties real-time access to suppliers' inventory. The sound e-collaboration makes the hotel managers focus on the day-to-day issues more and saves the hotel 8 percent to 15 percent (Higley 2004).

Better Communication

E-collaboration enhances inter-organizational relationships. Though reduction in face-to-face contact and an increase in the opportunities for dispersed or paperless offices and people-less factories that have proved to be largely unfounded (Clegg et al 2001), e-collaboration does allow managers/staff to share information dynamically and far more quickly than previously. It enhances the gain from face to face meetings and other types of communication.

Fewer Cultural Conflicts

As more collaborations are made, defining company culture is critical, especially when companies come from different countries. The social cultural environment will impact the company. While e-collaboration is based online, whether to customers or managers, it is more virtual than physical. Communicating while not working and meeting face to face day to day. Emotion and behavior interference will be less .

Key Problems

Collaboration offers a way out of the fierce competition but it is not a universal key. Without good understanding and preparation, e-collaboration can also damage business. Not all collaboration or alliances or cooperation are successful.

America's Tribune newspaper (2003) has reported a trend of hotel operators breaking away from their franchises and going it alone without big brand backing. The following are several key problems exist in e-collaborative relationship.

Unequal Resource Commitments

Perhaps the most critical thing in collaboration is the degree to which the partners' contributions are committed and complementary (Stern & Hicks2000).

Timothy (2000) pointed that the commitment on the part of individual nations to giving up absolute control in some areas is lack, because national interests nearly always outweigh cross-national interests when he talked out the collaboration between countries. It is a common problem throughout the world where collaboration is being undertaken no matter it is a horizontal collaboration, vertical collaboration or diagonal one.

Unbalanced Management and Power

Unbalanced management and power results from unequal commitment. But no party wants to be at a disadvantage in cooperation. The unbalanced situation sometimes leads to inefficient if dealt wrong.

Different Maintenance of Quality Standards between Partners

Every tourism industry player has different internal needs for different technological and organizational systems and external needs for connectivity and shareability of messages, data, applications and processes (Stern & Hicks 2000). But once collaborated, the reputation and services of each collaborator are bounded together. One comparatively worse website or service will lead to the poor impression of the whole group to customer. And also because of the collaboration of huge database, the difficulty of maintenance is increasing (Bernel *et al* 2002).

Losing the Opportunity for a Creative Solution

Problems are sometimes unavoidable no matter what product and what life stage. When an enterprise meets conflicts or problems entering a market, it might find its own way to solve itself. E-collaboration may need certain managers to negotiate with those who have been in the market and link their websites and database to bridge the markets.

Suggestions and Conclusions

E-collaboration is a very vital strategy for tourism industry players in today's business world. Vertical and horizontal e-collaboration is more often to see in tourism industry than diagonal collaboration. But this type of e-collaboration will be a trend when vertical and horizontal collaboration have developed well. Cooperation between different industries will enhance each other and help each industry's development. Smartly using this strategy can avoid the fierce competition between hotels, travel agencies and travel operators. As discussed above, e-collaboration can help to widen market, enhance competitive position, add value, reduce cost, bridge communication and lessen cultural conflicts. It is a great strategy more SME to compete with stronger competitors. But Zaid Ismail (2003), senior director of the National Chamber of Commerce and Industry of Malaysia (NCCIM), said though many small and medium size companies have their own websites, not all of them are aware of the benefits of e-business and fully utilize this tool.

Either to small business/tourism organisations or multinational enterprise, to take successful e-collaboration strategy to compete in the global market, the following suggestions should be considered:

- Choose your partner carefully. Every enterprise should know clearly its own strengths and weaknesses before collaborating, and then smartly look for partners that can fit its wants.
- Necessary information technology. The information that an organization communicates with its supply chain partners is among the most critical of its assets. Powerful, integrated collaborative technology is the backbone of an e-collaboration (Vlachopoulou and Manthou 2003). Protection must be provided against external threats and from internal abuse (Kolluru & Meredith 2001). The data that is shared between the partners and customers engaged in these different types of relationships varies widely in its criticality, thus requiring different levels of security.
- Managing the balance of power and dependence. Normally a partner who brings differentiating contributions of a more sustainable nature — such as a leading brand— will enjoy a more sustained influence. And the smaller partner is comparably more dependent. The dependence comes from commitments. As the commitments are irreversible, more specific commitments should be done so that every partner is very clear about its role and contribution, for example, the service standard, price, credit policy, service level performance, response time, image and etc. The trust between partners should be well set up as the basis of enduring collaborative relationships.
- Monitoring the quality. Quality is the life core in any industry. Service, price, credit policy, response time, and legal issue

warranties and so on detailed things should also be considered carefully. Online service and face-to-face service should be both monitored. Keeping a sustainable good quality can enhance customer's loyalty and then raise the company's reputation.

- Hiring intelligent and empowered employees. Managing e-collaboration will be more difficult than traditional management activities, as the systems become potentially more complex, more tightly coupled, and increasingly involve complex interrelations between people, organizations and technology (Timothy 2003). Companies need more than just good technology to make the most of the Internet (Cairncross 2000).

Evaluation can also not be forgotten while using e-collaboration strategy. Individually, jointly and publicly evaluation all are important to keep the process on its way to success.

This paper addresses the relevant theories on e-business and internet to the specific tourism industry. But as time and resources are limited, no particular case study is offered to support the researcher's ideas. E-trading is the industry witnesses the technology information development first and reacts first. The theories and practice in this industry can be studied more to contribute to tourism. A further research of comparing and analysing the similarities and differences between these two industries, especially the e-market place and online travel agencies can be carried out. What's more, the research of the trend of diagonal e-collaboration in tourism industry is also worth researching.

Interorganisational Collaboration in Tourism

Collaboration between organisations involved in the tourism industry is a widely established practice. Many of the benefits of such participation have been widely reported. For example, organisations have been known to co-ordinate their activities to cope with the turbulence and complexity of their environments, to solve environmentally-related problems, and to enhance sustainable development. Forming such relations, however, is not a simple process.

Frequently, difficulties are confronted. These difficulties derive from the complexity of the 'industry' for it actually involves a collection of businesses, from different sectors, all marketing travel-related services (Leiper, 1990). These tourism organisations, while diverse, are interdependent. This means that any developments or changes in one industry or firm will, in turn, affect another to a greater or lesser degree.

To clearly understand the characteristics of this industry, Leiper (1979) suggested that we should view it as a system. This conceptualisation is laudable as it captures the highly interdependent nature of organisational relationships in tourism. Implicit in this systems explanation is the need for close organisational coordination if tourism activities are to succeed. Leiper (1979: 404) explains:

The behavioural element, (1) tourists, are represented leaving (2) generating regions, travelling to and staying in (3) destinations, and returning home. The tourist industry element is represented within all three (4) geographic elements. Also symbolic is the representation of part of the tourist element outside the (5) industrial element, signifying the partially industrialised characteristics of the process.

Propositions about Collaboration Environmental Forces

Growth in Tourism

Collaborative marketing was developed to take advantage of growth opportunities and in an attempt to gain sufficient return on investment for stakeholders in tourism development.

Demand Uncertainty

Any problem domain, such as demand uncertainty, of concern to all stakeholders that cannot be satisfactorily managed by a single organisation, will lead to the formation of collaborative marketing.

Growth of Tourism Organisations

The growth of any tourism organisations or associations will facilitate the development and/or initiation of larger-scale collaborations in tourism destination marketing.

Motives

Perceived Benefits : Collaboration will not occur unless two conditions are satisfied: (a) stakeholders share at least one common interest in relation to the proposed collaboration and (b) they recognise the individual and mutual benefits of being involved in collaboration.

Perceived Interdependence

Collaboration in tourism destination marketing requires a recognition of the high degree of interdependence. The formation of any collaboration is enhanced by an initiator or convenor who emphasises the shared responsibility of all stakeholders as well as the potential negative effects of a lack of collaboration in marketing destinations.

Extendedness of a Relationship

Stakeholders will be motivated to collaborate by their expectation of extendedness in a future relationship.

Commitment

Collaboration will require a certain degree of commitment between a firm and its partners.

Legitimacy

An organisation's motives to gain future recognition from other stakeholders is positively related to their decision to participate in collaborative marketing activities.

Trust

Collaboration will be enhanced when stakeholders have trust and/ or confidence of the tourism association's ability to market the destination as a whole.

Conditions

Organisational Factors

Organisations with a small budget will collaborate where their budget allows them room to manoeuvre.

Problem Domain

Domain focus and domain consensus facilitate the formation of collaboration. The degree to which this occurs is related to the degree of acceptance of other's claims to specific goals and functions.

The Referent Organisation

A convenor and/or bridging organisation are required to initiate and facilitate collaboration in tourism destination marketing. The role of the convenor is to identify and bring all legitimate stakeholders to the table.

Any effort to involve all stakeholders in the development of collaborative marketing in tourism is likely be thwarted by divergent stakeholder views.

e-Tourism

e-Tourism is a subset of Travel technology with a particular focus on the tourism industry. In June 2003, the United Nations Conference on Trade and Development, UNCTAD, established a Task Force on Sustainable Tourism for Development that proposes the use of the concept of e-tourism as part of a strategy to build sustainable and locally rooted tourism industries. The e-Tourism Initiative aims to promote ICT-driven growth through a participative strategy that includes networking and competitive collaboration for the tourism sector of developing countries.

e-tourism: An Innovative Approach for the small and Medium-Sized Tourism Enterprises (Smtes) in Korea

The definitions of tourism innovation (*e.g.* product, service and technological innovations) remains unclear, with the exception maybe of the Internet. New technologies can produce an essential contribution to tourism development.

For tourism businesses, the Internet offers the potential to make information and booking facilities available to large numbers of tourists at relatively low costs. It also provides a tool for communication between tourism suppliers, intermediaries, as well as end-consumers. OECD (2000) revealed that the advent of Internet-based electronic commerce offers considerable opportunities for firms to expand their customer base, enter new product markets and rationalise their business. WTO (2001) also indicated that electronic business offers SMEs the opportunity to undertake their business in new and more cost-effective ways.

According to WTO, the Internet is revolutionising the distribution of tourism information and sales. An increasing proportion of Internet users are buying on–line and tourism will gain a larger and larger share of the online commerce market. Obviously, the Internet is having a major impact as a source of information for tourism. However, the SMTEs are facing more stringent impediments to the adoption of new information technology, in particular, e-business. Part of the problem relates to the scale and affordability of information technology, as well as the facility of implementation within rapidly growing and changing organisations. In addition, new solutions configured for large, stable, and internationally-oriented firms do not fit well for small, dynamic, and locally-based tourism firms.

Despite these challenges, SMTEs with well-developed and innovative Web sites can now have "equal Internet access" to international tourism markets. This implies equal access to telecom infrastructure, as well as to marketing management and education. According to a UN report (2001), "it is not the cost of being there, on the on-line market place, which must be reckoned with, but the cost of not being there." It is certain that embracing digital communication and information technology is no longer an option, but a necessity. Thus, one of the most important characteristics of electronic commerce is the opportunity and promise it holds for SMTEs to extend their capabilities and grow.

Recent Research on e-Commerce in Tourism Industry

The study of e-commerce in the tourism industry has emerged as a 'frontier area' for information technology. The literature on e-commerce in the tourism industry was critically reviewed with a view to developing a framework suitable for this study. E-commerce is defined as the process of buying and selling or exchanging products, services and information via computer networks including the Internet. However, adoption of Information and Communication Technologies (ICT) is only part of the story. In particular, network access costs, dissemination of information on electronic commerce, training, skill development and human resources provide big challenges for smaller companies.

The difficulty in addressing issues of trust and confidence also makes SMTEs more vulnerable than large firms to problems linked to authentication/certification, data security and confidentiality and the settling of commercial disputes.

However, a SME Electronic Commerce Study done by APEC reported that "Small and medium enterprises are significant players in business-to-business electronic commerce, which constitutes more than 80 percent of all e-commerce activities. SMEs that can demonstrate their capabilities to use e-commerce will have a competitive advantage in the e-commerce marketplace."

Most research suggested that government plays an important role in facilitating the use of electronic commerce for the tourism industry and in increasing their ability to reap the benefits, (*e.g.* via awareness building and training programmes). Governments in partnership with the private sector should establish a more comprehensive and consistent policy approach to the tourism industry and electronic commerce, and apply evaluation mechanisms to assess what works and does not work (UN 2001, OECD, 2000, Korea Information Society Development Institute 2000, APEC-TEL 1999).

Key Factors for Successful e-Commerce for SMTEs

Research was performed to collect the secondary data regarding e-commerce for the tourism industry. Based on those data, a questionnaire was developed to get information on the challenges and opportunities faced by the tourism industry. The survey covered e-commerce activities, benefits, barriers and key success factors. It covered essentially the Korean SMTEs. SMTEs are defined as businesses that have 300 or fewer employees or sales from USD 2 million to 20 million, depending on the characteristics of business.

Benefits of e-Commerce for SMTEs

Respondents considered that the main benefits of e-commerce for tourism enterprises are 'providing easy access to information on tourism services,' 'providing better information on tourism services,' and 'providing convenience for customers'. This result implies that respondents are less aware of many other benefits of e-commerce, such as 'creating new markets,' 'improving customer services,' 'establishing interactive relationships with customers', 'reducing operating cost', 'interacting with other business partners', and 'founding new business partners'.

Barriers of e-Commerce for SMTEs

There are a number of barriers for SMTEs in adopting e-commerce in Korea. These barriers include 'limited knowledge of available technology,' 'lack of awareness,' 'cost of initial investment,' 'lack of confidence in the benefits of e-commerce,' and 'cost of system maintenance.'

These barriers also include 'shortage of skilled human resources,' and 'resistance to adoption of e-commerce.' In terms of market situation, one might also mention 'insufficient e-commerce infrastructure,' and 'small e-commerce market size'.

Factors for Successful SMTEs E-Commerce Practices

The two main factors for conducting successful e-commerce are 'security of the e-commerce system' and 'user-friendly Web interface', thus recognising that building customer trust and convenience for customers are essential to succeed. 'Top management support,' 'IT infrastructure,' and 'customer acceptance' were also considered as important factors. On the other hand, most SMTEs do not recognise the importance of 'sharing knowledge and information between SMTEs' and 'business partnerships' as e-commerce successful strategies.

Importance and Performance of SMTEs' e-Commerce

The study used Importance and Performance (IP) analysis to examine e-commerce strategies. For 'Importance' respondents indicated the importance of each of the 16 proposed factors for a successful implementation of e-commerce by SMTEs. For 'Performance,' respondents indicated how well their member economy performs regarding e-commerce, in relation to their response to 'Importance.'

Four IP categories emerge from this analysis. The 'Keep up the good work' category means that both 'Importance' and 'Performance' are high. The category 'concentrated efforts' refers to 'high importance' and 'low performance' responses. The 'low priority' category refers to 'low importance' and 'low performance' responses. The 'Possible overkill' includes 'high performance' with low importance".

Keep up the Good Work

Respondents considered the following factors as important; 'Security of e-commerce,' 'User-friendly Web interface,' 'IT (Information Technology) infrastructure,' 'Level of trust between customer and company,' 'Customer acceptance.' All factors are strongly related to consumer issues such as security and user convenience. These factors were also considered as relatively well-performed.

Concentrated Efforts

The factors in this category include 'Top management support' and 'Skilled human resources'. These factors are considered as very important for implementing e-commerce but are considered as performed insufficiently. Thus, more efforts need to focus on these factors.

Low Priority

'Government support,' 'Sharing knowledge and information between SMTEs,' 'Integration with the existing corporation,' and 'Relationship with other business partners.' received low marks in importance and performance. These factors, however, are actually critical to successful e-commerce of SMTEs. This implies that managers have limited information and knowledge on e-commerce. More information should be delivered to entrepreneurs about the importance of those factors.

Possible Overkill

'Market situation' falls in the 'Possible overkill' category. According to the survey results, managers of SMTEs utilise the Internet for market analysis (may include competitor analysis) but do not consider this factor as important. Researchers believe that this result has some discrepancy with previous reports that SMEs (Small and Medium-Sized Enterprises) usually do not use the Internet for market research.

Remainder

Three factors including 'Specific tourism products or services for e-commerce,' 'Corporation knowledge, culture, and acceptance,' and 'Internal communication' fall somewhere between 'Low Priority' and 'Possible overkill.' One factor, 'Cost of establishing and maintaining e-commerce system' is between the 'Concentrated efforts' and 'Keep up the good work' categories. These factors were assessed relatively similarly as 'low importance' and 'middle performance.'

E-Commerce Strategies for Innovation of the SMTEs

For Rayport and Jaworski (2002), e-commerce strategy should be implemented with the four critical forces: technology, capital, media, and public policy infrastructures. An infrastructure is defined as the foundation of a system. E-commerce strategies refer to these four infrastructures:

- The technology infrastructure means the technological foundation of the Internet, which enables the running of e-commerce enterprises, including the hardware of computers, servers, routers, cables, network technologies, software, and communications. Understanding technology infrastructure – and thus understanding what is and is not achievable – is essential to formulating travel and tourism's vision and strategy.
- The capital infrastructure relates to how to secure funding for an e-business and subsequently value that business.
- The media infrastructure is an important issue for all e-commerce managers because the Internet is a mass communication platform. Managers who run on line enterprises must learn to manage a staff responsible for design interface, stylistic choices, and editorial policies, and content choices associated with the new communication venue. Therefore, the e-commerce manager is now a publisher of digital content on the Web. He/she should make choices about the types of media employed (*e.g.* print, audio, video), the nature of the media, and editorial policy, including style, content, and look-and-feel.
- Finally, all of the decisions related to technology, capital, media, and strategy are influenced by laws and regulation, that is, public policy decisions. The public policy infrastructure affects not only the specific business but also direct and indirect competitors. E-commerce managers should understand both the current laws and how the laws may affect their businesses and

those around them. This paper suggests different strategies according to the e-commerce infrastructure of the business and stage of e-business development:

- Internet start-up SMTEs should adopt a business model appropriate for their own e-business objectives and environments. External service providers have great potential for them. Marketing should be done selectively. Earning a good reputation in the local market should be the top-priority. Internet start-up SMTEs can develop a strategy to access international markets directly to sell their tourism products and services.
- Established SMTEs should focus on two key strategies: 1) expanding the range of services and products and 2) upgrading their quality. They should redesign their Web sites to focus more on 'customer retention' than 'customer acquisition' to ensure quality of service. The Internet is a useful tool to reach international markets. E-partnerships between SMTEs or large firms are important. They should utilise their resource to build an e-community.

Their e-business strategies should be formulated according to their business environments. Linkage to a site of destination management organization (DMO) is critical to success. Development of an online booking system is the most important technological aspect. Various measures to overcome lack of trust and confidence of consumers should be taken, such as utilization of 'about us,' 'frequently asked questions (FAQs),' and 'call center' services.

Established SMTEs should consider e-strategy issues, including; 1) target market segments, 2) building trust and confidence of e-consumers, and 3) expanding e-commerce activities.

Implications for Tourism Policy

The role of government is very important. The key principle is that the private sector leads the market. The government should avoid creating undue obstacles to e-commerce and its aims should be to support and enforce a predictable, minimal, consistent and simple legal environment if governmental involvement is needed. Active government support to foster an entrepreneurial culture is important. Key policy agendas include; 1) improving the legal and regulatory framework, 2) moving government procurement on line, and 3) facilitating e-transformation in industry sectors.

Legal and regulatory issues should consider consumer protection, legal resource mechanisms in disputes (*e.g.* e-commerce mediation committee), intellectual property protection, and validity and enforcement of contracts. The policies cover issues such as what taxes should apply to Internet transactions, the identification and residence of users, and the problem of tax avoidance. The guidelines of international organisations such as APEC and OECD can be a basis for e-commerce laws and regulations. To support consumer trust and confidence, a programme of e-trust certification could be effective. Online government procurement and government participation in e-transformation of industry sectors should be planned and implemented in the medium-and long-term. Government support can be provided in tax reductions, monetary support, and sharing of knowledge and information between industries and research organisations.

In Korea, a pilot project aims to construct a B2B network in all key industries. The government has also implemented a 'System to Certify Venture Tourism Business,' which indirectly supports the industry. In 2001, 11 companies were selected as venture tourism businesses and can receive support and benefits. Applications for the status of venture tourism are evaluated twice a year. Most domestic software companies in Korea do not have distribution channels of their own.

Therefore, they pay a commission of almost 40% to distributors of their products. This is a major disadvantage in the competitive market. To solve this problem the government established a software cybermall. The Internet shopping mall, which opened in 1998, provides product demonstrations and the ability to purchase products electronically. The mall is linked to the sites of many vendors.

Finally, government could help the growth of e-commerce in various ways through, planning, creating the legal and regulatory framework, building capacity in information technology infrastructure, skill formation and manpower planning, and also undertaking promotional and incentive measures. The government should function as a facilitator, promoter, educator, and 'anchor tenant' for testing and pilot deployment of new applications. It is expected that OECD member countries facilitate international strategic alliances at government-to-government (G2G) and industry-to-industry (I2I) levels and help local firms to grow, regionalise and also globalise. Government can also help create markets in emerging areas at the initial stage and help remove regulatory obstacles that may impede the growth of markets and businesses. Again, the ultimate objective of the government remains the promotion of private sector initiatives in e-commerce development (Kahn, 2002).

Conclusions: Recommendations for e-Tourism Innovations

In conclusion, this paper suggests some recommendations for decision makers, entrepreneurs and practitioners in the tourism industry field, particularly for SMTEs. These recommendations are made to the Korean e-tourism market, however, they can probably apply to the tourism industries in other countries.

The government should develop a national vision, a strategic plan and policy guidelines for SMTEs e-commerce activities. The development of e-commerce strategies should involve all tourism stakeholders. The policy makers are also responsible for establishing the appropriate laws, regulations and service standards that will enable to build trust and consumer confidence.

Entrepreneurs need to adopt business models which are tailor-made for their own e-business objectives and the SMTEs environment. SMTEs can combine various e-business models. External service providers have great potential to assist SMTEs.

Stakeholders should also find ways to integrate SMTEs into industry-wide associations. This will encourage SMTEs to stop competing at the destination level, and to develop networks for mutual benefit. In line with this co-operation, they need to formulate and implement networking or strategic alliances through partnerships with other SMTEs or large firms, especially in the area of brand management, customer relationship management, and human resources management.

As regards marketing, association with e-shopping will allow SMTEs to conduct Internet-based e-commerce without bearing all the start-up costs, improvements cost, advertising and technical difficulties, which could be shared by all the merchants in the mall instead. Associations of e-shopping will provide SMTEs with the opportunity to take advantage of e-commerce systems *e.g.* interactivity, mass customisation, real time and a database of customers.

In the established stage, SMTEs may need to redesign their website to focus more on 'customer retention' than 'customer acquisition'. They should also try to develop and manage their own digital brand. Brand power is more important on line than off line because the main stage of e-business is the virtual world where consumers are more dependent on recognised brands. Finally, both the policy makers and the entrepreneurs should work together to raise awareness of e-commerce through training and education for stakeholders, employees and consumers. E-commerce cannot be implemented without empowering and enabling tourism stakeholders to take advantage of new Internet and e-commerce technologies.

Helping Developing Countries to become Autonomous

Tourism is one of the main exports of the 50 least developed countries (LDCs). But at the same time, leakages (repatriation of profits) in this sector total up to 85 percent in some African LDCs, more than 80 percent in the Caribbean, 70 percent in Thailand and 40 percent in India.

In order to minimize leakages and to promote sustainable growth and poverty alleviation, it is now essential for tourism destinations and local small and medium-sized enterprises (SMEs) to increase their autonomy, and to include all tourism stakeholders. To deal with this issue, UNCTAD has developed the e-Tourism Initiative, with the aim of helping developing countries, and particularly the LDCs, to make the most of their tourism potential.

Launched at the eleventh UNCTAD quadrennial ministerial conference in Sao Paulo, Brazil, in June 2004, the E-Tourism Initiative is part of UNCTAD's task force on sustainable tourism for development. The Initiative is part of the UNCTAD XI Information and Communication Technologies for Development Partnership. This partnership encompasses activities in the areas of free and open-source software, e-tourism, ICT policies, e-measurement, ICT indicators and e-finance.

Linking sustainable tourism and ICTs for development, the demand-driven E-Tourism Initiative will strengthen developing country capacities to promote their tourism product and dynamically match it to worldwide demand.

The Initiative focuses on the development and implementation of ICT-based tools that will help communities tap the international market by strengthening and including local institutional and human capacities in the global market and promoting local involvement and ownership.

Purpose of the Initiative

For many developing countries, and particularly the LDCs, the small economies and the island developing States, tourism provides a significant potential for poverty reduction, economic growth and development. It is often their primary source of hard currency and is also one of the largest sources of employment.

ICTs can make developing countries more autonomous and self-sufficient in constructing their own brand images and promoting their own tourist attractions. In maximizing their comparative advantage in this sector, developing countries can adjust their tourism services to suit their own development strategies and become better integrated in the world economy.

The target population for this project is composed of ministries of tourism, national tourism boards, destination management organizations, local tourism stakeholders and other relevant partners.

The immediate objective is to design, create and establish a steady e-commerce market place by identifying, promoting and integrating the providers of national goods and services with regard to international business. Other objectives are to enable destination countries to organize their tourism services, to develop new tourism products, to improve the quality of their services and foster public-private partnerships to improve the competitiveness of the sector.

A Package

The E-Tourism Initiative is structured around a tool, a method and a partnership-building approach.

The tool is a country platform aimed at helping developing countries identify, standardize, coordinate and propose tourism services in response to varying world demand.

The Initiative also provides a method for collecting the relevant information, standardizing it and disseminating it on the Internet. The aim of the method is to encourage active cooperation among partners, and learning and capacities enhancement, in order to promote sustainable development.

Partnerships will enable all concerned stakeholders to coordinate their resources and objectives. They may be formed in the private sector (private-private), in the public sector (public-public) or between the private and public sectors.

A Tool

Technically, the tool is a *web-site generator*, which is reproducible and adaptable, and which builds around a group of databases and multi-criterion search engines. This genuine decision-making, management and promotional tool will offer visibility to the destination countries in the global market place.

Designed to be inclusive, decentralized and commercial, this tool contributes to the organization of national markets by encouraging organizational and functional links between private and public entities in the sector, and allows tourism services to be promoted in accordance with countries' development objectives.

The electronic platform acts as a virtual travel agent and offers personalized information. This tool aims at increasing the online consumer rate. It has the potential to give a real boost to national growth, notably among SMEs, by shaping a national identity for destination countries. Developing countries will be able to promote their products and services and diversify their economies.

A Method

As well as providing an Internet platform, the Initiative provides a method and relevant mechanisms for collating the relevant information, standardizing it and disseminating it on the Internet.

As the approach is business oriented, it includes a corresponding generic business model, educational material, various guides and related road maps for building user skills, with the aim of strengthening national capacity in this field. The business model is adapted to conditions in the country to ensure the platform's sustainability.

A guide that gives full directions for using the portal, and special records for the various entities, operating in the sector will be produced and distributed. Each participant is responsible for its own part and is given a road map and blueprints for measuring and evaluating results. At the end of the project this informal arrangement should be firmed up and kept in operation in accordance with the associated business plan.

The success of such an initiative depends on the involvement of local entities, from the start, in taking ownership of the project and jointly defining its framework. Their responsibilities towards each other should be clearly understood, accepted and followed up. This is, in the long run, the purpose of the awareness-raising seminar planned for the start of the project.

13

Modern Tourism in New Era

Introduction: Need for Global Economic Development

The theme of the 2001 IAF Congress was "Meeting the Needs of the New Millennium", reflecting the fact that humans' most urgent need at the start of the 21st century is undoubtedly the continuation of economic growth. This is the only means by which the great majority of the world population can lift themselves out of the poverty in which they live.

The conventional definition of economic growth has been justly criticised. In order to be more useful it needs to be improved by including the preparation of national balance sheets and government accounts according to standard accounting principles, the use of factors to measure 'quality of life', the valuation of unpaid domestic and child-rearing work, accounting for environmental destruction, adjustment of market exchange rates to allow for 'purchasing power parity', and other improvements. New measures such as the "Genuine Progress Indicator" (GPI) are being developed, but they require further work before they can be relied upon.

Although economic measures may not yet be a satisfactorily precise definition of the standard of living, large-scale differences such as that between 'G7' countries with average incomes of about $20 000/yr and developing countries with average incomes of $1000 or less per year are undeniable. As a result of worldwide economic growth to date, more people live at higher standards of living than ever before; middle-class populations in many previously impoverished countries are growing rapidly; and average life spans have grown rapidly in every country in the world over the past two decades. However, this is not a cause for complacency since, thanks to unequal distribution of income and population growth, very large numbers of people still live in poverty.

The longterm effects of economic growth are impressive: in round figures, growth at 2 3% per year raises incomes by 100% in 25-35 yr, and by 1000% per century. Poorer countries growing at 7% per year can double their average incomes in just 10 yr, and grow by nearly 1000% in a single generation. However, achieving continuing economic growth in the world economy requires appropriate policies in both poorer and richer countries.

Unfortunately, governments in both democratic and non-democratic countries are continually tempted to follow policies that hinder economic growth, as analysed in depth in recent decades in the field of 'Public Choice' economics.

In particular, politicians in democratic countries can often win electoral popularity by implementing policies to 'protect' companies in difficulties. The economic effect of such policies is strongly negative: instead of flowing to new activities with good growth prospects, resources are wasted preserving economically incompetent companies that should be reorganized-thereby delaying needed restructuring of the economy.

This problem has been particularly notable in Japan where, during the 1990s, the government borrowed more than $1 trillion to support a large number of unprofitable companies. As a result there is substantial overcapacity in 'mature' industries such as construction, department stores, real estate, retail banking, car-making, steel-making, shipbuilding, distribution and others, while the number of new companies has declined substantially since 1990.

Predictably, this has aggravated the recession caused by the bursting of the economic 'bubble' of the late 1980s to become the worst recession in 50 yr-with continuing deflation, shrinking of the economy and ever-rising unemployment. In order to understand what policies would be more effective in sustaining economic growth, it is useful to understand the pattern of global economic development.

Pattern of Global Economic Development

While there are many details that are the subjects of ongoing research, the large-scale pattern of business and economic development through the 20th century is not the subject of significant dispute. One of the most fundamental underlying trends is that as poorer countries develop economically they progressively 'take over' industries in which low labour costs are a significant advantage, and export their products to richer countries. Employment in these relatively low-productivity activities is thereby lost from the rich countries. In parallel, the familiar processes of automation and improving business practices continually reduce the number of employees needed to produce a given quantity of goods and services. However, these trends have not caused rising unemployment overall because the displaced employees are reemployed in new industries which are continually being created.

The process of global economic development is thus one of continuous change, involving the decline and failure of companies as well as the birth and growth of new ones. As a consequence, for most people it is not possible to improve their standard of living without accepting change in their working lives. In addition, the timing of economic booms and recessions depends on many factors including chance discoveries leading to innovation, the whims of entrepreneurs and the vagaries of political decisions. Although economic growth can be hindered by government policies, the underlying process cannot be stopped-at least not without preventing people from trying to improve their standard of living which is not desirable. In the simplest terms, some people use their heads to work out ways of achieving the same results with less effort. This human creativity, specifically in inventing machines improving business practices (including expanding trade), and developing new popular services makes the productivity of work grow continuously, decade after decade, enabling everyone's incomes and standards of living to rise progressively.

World economic growth also requires international flexibility and agreement on rules of 'fair play'. For example, the rapid economic growth achieved by Japan from the 1960s until the 1980s caused considerable trade friction with the then more advanced countries as it changed the pattern of global specialisation-even leading the French Prime Minister Cresson to describe Japan as "France's number one enemy". Thus Japan's rapid growth depended on the richer countries' willingness to make adjustments to facilitate it, which Japan in turn is now required to show towards later developing countries.

However, as a measure of how much more adjustment in the structure of the world economy is going to be required, note that the combined populations of India and China are 20 times the population of Japan, and their average wages are just a small percentage of Japanese wages today. Consequently the adjustments in the pattern of global specialisation that will be required to accommodate the growth in these countries' shares of world trade will be proportionately many times larger than was required for Japan. The recent rapid growth of exports of clothing from both countries, and of food products, light manufactured goods and motorcycles from China, and bicycles and software from India, is just the beginning of this long process of adjustment. In principle the growth of exports resulting from such differences in labour costs will not end until average incomes in these countries reach broadly the same level as in the richer countries. (The current loss of competitiveness of certain industries in Korea Taiwan and other southeast Asian countries, as their average incomes rise relative to those in China, are examples of this process.). For humanitarian reasons, as well as from the wish to reduce friction between richer and poorer countries, we must hope that poorer countries' economic development continues successfully. But, as an inescapable corollary, to the extent that these countries' participation in the world economy grows through the 21st century, proportionately greater innovation of new industries will be required in the currently more advanced countries. If this is insufficient, unemployment will increase very substantially, and/or average incomes will fall proportionately because of inexorable competition from countries with lower average incomes.

Overall, as the human effort needed to produce the same output of goods and services becomes less and less through technical and managerial progress, and unless humans generate more total output and consume more goods and services, the total amount of work needed will fall. In this case, unless the remaining work is shared out through shortening average working hours (and reducing wages proportionately), more and more people will become unemployed. During the 20th century demand did not reach such a limit; instead, although employment in many older industries shrank drastically in the richer countries, the continuation of economic growth was stimulated by the creation of new industries.

Creation of New Industries

During the 20th century, as the number of people in economically more advanced countries who worked in such fields as agriculture, horse-drawn transport, steam-engines, mining, textiles, clothing and many other traditional activities declined, a wide range of new industries arose which re-employs those displaced. These included car manufacturing and associated activities (such as oil production, refining and distribution and road construction and maintenance), electricity generation and distribution, the film, radio, television and video industries, aircraft manufacturing and operation and associated activities (such as airport construction and operation and air traffic management), telecommunications, computers, tourism and an ever-growing range of leisure industries, including many sports activities.

During the 20th century also, government activities expanded from <10% of GNP to some 40%-though this trend has more-or-less stopped or even begun to reverse in most countries with the recent moves towards privatisation. This new trend has been stimulated by work in the field of 'Public Choice' economics, which has provided the theoretical explanation for the fact that, in general, government activities are economically very inefficient, as outlined for instance in.

It is a sine qua non for continuing economic growth in the 21st century that the rich countries continue this process of creating new industries which will employ people displaced from older industries as they progressively automate and migrate to lower-cost countries. During the 20th century this process created high-productivity employment for hundreds of millions of people around the world, and enabled many more people in developing countries to gain employment in exporting and importing businesses, thereby facilitating their economic growth. It is a key desire of companies in poorer countries today to be allowed to increase their exports to richer countries, but these are restricted by international treaties designed to protect relatively uncompetitive activities in the richer countries, in order to reduce local unemployment. For example the governments of the USA and the EU subsidise the production of many agricultural products, thereby reducing the market for imports from cheaper countries, and they also subsidise the export of agricultural surpluses, providing a second blow to poorer countries' price-competitive agricultural industries. The G7 countries also limit clothing and textile imports from poorer countries.

The development of new industries has another important aspect, namely the 'leading sector' effect: as investors anticipate the future profits that they expect to be earned in new industries, market prices of relevant companies' shares rise. This attracts more investment to these companies, helping them to grow faster, while the 'wealth effect', whereby shareholders spend their new (anticipated) wealth, spreads the benefits of expansion to other sectors of the economy.

This process was seen particularly clearly in the late 1990s in the USA, when share prices of many companies related to the major innovations of the Internet and World Wide Web grew by hundreds and even thousands of percent. As shareholders became wealthy, at least 'on paper', they increased their spending on a wide range of goods and services including houses, cars, restaurants, travel and leisure, thereby greatly stimulating the general economy. Unfortunately, in this particular case, much of the rise in share prices of 'new economy' companies was distorted in an economic 'bubble' in which investors had become unrealistically optimistic. Consequently the companies in question did not achieve the high level of profits that stockbrokers' analysts were predicting, and their share prices have since fallen steeply to date, destroying several trillion dollars of the 'wealth' that had been anticipated. (Controversy continues over the relative blame attributable to failures of business ethics, stockbrokers' conflicts of interest, auditors' standards, market regulation, media reporting, economic policy and investor caution.)

Today the need for new industries is particularly urgent because of the serious imbalances in the world economy. These include the decade-long recession that has led to the highest unemployment in Japan for 50 years, with continuing deflation and negative economic 'growth'; continuing double-digit unemployment in much of continental Europe-as well as in Russia, Southeast Asia, South America and many other countries; and a deepening recession combined with an unsustainably high trade deficit and private indebtedness in the USA. The fundamental reason for this deflationary condition of the world economy is the excess capacity in many older industries and insufficient investment in the establishment and growth of profitable new industries, which alone can create new employment for those no longer needed in mature industries. The record US trade deficit of more than $1 billion per day, first reached during the 'Clinton bubble', is a measure of many US industries' lack of economic competitiveness: toys, clothing, electrical goods, steel, televisions, personal computers and mobile telephones are just some of the industries in which fewer and fewer US-based manufacturers can match global competition. The only way in which the currently richer countries can maintain higher average incomes than currently less-developed countries is through working with higher productivity: people earning higher incomes cannot compete with people using the same technology and know-how but working at significantly lower incomes. The solution to enabling those in already rich countries to maintain or increase their standards of living while also enabling poorer countries to grow rapidly, is for companies in G7 countries to work at newer activities that poorer countries cannot yet perform. The need for this was explicitly recognised in a 2001 article in the Washington Post: "What this country needs is a really good $500 billion technology-something to reignite popular enthusiasm and the economy".

What, then, are the new industries that are expected to generate new fields of large-scale high-productivity employment? It is important to note first that commentators' inability to predict future industries is no evidence that they will not arise: almost no-one in 1902 could even imagine, let alone predict, the rise of passenger air travel, nor a fortiori its growth to its current world-changing scale. Economic commentators today predict growth in employment in many areas of the information industry (although it is important to recognise that the growth of the Internet is also eliminating work in many related fields); in biotechnology, including the use of genetic information in agriculture and medicine; and in activities aimed at environmental preservation.

Many new opportunities could also arise through restructuring the incentives created by the government-imposed pattern of taxation and subsidies. For example, in many countries employment is heavily taxed and large companies are subsidised, while the use of non-renewable resources and environmentally damaging activities are lightly taxed or even subsidised. Reversing these undesirable distortions could increase the quantity of employment in many different fields, including particularly recycling activities. An important clue to the identity of other fields in which new jobs will arise in rich countries can be found in the 'Engel coefficient', which is defined as the proportion of peoples' income spent on food (although alternative definitions based on expenditure on 'necessities' are also used). The average Engel coefficient in any country falls progressively as it develops economically; in G7 countries it is now typically <25%. Further economic growth in such rich countries depends less on providing for consumers' real 'needs' and more on satisfying their 'wants'. Broadly speaking, this explains the relatively rapid growth of leisure-related industries. Although many people feel that there are more 'important' things in which to invest than leisure industries, once average productivity reaches the level in the G7 countries, most basic needs of the society can be satisfied by a fraction of the workforce-for example agriculture typically employs <5% of the workforce. Thus there is no longer enough 'essential' work to employ more than a fraction of the population in richer countries.

One problem that arises in low-Engel-coefficient societies is that the demand for nonessential goods and services is relatively unstable, since by definition their consumption can readily be cut if necessary.

This inherent instability is seen clearly in the demand for tourist air travel which periodically falls sharply as a result of heightened concern about the risk of terrorism. Another example of this instability is that as the number of two-, three-and four-car families increases, sales of used cars can grow rapidly at times of recession, leading to dramatic falls in the demand for new cars.

The truth of the 'human condition' at the start of the 21st century is that economic development has progressed so far in the G7 countries that, if the average standard of living is to continue to rise, there is an urgent need for the growth of major new industries, most of which will probably be leisure services broadly defined. The reason for this is that in order for a new industry to grow to large scale it must provide services that will be purchased by a large proportion of the middle-class population-most of whom already possess most of the goods they 'need'.

Arguably the most significant industrial development of the 20th century was the development of passenger air travel from zero in 1900 to 1.5 billion passengers per year in 2000. Among other effects, this development has helped the hotel and restaurant industries to reach their present scale, employing some 60 million people or 3% of the world's total labour-force, and some 6% in Europe. As a pointer to the future growth potential, a survey performed in 2001 showed that the majority of middle-aged and older Japanese do not wish to purchase any more goods; the main service they wish to buy is foreign travel-which has notably been booming even during the current recession.

Until 2001 the aviation industry was predicting 100% growth over the next 20 years, although airlines' increased costs for security and customers' fears of terrorism may reduce this. However, it should be noted that tourism is already having damaging environmental impacts as a result of ever-growing numbers of tourists visiting popular destinations. It is not clear that this activity can reasonably grow by a factor of 1000% as would be necessary by the time-perhaps 2100?-when most of the world population attains a middle-class lifestyle which includes foreign travel.

Some commentators, mostly in the richer countries, take the view that most of those living in the presently poorer countries will remain poor forever. However, living standards are rising in every country, and the desire for material comfort is strong everywhere that living standards are low. While attaining a 'middle-class lifestyle' in the same form as seen today in G7 countries for a world population of perhaps 10 billion people would cause many industries-energy, construction, cars, agriculture, waste disposal-to degrade the environment severely, it must be anticipated that technological progress will greatly ease currently foreseeable problems. The application of even only presently foreseeable advances in already existing fields-such as genetic engineering and hydroponics in agriculture, energy efficiency and non-fossil (solar) energy, city planning, and Internet-based tele-commuting, to name but a few-holds such clear promise that simple extrapolations based on multiplying existing economic activity by increased population numbers without allowing for technological improvements are unrealistically pessimistic. As a result it may be that the main limits to the potential for terrestrial economic growth are political ones. It is clearly in the self-interest of the already-rich countries to try harder to help overcome these in order to reduce the friction that would be inevitable in a globalized world with continuing gross inequalities in living standards.

Whatever the longer term future, assuming that economic growth will continue for at least a few more decades, the popularity of leisure travel in low-Engel-coefficient societies raises the question of what other newer destinations people could travel to. Tourist destination development is proceeding rapidly around the world, but a new possibility which has received ever-increasing attention is passenger travel to space, or 'space tourism'. It is now clear that this idea is not only not fantasy, but it is a promising candidate to grow into a major new activity as economically valuable and socially significant as passenger air travel.

Economic Potential of Passenger Space Travel

On the 'demand side' of passenger space travel, market research performed in Japan, Canada, the USA, Germany and the UK, and summarised in has shown that there is enormous pent-up consumer demand. It is sometimes suggested that this demand is fictitious; for example a recent letter to Aviation Week & Space Technology stated: "People were already travelling in the early days of aviation-by trains boat and car. They had a reason for travelling and infrastructure to support them when they reached their destination. The aeroplane became another mode of transportation. The reasons for travelling do not exist for space. No one is visiting relatives, emigrating nor going to business meetings. And there is no infrastructure in space".

However, it is a mistake to have preconceived ideas about people's reasons for wishing to travel to space, which are obviously different from reasons for travelling on Earth. The market research referred to above shows consistently that a large proportion of the middle class population of the richer countries does want to go to space, and that their major reason for wanting to do so is to be able to look back at the Earth. The fact that all of the 400 people who have been to space to date say that it was the greatest experience of their lives probably has some connection with this immense popularity. While there is a great need for more market research, and it will remain uncertain how many people will actually travel to space until the service becomes widely available, there is no justification for denying facts shown by market research.

Furthermore, contrary to what the above letter states, there is infrastructure to support travellers-a partly assembled space station which was sufficient for the first customer, Dennis Tito, to describe the Russian section as "paradise". The second piece of infrastructure for space travellers, Mir Corp's 'Mini-Station', is due to become operational for an investment of $100 million. And as launch costs fall to a few hundred dollars/kg as passenger traffic grows, it will be possible to assemble even very large accommodation facilities in orbit at a cost acceptable to hotel companies.

On the 'supply side' of passenger space travel technical studies by the Japanese Rocket Society (JRS), Dietrich Koelle, Ivan Bekey, Bristol Spaceplanes, Buzz Aldrin and others have shown that the cost of developing the required vehicles and infrastructure would be a small fraction of the $25 billion that G7 taxpayers already pay every year for government space activities. The great potential of passenger space travel for 'space commercialisation' has also been acknowledged in reports published by Nasa; the American Institute of Aeronautics and Astronautics (AIAA) which concluded: "In light of its great potential public space travel should be viewed as the next large new area of commercial space activity"; and the Japan Federation of Economic Organisations, among other organisations.

One particularly interesting conclusion of the Nasa report namely that "generally available trips to orbit and weeklong stays in low Earth orbit hotels now can be seen as certainly feasible" gives a further indication of how large the economic impact of space tourism may become. This is because in all market research to date most people say they would like to spend several days or a week or more in orbit, rather than only a few hours or a day. Thus in addition to economical launch vehicles the demand for space tourism will also drive the construction and operation of accommodation in orbit-that is space hotels.

The only detailed professional study of the potential development of passenger space travel published to date is that of the Japanese Rocket Society (JRS) briefly reviewed in. (A large number of other papers from the pioneering JRS study are available in the library of the six major JRS reports published as of 2002 are available only in Japanese.)

According to the JRS scenario, the number of customers would reach 700,000 per year 17 years after starting the development of the ' Kankoh-maru' passenger vehicle, with a return flight price of some $20,000 per passenger.

The JRS cost estimates are in line with those of Koelle and Bekey. Extrapolating from this, when the number of guests reaches one million per year after perhaps 20 years, there will need to be accommodation for more than 10,000 people in orbit, and several thousand staff will work in orbit. Since no one has identified any other space activity that offers anything approaching this level of demand, we reach a conclusion that is still not widely appreciated-the hotel industry will probably become the largest employer in space.

From the economic point of view it is very significant that the development of orbital accommodation will lead to the participation of a wide range of associated industries, thereby greatly expanding the number of different industries involved in space activities including particularly such consumer-oriented activities as construction, interior design, hotel management, catering, fashion, entertainment and sports.

This will have the effect of bringing the economic energy of the consumer economy to bear on space activities, which are cutoff from this source of economic growth, except for certain information services.

In addition to stimulating innovation in these many different fields, the growth of space tourism in this way could also exert a 'leading sector' effect, whereby an expansionary economic influence will diffuse through the economy as direct investment and optimism lead to increased shareholder wealth. Furthermore, the increase in employment and economic growth which the development of passenger space travel causes directly in more advanced economies will in turn reduce the pressure for protection against imports from less developed economies. Such a scenario is strikingly different from the effect of existing governments' non-science space activities which, sadly, contribute very little to the economy or employment, despite the very large financial resources they consume.

Low Economic Value of Space Agencies' Activities

The desirability of initiating passenger space travel might be less if space agencies were engaged in work that was of great economic value or urgency-but they are not. Some 20% of their budgets are typically used for scientific research, including astronomy and Earth observation, which can be assumed to have value per se. However, the remaining 80%, some $20 billion per year, is used for the development of technological systems and technologies for such purposes as "space infrastructure development". The economic value of the results of this expenditure can be considered in two parts, direct and indirect.

Direct Economic Value

The definition of economic value is the present value of future profits to which an activity gives rise. Since space agencies' investment mostly does not lead to commercially profitable activities, it has far less economic value than normal business investment. The difference between commercial activities and space agencies' activities is shown in Figure below. In round figures when a company invests $1 billion it typically generates commercial sales revenues of some $1 billion per year, from which the cumulative profits over several years exceed the initial investment by a sufficient margin to satisfy investors and increase the assets of the company. (For example, $1 billion investment might generate profits of $3 billion over 10 years, from which $2 billion would be repaid to investors, and $1 billion would add to the company's assets.) By contrast, the expenditure of some $20 billion per year by government space agencies on non-science activities generates little or no increase in commercial space activities: employment in space activities is currently shrinking, rather than growing cumulatively, as would result from commercial investment on this scale.

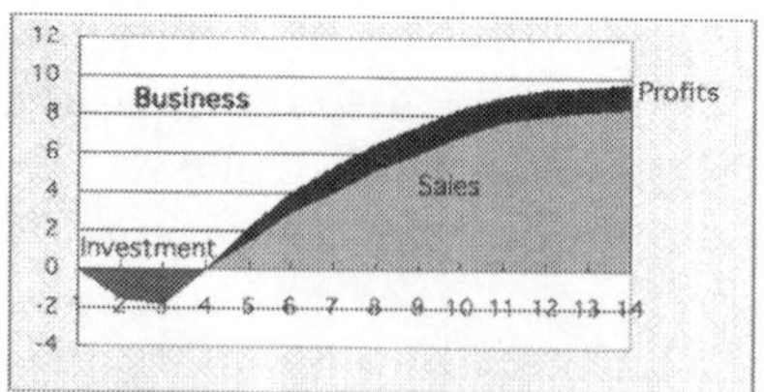

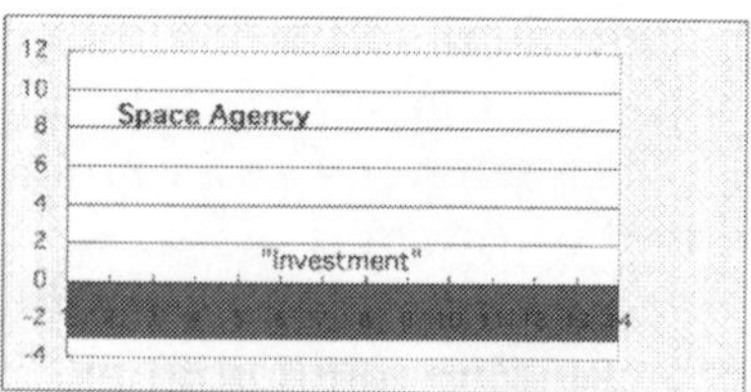

Figure: *Contrast between Business and Space Agency Activities.*

For example, the development and operation of expendable launch vehicle systems are heavily loss making; such launchers never repay their development costs, and depend in many cases on continuing government funding of periodic 'upgrades'. At the time of writing, the most recent of many articles describing the lack of demand for satellite launch services states that, of the three main launch vehicle manufacturers: "Arianespace, the only company that discloses its annual earnings, posted a loss in 2001 for the second straight year..." and predicts that because "the market could remain flat for the next 10-20 years..." one of the three companies may disappear in the anticipated 'shake-out'.

Following the conventional definition of economic value given above, the ' International Space Station' (ISS) project has very little economic value: almost no companies want to pay to use its facilities, and their total contribution will represent a small fraction of its running costs alone, let alone repaying taxpayers' investment of some $50 billion. The probability of researchers on board the station making a valuable scientific discovery must also be judged to be low: research in microgravity has been underway for more than 30 years, and there is little expectation of any major discoveries in the near term, particularly since the microgravity environment on board the station will be of low quality. This and the station's very high cost led many science research bodies, including the US National Science Foundation and the British Science Research Council, not to support the project. In 2001, as the latest step in the ISS's ever-growing cost and ever-shrinking capabilities, Nasa's announcement of further 'cost growth' of $5 billion led to it becoming the subject of a special investigation by the US government's General Accounting Office. Upon the departure of its then administrator it was decided to appoint the deputy director of the Office of Management and Budget (OMB) as his replacement. (It is perhaps worth noting that accounting is not a mysterious activity. When the managers of a $15 billion per year organisation choose to use accounting systems that allow them to be 'surprised' by cost over-runs as large as $5 billion, this is surely not accidental-it is done because it is in their economic interest to obscure the truth.

In this, space agency managers' behaviour is entirely consistent with the economic analysis of government bureaucracy pioneered by Niskanen. Because of the incentives which a bureaucratic organisation creates for its staff, they are motivated primarily to increase their budget; they have no motivation "either to know or seek out the public interest or to act in the public interest". Until the 'crisis' of 2001, successive Nasa administrators' policy of having such inadequate accounting information was successful in preserving its budget; and it seems very unlikely that Nasa or its management will suffer any significant cost-certainly nothing approaching that experienced in commercial companies when their accounts are revealed to be untrustworthy, such as the 'carnage' among 'new economy' companies in the USA in 2001-2002.)

Indirect Economic Value

Advocates of larger budgets for government space agencies frequently argue that government spending on space is much more beneficial for the economy than other forms of economic activity, thanks to the useful inventions arising from the development of space-related technology. The original source of this idea was a study performed during the 1970s by Chase Econometrics, which claimed to find such an effect. In a recent citation members of the US Congressional Research Service in 1998 wrote: "Studies by Chase Econometrics Inc., and the Midwest Research Institute in the late 1980s determined that every Nasa R&D dollar produced \$5-\$9 in economic activity".

However, it is rarely reported that when Chase Econometrics tried to reproduce their work in 1980 they concluded that: "productivity changes from Nasa R&D spending proved not to be statistically different from zero". Hertzfeld studied the issue in detail and concluded: "due to theoretical and data problems with the macroeconomic model and data sets available, this approach to finding aggregate economic returns to R&D expenditure is difficult at best, and probably impossible". Other studies of particular technologies developed at Nasa which have subsequently been used in new products are said to have shown reasonable rates of return. However, such studies do not enable any conclusions to be drawn concerning the relative value of alternative innovations that would have arisen if the same funding had been applied in other fields, such as marine engineering, electrical engineering etc.

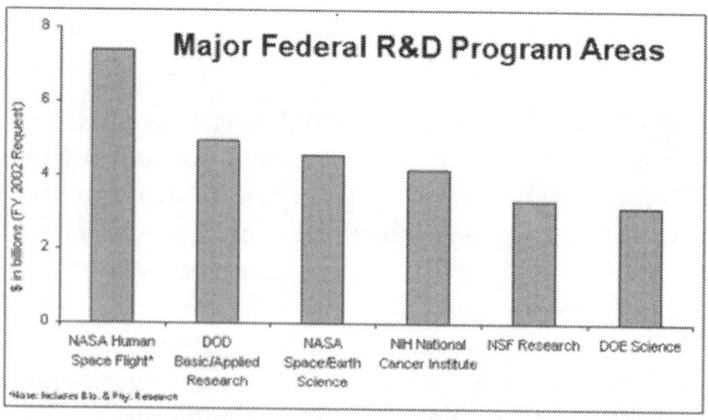

Figure: *Major U.S. Federal R&D Program Areas*

In this context the bar chart presented to the US Congressional Science Committee by Sean O'Keefe, when Deputy Director of the OMB during 2001, is of interest. This shows that Nasa's budget of $15 billion per year is twice the combined research budgets of the US National Science Foundation (NSF) and the US National Cancer Institute (NCI). Since scientific research funded by these organisations has contributed to many of the Novel prizes and scientific advances which US researchers generate, the lack of Novel prizes or major technological advances arising from Nasa's work-let alone twice the annual output of the NSF and NCI combined-is striking.

Seen in this light, the claim that US government spending on Nasa projects (including the $5 billion cost-growth during 2001) is particularly valuable for the economy is not credible. It appears rather to be a convenient myth that serves the economic interests of the government-funded space industry. Much more credible is the 'common sense' view that Nasa's expenditure of more than $100 billion during administrator Goldin's 1992 2001 tenure, during which employment in the space industry grew not at all and passenger space travel was starved of research funding (as discussed below), was a serious misuse of economic resources which could have been used much more productively on other activities.

Space Agencies' Anti-space Tourism Policy

In view of the low economic value of space agencies' current activities, it is very unsatisfactory that they are making no attempt to realise or even evaluate passenger space travel. In this the agencies do not simply show a lack of enthusiasm-they appear to have deliberately delayed progress towards this economically valuable objective, and even to have concealed valuable information from the public.

For example, the largest government space agency, Nasa, is required by US federal law to "encourage, to the maximum extent possible, the fullest commercial use of space". In its 1998 report, 'General Public Space Travel and Tourism', Nasa confirmed that space tourism is a realistic objective; that most people will be able to take a trip to space; that suborbital space travel (similar to that experienced by the first American to travel to space, Alan Shepard) is easily feasible using long-available technology; and that passenger space travel is likely to grow into a major commercial use of space. The report also included a long list of recommendations as to how to encourage this commercial use of space. However none of the recommendations in this report have been implemented, and no funding at all was allocated to advance the possibility-out of the $56 billion that Nasa has spent between that report's publication and time of writing. This behaviour is clearly contrary to Nasa's obligation to "encourage, to the maximum extent possible, the fullest commercial use of space".

It is worth noting that Nasa's 'space tourism report' can be judged the most economically valuable report Nasa has ever published, since it describes what is likely to become the largest commercial activity in space, and steps to realise it. It is therefore of particular interest that the then Nasa administrator Goldin refused to allow the report to be made available via Nasa's website for over 3 years. The author spoke to both Goldin in 1999 and then deputy associate administrator Graver in 2000 at public meetings at which they both stated (in recorded sessions) that NP-1998-03-11-MSFC would be put upon the Nasa website. However, this simple step did not take place until 2002.

Early in 2001 Nasa administrator Goldin attempted unsuccessfully to prevent the US citizen Dennis Tito visiting the international space station; his high-profile campaign was widely reported in the media. Yet the 80% popular support shown for Dennis Tito in US opinion polls provides a good indication of the great popularity of passenger travel and the misguidedness of Nasa's stance on this matter. Subsequent events during 2001 included the announcement that Goldin would not continue as Nasa administrator; testimony requested by the Subcommittee on Space and Aeronautics of the Congressional Science Committee from Nasa deputy associate administrator W. Michael Hawes on 26 June concerning Nasa's work relating to space tourism; and the appearance on Nasa's internet website of its space tourism report after over 3 years delay. Also during 2001 newly appointed Nasa Chief of Staff Courtney Stand drafted a plan for the agency under which it was proposed that Nasa would "provide commercial projects with engineering support for private-sector development of commercial manned spaceflight vehicles for commercial space tourism". (It is perhaps worth noting that the main supporter of space tourism in the US government today is the associate administrator for Commercial Space Transportation in the FAA. As the first head of the then Office of Commercial Space Transportation within the Department of Transportation Stand could be expected to take a more commercial approach.)

The selection of Nasa during 2001 as the fourth-worst-managed activity within the US government, and the recently initiated probe into its extraordinary mismanagement of the ISS project provide further testimony to the very poor value-for-money that US taxpayers receive in return for $15 billion per year-over and above Nasa's deliberate delaying of the development of passenger space travel services. The growing political disenchantment with this behaviour is reflected in the recent comment that "space spending is moving from the back burner to completely off the stove".

Other Countries' Activities

Other countries' government space agencies also have responsibility for commercialisation of space activities, but they take a similar stance towards passenger space travel. For example the European Space Agency (Esa) joined Nasa's unsuccessful attempt to prevent Dennis Tito visiting the international space station, and has likewise provided almost no funding whatsoever for research on the economic potential of passenger space travel. The senior staff of Esa and their political paymasters do not want to know about the commercial potential of passenger space travel, any more than their counterparts in Nasa and the US Congress, exactly as Niskanen's work describes.

Uniquely among G7 countries' space agencies, the British National Space Centre (BNSC) invests in neither expendable launch vehicles (such as the European Ariane) nor the international space station, since it is required to focus on space science research and activities with potential to be commercialised. However, in 2000 it was criticised by the UK Parliamentary Trade and Industry Committee for investing some 1 billion Sterling over the past decade in remote sensing systems that have generated far less commercial revenue than planned, and for actively discouraging any British government investment in research aimed at realising passenger space travel. The BNSC staff responsible for this stance, Director-General Colin Hicks, Deputy Director-General David Leadbeater and Director of Policy and Finance Alan Cooper, ignored the Committee's suggestion to perform some analysis of its feasibility. They have still provided no justification for their decade-long prevention of funding of work towards passenger space travel-which is clearly contrary to the BNSC's stated objective "to help industry maximise profitable space-based business opportunities".

Space agencies' negative behaviour towards the largest commercial opportunity in space can be termed a 'Conspiracy of Silence'. The economic reasons for their acting so strongly against the public interest in this matter are discussed in, and some of the 'cultural' reasons why the heads of space agencies unanimously refuse to permit any work to facilitate passenger space travel are discussed in the appendix to. Because of government space agencies' organisational structure making them responsible for commercialisation presents a conflict of interest with their own economic interest in survival and expansion, since it would mean handing over some of their operations to private companies.

They resolve this conflict, predictably, in their own interests by suppressing the most promising commercial application, which is ipso facto also the most threatening to their own interests. Nasa, Esa and other countries' national space agencies also exert a strong influence on the news media, being a near-monopoly source of information about space activities. This has helped to delay, though not to prevent, the growth of interest in passenger space travel in the mass media.

By contrast, Russian companies have now already profitably carried two space tourists to orbit, and are currently planning an orbiting 'mini-station' for tourism accommodation at a cost of $100 million. This is particularly noteworthy since, at the time of writing, Nasa's mobile exhibition 'Starship 2040' is publicising the idea of a small module being feasible for space tourism in 2040. 'Starship' is smaller than the first US space station 'Skylab' that operated 70 years before this date. Together with the suppression of the 1998 Nasa space tourism report until July 2001, this can only be seen as deliberate 'disinformation' designed to mislead the US public, media, government and others about the potential for space tourism. In view of the potential for passenger space travel described above, it is clearly greatly against the public interest that space agencies are knowingly resisting progress in these ways in favour of continuing their existing activities despite their low economic value.

Future Scale of Space Tourism Industry

As discussed above, meeting the needs of the new Millenniums, or at least of the early 21st century, requires the development of major new industries in the more advanced countries.

Failure in this would lead to a further rise in the already high levels of unemployment worldwide, with corresponding undesirable social effects. In view of this need for new industries to facilitate continuing global economic growth, it is interesting to consider how large a scale passenger space travel might eventually reach and how much it might ultimately contribute to world economic growth. As described above, the unique potential of passenger space travel was acknowledged by Nasa, the AIAA and the Keidanren as long ago as 1998. Since none of these organisations has made any further attempt to investigate or assess the scale of this opportunity during the four years since these reports were published (during which time government space agencies have spent a further $100 billion on economically unprofitable activities), the author outlines a simple estimate in this section.

Although some critics have claimed that space tourism will be no more than a pastime of the very rich, the basic scenario of the Japanese Rocket Society is aimed firmly at serving the middle-class market, and leads to some 700,000 passengers paying a little more than $20,000 each for return flights to orbit in the 17th year. Further growth to reach, say, 5 million passengers in the 30th year as discussed in would require an annual growth rate of some 16% which is not unrealistic by comparison with growth rates seen in other popular services. This would give a scenario like that shown in Figure.

Several comments are worth making about this figure.

(1) On this scenario, some 40 million people would have visited space by 2030, that is perhaps 2% of the middle class of that time-yet market research has shown that most middle class people (that is, more than 50%) would like to make a 'space trip'. Consequently this scenario certainly does not seem over-optimistic in relation to the potential market.

(2) The cost to taxpayers to realise this scenario would be far less than the $750 billion that they would have to pay through 2030 for space agency activities on their existing budgets, since most of the investment would come from the private sector. The economic value of the scenario, based on the difference in expected profits, would be about $1 trillion higher.

(3) Several million people would be directly and indirectly employed in related activities, and tens of thousands of people would work part-time in space as hotel staff.

(4) Such a scenario makes some people uneasy as they think that leisure industries are not 'important', and that people should be doing more 'serious' work, like making machines or buildings. But, as described above, the G7 countries have made such progress that producing necessities does not keep many people busy: a smaller and smaller proportion of the population can produce all that is needed, and a growing proportion work to provide services that are 'wants' rather than true 'needs'. The growth of service industries in turn creates demand for manufactured products-as the demand for tourist air travel

creates a massive market for the aerospace manufacturing industry. Thus the growth of passenger space travel as shown would stimulate a genuine 'renaissance' of the space industry, after the post-cold-war period of stagnation and shrinkage.

In addition to its economic value as a popular consumer service, making space travel available to the general public would have great social value. Thanks to its well-known inspiring and educational value it would seem highly desirable in comparison with many other 'unnecessary' activities that are proliferating in rich countries, such as the use of recreational but often addictive drugs, gambling and pornography, to mention a few. For some years there has also been talk of a "crisis in aerospace" because of the sustained decline in interest among young people in working in the industry. The author's proposal that the development of passenger space travel would also resolve this problem by putting work in space engineering at the forefront of a popular new industry was published as a 2001 editorial in Aviation Week & Space Technology. For simplicity, if it is assumed that the progressive fall in service price thanks to increasing scale of operation is balanced by growth in demand for more expensive services, average expenditure of $20,000 per passenger would give a turnover of some $100 billion in 2030. How much further passenger space travel services might grow depends on many factors; however it does not seem likely to be limited by a lack of demand in the foreseeable future. In addition to the great popularity of the activity itself, there is enormous scope for provision of even more interesting experiences in space with the development of progressively more advanced hotels, orbiting sports centres, lunar hotels and other facilities, as discussed in the references in. As an example, growth of 8% per year after 2030 would lead to a turnover of $1 trillion per year in 2060, that is some 50 million passengers per year (less than two weeks' of air travel passengers today). As a different way of looking at the potential, a rough estimate of the potential cumulative market.

Cumulative revenue of $40 trillion is equivalent to some 2 billion people travelling to space once each. Although this may seem a large number, we note again that aviation has already reached 1.5 billion passengers-i.e. equivalent to one quarter of the world population every year. Criticism of this suggestion by staff from government space agencies, by those indirectly funded by space agencies or by others in such terms as that it is "unconvincing" or "pure guesswork" could of course be readily answered if agencies were to devote even as little as 1/10 000 of their annual budgets to study the possibility. It is also interesting to consider how a correct prediction made in 1902 about the future scale of passenger air travel during the following century might have been received, at a time when the main form of transport was still horse-carriage, and no one had even flown in an aeroplane. Talk of "millions of passengers per day" and "one billion passengers per year" would surely have been dismissed not as "guesswork" but as sheer madness. Yet, by contrast to the nonexistence of aviation in 1902, crewed space travel has been under way in 2002 for more than 40 years already, making the projection of future passenger space travel services-based on known technology and market research data-far less uncertain.

The low cost of access to space that would be brought about by such large-scale space tourism would also lead to other forms of economic development in space which are not possible at present high launch costs. Many writers of both fiction and nonfiction have described futures in which human activities spread far beyond Earth-a genuine 'Space Age'. The fundamental reasons why this has not happened yet are because the cost of access to space is too high, and there is very little demand for the services utilising space that are currently being offered. By bringing costs down by providing services for which there is known to be a very large consumer demand, space tourism uniquely offers the promise of realising these longterm possibilities. Even if the possibility of realising this scenario was estimated to be only 1%, space agencies should still be investing tens of millions of dollars/year to investigate it. The fact that they devote nothing to this work is proof that they are not trying to maximise the growth of commercial space activities, despite their legal responsibility to do so.

'Opening the space frontier' is a phrase used in the literature published by government space agencies-but despite spending $25 billion per year they offer taxpayers no such prospect. The research-oriented activities funded by government space agencies are of little value for commercialisation, which is the key to enabling space activities to contribute to economic growth. The fact that the development of consumer-oriented commercial services in space is likely to be far more effective than government 'space development' activities at bringing about economic development in space should not be surprising-and it should be particularly obvious to economic policy makers.

Imperative for Economic Policy

Space activities generally receive little or no attention from economic policy makers for a number of reasons: they are very small-scale by comparison with commercial industries; they are largely government-funded; and they show little prospect of significant growth-at least according to government space agencies' forecasts. In truth, economists should know better than to rely on the views of government monopoly organisations concerning either costs or future prospects, since they have a well-understood tendency to have excessively high costs, to avoid risks, and to resist innovation, in pursuit of their own economic interests. However, although these problems of government organisations are well-known within both business and the economics profession, it is easy for government organisations that use large budgets for public relations to appear impressive and authoritative to non-specialist members of the public, including many journalists and politicians. And it is notable that both journalists and politicians-and indeed most of the general public-tend to accept the statements of space agencies as definitive even in matters of cost.

Sadly, government space agencies have avoided proposing that space activities could have economic value commensurate with their costs. On the contrary, the way in which they are structured and funded gives them a strong economic interest in exaggerating the difficulty of space activities, playing down future prospects, avoiding risks, and minimising the public's expectations by such means as ignoring proposals for passenger space travel, in line with Niskanen's description. Before being appointed Nasa Administrator, O'Keefe himself drew attention to the unsatisfactory form of many of Nasa's stated objectives, such as to "chart our destiny in the solar system" which do not allow the measurement of success or failure. In this way, by reducing the likelihood that they will receive criticism for having 'failed' in their work, space agencies thereby maximise the likelihood of continuing to receive funding.

To date, government space agencies have spent some $1 trillion of taxpayers' money. But whereas commercial investment on that scale would have created businesses earning revenues of some $1 trillion per year, commercial space activities today are roughly one 50th of this. Even allowing for the fact that 10-20% of this funding is for scientific research, and perhaps $1/2 trillion spent in the early decades was explicitly for political purposes, the return on investment is still < 10% of what commercial activities would achieve. If space agencies were genuinely motivated to achieve economic benefit for taxpayers, then in view of this extremely poor economic performance they would be urgently investigating potentially promising new commercial opportunities. Since passenger space travel is recognised to have the potential to grow into a major new service industry similar to passenger air travel space agencies' unanimous refusal to investigate it, despite being required by law to promote commercial space activities, shows that space agency leaders do not want to know about the potential of passenger space travel, and moreover that they do not want the public to know about it either.

In view of space agencies' economic interest in maintaining government funding of their existing activities, it seems likely that they will continue to refuse to do anything to help the development of passenger space travel until they are compelled to do so. Unfortunately the interests of the politicians who control their budgets are very similar to those of the agencies themselves, as Niskanen explains. Consequently reform will require intervention from outside existing arrangements, which will take time.

From the economic point of view, a particularly damaging effect of the present situation is that, until such change occurs, it will remain very difficult for private companies to raise funding to develop passenger space travel services. Major aerospace companies are 'captives' of space agencies, in the sense that they cannot do any independent work that might jeopardise their chances of continuing to receive large, low-risk contracts from them, while small companies lack the credibility to raise the funding they need in financial markets, since financiers tend to accept the 'conventional wisdom' about space which comes from government space agencies. This problem has been documented in such cases as Beal Aerospace Inc. Stopping their project to develop a lowcost satellite launch vehicle in 2001 because of competition from Nasa, and difficulties caused for other companies trying to raise funding for similar projects by public comments from space agencies.

Macroeconomic Viewpoint

From the macroeconomic point of view, in the absence of detailed analyses demonstrating errors in the Nasa report and similar published work, it is clearly desirable that passenger space travel services should be developed as soon as possible. This is because in 2002 the major blocs of the global economy are sinking into recession simultaneously, and the severe overcapacity in many older industries, combined with a serious lack of profitable new industries creates a real risk of a prolonged depression.

Historians and economic policy makers must not forget that the slide towards the second world war gathered pace through the depression of the 1930s when unemployment reached 20% in many countries. If current high levels of unemployment rise even higher in the coming years, they may lead to dangerous impatience in many regions of the world. It is already clear that in some of the poorest countries religious extremism can seem attractive by comparison with a life of impoverished unemployment, from which escape is hampered by G7 countries' protectionist trade barriers against their cheap exports. These trade barriers are motivated by the high unemployment in richer countries caused by the lack of new industries (as discussed above).

It would be economically beneficial to taxpayers if economic policy makers insist that our accumulated space engineering capabilities be used for activities with greater economic value than government space agencies' current unprofitable ones. As they operate today, instead of contributing to economic growth, government space activities are a hindrance to it-by using $20 billion per year of taxpayers' funds on activities which have an annual rate of return close to minus 100%; by indirectly preventing companies from developing lower-cost launch vehicles; and by deliberately hindering the growth of the activity which they have themselves confirmed is the most economically promising use of space-passenger space travel.

As described above, if present budgets continued and passenger space travel services were not developed as proposed in Figure above, the net loss to taxpayers from continuing the present pattern of government space activities for several more decades would be around $1 trillion. This would be a terrible miscalculation of economic resources-particularly at a time of inadequate economic growth-and the quicker it is remedied by prioritising the development of passenger space travel the more the space industry will contribute to world economic growth, and thereby to 'Meeting the Needs of the New Millennium'. In addition to this economic cost, there would also be an incalculable human cost: in unnecessarily prolonging the poverty of hundreds of millions of people in late-developing countries; in postponing the development of an exciting new goal for the young in the currently richer countries; and in aggravating the risk of global conflicts through high unemployment. If government space agencies were genuinely trying to "encourage, to the maximum extent possible, the fullest commercial use of space" they would obviously investigate this potentially major new business opportunity in depth. But instead, they are currently suppressing discussion of this possibility by refusing to provide even the smallest funding to study it, despite having endorsed it in print. Economic policy makers should act to correct this serious policy failure as soon as possible. Another cost of this policy of deliberate neglect is that it ensures that there will inevitably be a further delay before passenger space travel grows to a large scale. Although it seems possible that passenger space travel could grow to reach a scale of $1 trillion per year later in the 21st century, turnover during the next 10 years will clearly be limited, and even with vigorous growth it seems unlikely to be measured in more than tens of billions of dollars by the 2020s.

How best to stimulate the development of passenger space travel services is a separate question, which has been discussed elsewhere. Some preliminary actions can be simply described: following the first recommendation in senior staff of space agencies should speak formally, positively and often about the economic importance and social value of developing a vigorous, commercial passenger space travel industry; they should also establish well-resourced offices tasked with encouraging the development of passenger space travel; and they should collaborate closely with the aviation industry in realising this goal. The latter action will require significant restructuring since government space activities have little relevant contact with aviation. Yet the vast experience of the airline industry is essential to realising passenger space travel. To the extent that space agencies do not participate effectively in implementing these and other economically beneficial changes to their existing activities, taxpayers will benefit economically if space agencies' budgets are cut-both directly by making large savings in subsidies to high-cost activities with little economic value, and indirectly by reducing misinformation about the potential for space commercialisation in general and passenger space travel in particular.

The chapter has described the potential economic benefits from developing passenger space travel services, which could contribute greatly to the continuation of peaceful world economic growth. By contrast, the vision of the future offered by government space agencies, based on continuing government domination of space activities centred on a crewed mission to Mars, is tragically narrow-minded and would merely preserve space agencies' near-monopoly status rather than contribute to economic growth. In view of the potential economic importance of passenger space travel in creating a major new field for economic expansion it is most unfortunate that little progress is being made today in developing this promising new consumer service industry, mainly because governments spend some $20 billion per year on a range of unprofitable 'space development' activities and nothing at all on work that would help to realise passenger travel. Claims by space agency leaders that they are fulfilling their legal responsibility to encourage space commercialisation are disingenuous at best.

The sooner that policies are implemented to accelerate the development of passenger space travel, the sooner the space industry will be able to claim honestly that it is contributing to meeting the needs of the 21st century-rather than holding back world economic growth by suppressing a new field with great business potential. For government space agencies and the politicians responsible for their budgets to continue to remain silent concerning their potential contribution in this area at a time of growing economic difficulty worldwide would be a shamefully wasted opportunity. It is highly desirable that economic policy makers should be informed of the opportunity for economic growth that is being wasted by government space agencies. They will then be in a position to implement policies to bring about the attractive future shown in Figure, thereby creating a wealth of new business opportunities for the innovative leaders who are so sadly lacking in space agencies.

Sampling and Non-sampling Error

Due to various constraints, the authors believe a small amount of sampling error exists in the survey data. First of all, error was introduced in the sample by interviewing the first person who answered the telephone on each call. Although, in many cases, the person who answered chose to pass the call on to another, in the majority of cases the initial respondent completed the survey. An example of the error that can be introduced by doing this is that, in western households, women are statistically more likely to answer the phone than their male counterparts. In order to produce a sample that better represents the population, one needs to select a respondent randomly from all the individuals who reside in each household. This can be accomplished, for example, by asking to interview the person in the house with the next birthday. This procedure or others like it, however, considerably complicate the survey procedure and increase the time needed to take the sample. A comparison of the sample taken in this study with national statistics of gender and age shows very little difference in composition, and therefore this type of sampling error is considered small. Further details concerning the representativeness of the sample are discussed later in the paper.

The largest source of sampling error in a telephone survey can usually be attributed to non-response. This arises because many people are not at home when called (54% of the numbers dialled), and many individuals (48% of those contacted) choose not to participate in the survey. This survey was administered during selected periods of time during the week: Monday-Friday from 5 pm to 9 pm, and on Saturday from 11 am to 7 pm. These set time-frames were chosen to reduce non-response due to refusals, and to increase the likelihood that more people in each household would be at home to answer the phone.

It is recognized however, that calling during specific time periods can exclude certain portions of the population who may be doing shift-work, or certain age-groups who may not typically be at home during these time-periods. Calling on Saturdays and also on the Labour Day holiday may have helped to reduce this error. Possible ways to determine if biasing is present include making call-backs to numbers where there was no answer, and interviewing individuals who refuse to do the survey on their first option by coaxing them with some type of reward. These measures however, were considered unnecessary in this case because of the nature of the survey. All in all, it is very unlikely that significant error has been introduced into the data with the sampling method used. Non-sampling error for this study is considered to be very small since the interviewing sessions were conducted in a highly controlled manner. The use of computer programs to dictate the survey text so that each participant received exactly the same information, as well as to collect, process, and analyse the data, decreased the possibility of error being introduced in these processes to a minimum.

The Survey

The survey consisted of 17 questions and took approximately four minutes to complete. Respondents who were not interested in travelling to space had a much shorter survey to answer that took only half the time.

The first section of the survey collected basic personal information on the respondent, as well as information concerning interests and travelling preferences. The second half of the survey began with the following space tourism concept statement: Consider for the moment that it is possible to travel to space as a potential vacation alternative. Imagine that people are able to go to there using a means of transportation similar to a planed The respondent was then asked would you be interested in travelling to space-yes or noway If the respondent answered no, they were queried as to why.

If they responded yes, the survey continued with more specific questions concerning a space trip. Several open-ended questions in the survey stimulated many interesting opinions and comments from the respondents, which suggests that many people have given considerable thought to the idea of travelling to space for themselves. In the future, a more detailed analysis of the results of this survey will be published, and those comments will be given further attention. For the present, the following paragraphs briefly describe the studious main findings.

Survey Results

Table below shows the overall distribution of the survey participants by age and gender, and compares them to the US population as a whole. (Adding the figure in the variant column to the corresponding age group yields the percentage of that group in the overall US population, census data-1990.

It has been assumed that the Canadian population distribution is similar.) The distribution by age matches the overall population very closely; none of the five age groups considered is over-or under-represented by more than 2.2%, confirming the representativeness of the sample in this respect. The distribution by gender, however, is significantly different, with women over-represented and men under-represented by 6.3%. In the following, wherever necessary, the figures are adjusted to compensate for this.

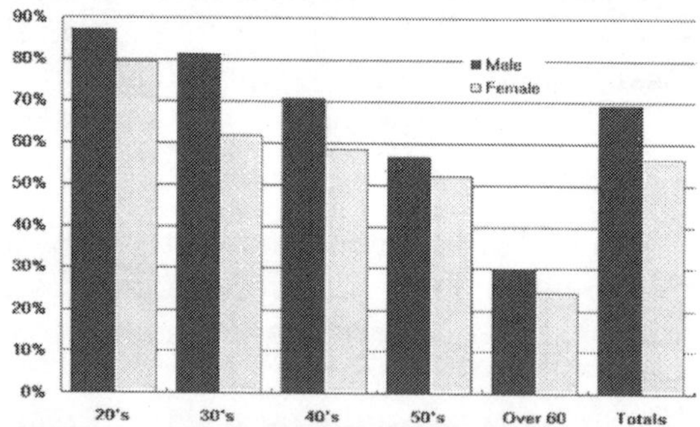

***Figure** : Percentage of respondents interested in travelling to space*

Figure shows the basic level of interest in travelling to space, broken down by age and gender. As an overall average, more than 60% of the population say they are interested, with a higher proportion of younger people being interested, as one might expect. The overall average figure is comprised of more than 75% of those under 40 years old; 60% of those between 40 and 60; and more than 25% of those between 60 and 80.

It is notable that in every age group men were more interested than women, the average difference being about 10%. This is rather different from the results of the survey in Japan, where no significant difference was found. This may be due to the fact that many US astronauts are military staff, whereas all the Japanese who have visited space are civilians.

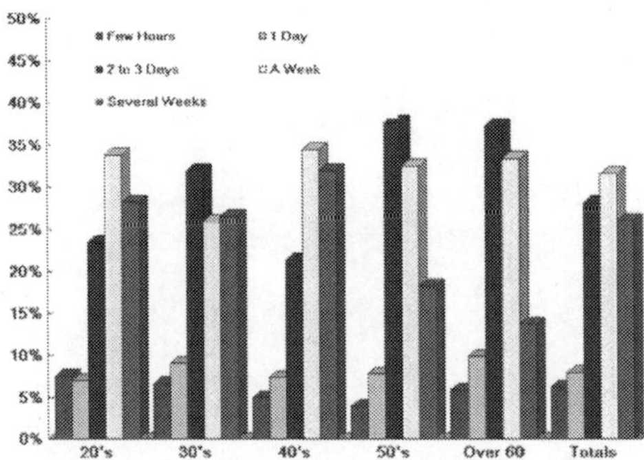

Figure: *Preferred length of space trip*

Figure shows the length of timc participants would prefer a space trip to be, broken down by age groups. A substantial majority of all age-groups say that they would prefer to go to space for either several days, one week or more. In all age-groups, no more than about 15% of the people say they would prefer a visit of a few hours or one day; the majority have a clear preference for a longer stay, some 30% of those under 50 preferring several weekdays.

The questionnaire did not discuss the relative price of different lengths of visit. In reality, a longer stay will be more expensive, but these results give no information on participants price-sensitivity. It seems reasonable to conclude that, in the absence of orbital accommodation enabling people to stay for a few days, the demand for space tourism will not reach its full potential. Figure displays the amount that respondents interested in travelling to space would be prepared to pay for a trip, expressed in months of salary. The first point to note is that there is little difference between the various age groups on this variable. At the upper end of the range, it is interesting that 2.7% of those wishing to visit space (representing almost 3 million people) say that they would pay three hearsay salary. Clearly for these people travelling to space is a very strong desire.

10.6% (representing 11 million people) say they would pay one year's salary, which is still a very substantial expense. 18.2% of participants (representing 19 million people) say they would pay 6 months salary, and 45.6% (representing 48 million people) say they would pay 3 months salary.

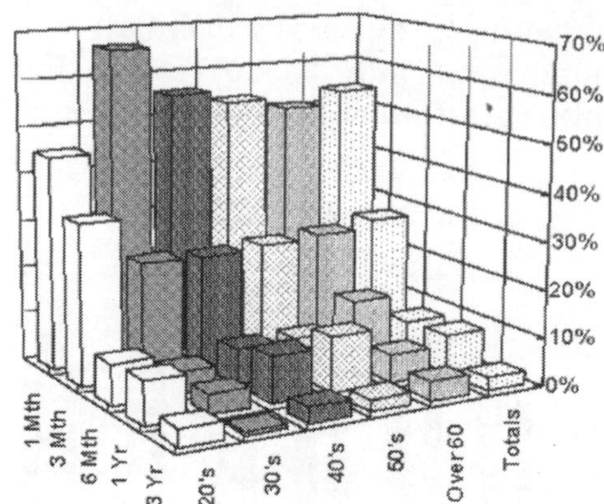

Figure : *How much people feel is the proper proportion of their income for a space trip*

In further analysis of the data, average income statistics for different age-groups will be used to derive a demand curve and study market segmentation for the North American market. For the present we simply note that the overall average income for North Americans is approximately $2,000 per month, or $12,000 for six months salary, and $24,000 for a year. In addition, two thirds of those wishing to visit space said that they would like to do so several times, not once only.

Consequently, even allowing for a substantial gap between consumerism intentions and their actions, space travel could clearly become a $multi-billion per year market in America alone. 10% of the above estimate is still more than $60 billion in funds that people say they are willing to spend on a space trip.

Bibliography

Blanton, D. : *Tourism Training in Developing Countries,* Annals of Tourism Research, 1981.

Buhalis, D. : *Information Technologies in Tourism, in E. Laws,*London, Tourism Society, 1997.

Chalazion, P: *Tourism and Cultural Change, Sunderland,* Business Education Publishers Ltd, 1996.

Davidoff, Donald M.: *Customer Service in the Hospitality and Tourism Industry,* Englewood Cliffs, Prentice Hall, 1994.

Douglas C: *Practical Tourism Forecasting,* Oxford, Butterworth Heinemann, 1996.

Elliott, James: *Tourism: Politics and Public Sector Management,* London, Retailed, 1997.

Foster, Douglas: *Travel and Tourism Management,* London, Macmillan Educational, 1985.

Ghimire, Krishna: *The Native Tourist*: Mass Tourism within Developing Regions, London, Earthscan, 2001.

Hoffman, Edward: *Project Management Success Stories: Lessons of Project Leaders,* New York, John Wiley & Son, 2000.

Hubert, B.: *A Host of Opportunities: An Introduction to Hospitality Management,* Chicago, Irwin, 1996.

Ireland, Lewis: *Quality Management for Projects and Programs,* Upper Darby, PMI, 1991.

Jakle, John: *Tourist, The: Travel in Twentieth Century North America,* University of North Nebraska, 1985.

Jitendra K. : *Contemporary Tourism and Hospitality Management,* Kanishka, Delhi, 2006.

Judi Radice: *Restaurant & Food Graphics,* Glen Cove, PBC International, 1994.

Klein, S. : *Information & Communication Technologies in Tourism,* Springer-Verlag, Wien-New York, 2000.

Kotler, Philip: *Marketing for Hospitality and Tourism*: New Jersey, Prentice-Hall, 1998.

Larkham, P J: *Building a New Heritage: Tourism, Culture & Identity in the New Europe*, London, Routledge,1994.

Marjorie, E.: *Careers in Travel, Tourism, and Hospitality*, Lincolnwood, VGM Career Horizons, 1997.

Nightingale, M. : *Tourism Occupations, Career Profile and Knowledge*, Annals of Tourism Research, 1981.

Nijkamp, Peter: *Sustainable Tourism Development*, Aldershot, Avebury, 1995.

Pantelidis, I.S. : *Evaluating the Consumer in Hospitality*, Annual Research Conference: London, 2010.

Peters, M: *International Tourism*, London, Hutchinson, 1969.

Powers, Thomas F. : *Introduction to the Hospitality Industry*, New York, Wiley, 1995.

Prentice, R: *Conceptualising The Experiences of Heritage Tourists*, 1997.

Robert C.: *Cases in Hospitality Marketing and Management*, New York, John Wiley, 1997.

Rosemary E.: *Managing Employee Relations in the Hotel and Catering Industry*, London, Cassell, 1995.

Rosenzweig, J. E.: *Organisation and Management*, New York, McGraw Hill International, 1963.

Sherman, Barry: *Telecommunications Management*, New York, McGraw Hill, 1995.

Slinn, Judy A: *Tourism: Management of Facilities*, London, Pitman: M & E, 1993.

Swarbrooke, J.: *Marketing Tourism, Hospitality and Leisure in Europe*, London, International Thomson Business Press, 1996.

Timothy R.: *Cases in Hospitality Management: A Critical Incident Approach*, New York, Wiley, 1995.

Tribe, J. : *Community and Commercial Interests in Tourism*, Developments in the European Tourism Curriculum, Tilberg, 1998.

Tribe, John *Corporate Strategy for Tourism, London*, International Thomson Business Press, 1997.

Umbreit, T. : *The Role of Education in the Tourist Industry*, Salt Lake City, University of Utah, 1987.

Var, Turgut: *Tourism Planning*, London, Retailed, 2002.

Weiler, B: *Ethnic Tourism*, Belhaven/Wiley, 1992.

William H.: *The Chef's Guide to Practical Restaurant Cookery*, New York, Van Nostrand Reinhold, 1988.

Williams, A: *Tourism and Tourism Spaces*, London, Sage, 2004.

Index

❑❑❑